Greater London
MURDERS

Greater London MURDERS

33 TRUE STORIES OF REVENGE, JEALOUSY, GREED & LUST

LINDA STRATMANN

The
History
Press

First published 2010

The History Press
The Mill, Brimscombe Port
Stroud, Gloucestershire, GL5 2QG
www.thehistorypress.co.uk

British Library Cataloguing in Publication Data.
A catalogue record for this book is available from the British Library.

ISBN 978 0 7524 5124 4

Typesetting and origination by The History Press
Printed in India by Replika Press Pvt. Ltd.
Manufacturing managed by Jellyfish Print Solutions Ltd

CONTENTS

Author's Note

I would like to thank everyone who has helped me with the preparation of this book, especially the staff of the British Library, Colindale Newspaper Library, the National Archives, and the Newham Local Studies Library. My grateful thanks also to the Metropolitan Police Historical Collection for permission to reproduce some of the pictures in this book.

My thanks are always due to my husband Gary, for his assistance, support and enthusiasm in all my endeavours.

This book is dedicated to my friends in the Forest Writers' group, who have listened to my readings with such patience, and made so many helpful and illuminating comments.

The Illustrations
Except where specifically stated, the illustrations in this book are from the author's collection.

About the Author

Linda Stratmann is a freelance writer and editor. She has a long-term interest in true crime and is the author of *Chloroform: The Quest for Oblivion*, *Whiteley's Folly: The Life and Death of a Salesman*, *The Crooks Who Conned Millions: True Stories of Fraudsters and Charlatans*, *Notorious Blasted Rascal: Colonel Charteris and the Servant Girl's Revenge*, *Gloucestershire Murders*, *Essex Murders* and *Kent Murders*. She lives in Walthamstow, London.

BARKING AND DAGENHAM

A Fight to the Death

In the 1840s, Dagenham was a rural village, largely populated by agricultural labourers. With the Thames estuary only two miles away, many men were tempted to supplement their low wages by smuggling. There was no Essex police force, and the area earned a not undeserved reputation for lawlessness. To combat the problem the Metropolitan police force established a small station in Dagenham which was manned by six constables and a sergeant, and provided with a horse. The police soon came into conflict with the criminal elements, and some constables received threats which were taken so seriously that it was decided to transfer the officers in question to other districts.

On 4 March 1846, PC Abia Butfoy was on patrol when he encountered a man he knew to be of bad character, carrying a bag. Suspecting that the bag contained stolen property, he insisted on seeing its contents. The man refused and this resulted in a scuffle. Later the man showed him what was in the bag, but departed with a threat to get even. In mid-May Butfoy was replaced on his beat with another constable, PC George Clark.

Clark had been in the police force only six months, and in Dagenham just six weeks. He was 20 years old, robust and well able to take care of himself, and had already impressed his superiors with his conscientious attention to duty. He was a quiet, good humoured and religious lad, who sang hymns as he walked along and carried tracts in his pocket. He had recently become engaged to be married.

The police patrol began every night at 9 p.m., with Sergeant William Parsons on horseback at the head of his men. At a crossroads known as the Four Wantz, where the roads led to Ilford, Barking, Dagenham and Chigwell, the men parted, setting off on their individual beats. They met up at set points and times

Old Dagenham.

during the night, returning to the station at 6 a.m. The lone policeman walking country roads in the hopes of deterring a band of armed cutthroats was poorly equipped. He carried a truncheon and a cutlass, and wore a thick greatcoat done up tightly at the neck with a stout leather stock to protect against being strangled. If attacked, he could alert his colleagues with a wooden rattle.

On Monday 29 June the men patrolled as usual, and Clark was at his appointed place at 1 a.m., but two hours later, he was missing. When the men returned to the station, Clark was absent. His colleagues retraced his route but found nothing, and started dragging ponds for a corpse.

On 3 August they reached the farm of Ralph Page and asked his wife, Elizabeth, for permission to drag the pond. Mrs Page remembered that at 3 a.m. on 29 June she had been awoken by the furious barking of dogs. She had thought she heard a distant cry for help, but the barking was so loud that she had not been sure. Once the pond had been dragged Mrs Page said that there was another further on, and sent her two boys to show constables Butfoy and Thomas Kimpton where it was. In a field a quarter of a mile from the main road, they became aware of a strong smell. Kimpton found a policeman's staff, bloodstained and very much cut about, and immediately recognised it as Clark's. A little further on he found Clark's cutlass, stuck in a hedge, and when it was withdrawn it was seen to be covered in blood, with human hair sticking to it. Half a dozen yards further on was the body of George Clark, and even after the previous two discoveries the two policemen could not have been prepared for the ghastly appearance of the corpse. 'Here he lies!' called Butfoy, while the children screamed so loudly their mother could hear them back at the farmhouse. Kimpton was too appalled to speak and Butfoy, who had a stronger stomach, added, 'you are a pretty cow-hearted sort of a policeman.' They called for Sergeant Parsons and PC Stevens, who were in the adjoining field. Stevens took one look at the body and fell back in a dead faint.

Clark was lying on his back, one hand tightly grasping a handful of wheat in the last spasm of death. There had been a fierce struggle, for the crops were trodden down for ten or twelve yards in every direction. The face and hands of the corpse were covered with blood and dirt. The wounds were appalling. There was a large opening in the back of the skull some six to eight inches in circumference. Part of the scalp had been cut off, probably with the cutlass, and was lying beside the body.

Local surgeon Mr Collins was sent for to examine the body, then it was removed to the ruins of a nearby cottage using a cart borrowed from Mrs Page. Whatever the motive for the murder it could not have been robbery, for Clark's money and watch were found in his pockets. His rattle was still in his greatcoat pocket, in such a position that he could not have got to it in time to give the alarm. Collins removed the leather stock, which was completely saturated with blood, and found a deep wound to the throat, cutting through the windpipe and the root of the tongue almost through to the vertebrae. Another wound under the right ear went completely through the neck and must have been inflicted with a sharp double-edged knife. The face and chest were heavily bruised. There were other superficial wounds, and one finger had been cut off, probably as Clark defended himself.

Late that night the policemen returned the cart to Mrs Page, and she invited them in for refreshment. As they chatted, Kimpton mentioned that Sergeant Parsons had not been on duty for the whole of the night of Clark's murder. At about midnight, the sergeant had said he was not feeling well and had asked Kimpton to take the horse and do his duty for him. This casual statement sowed the seeds of a major scandal which was to damage the reputation of the Metropolitan police force for several years.

At daylight, further searches were made at the scene of the crime, but there were no footprints, and though the wheat had been parted at the side of the field showing that people had passed that way, it was not clear from what direction they had come, or where they had gone. Broken pieces of Clark's skull were so deeply embedded in the earth that they had to be dug out with a knife. The newspapers were to report that the body had been flung down with such force that it had left an impression in the earth, but a more likely explanation was that Clark's corpse had been trampled by many feet.

£100 Rew

WHEREAS on the Night of the 29th
Morning of the 30th,

GEORGE CLA

Police Constable of the h Division of
Police, was brutally Murdered, when
some Person or Persons unknown,
the Parish of Dagenham, in the Coun
A REWARD

The inquest was opened on Saturday 4 July. The jurymen were obliged to view the remains, but many could barely glance at the body, and the smell made them feel nauseous and faint. Back in court, Abia Butfoy gave the name of a suspect, but this was not made public. Mrs Page was in court, and must have been astonished when Sergeant William Parsons gave evidence in which he stated that he had been on duty all night. The inquest was adjourned for a fortnight, and Clark's mother begged to be allowed to see the body. The coroner advised her not to do so, but reluctantly granted her request with the anticipated effect – she was overcome and had to be carried away, insensible.

Two detective officers from Scotland Yard arrived in Dagenham to conduct the investigation, questioning the inhabitants, visiting public houses and beer shops, and placing any known bad characters under surveillance. It was believed locally that Clark had been murdered after being mistaken for Abia Butfoy. The body was so far from his normal beat that he must have been deliberately lured there.

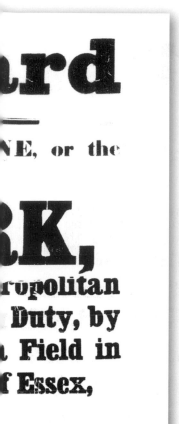

rd

NE, or the

RK,

ropolitan

Duty, by

Field in

Essex,

Wanted poster for the murder of PC Clark. (By kind permission of the London Borough of Barking and Dagenham)

At the next inquest hearing, Mrs Page revealed that she had been told that Parsons had been absent from duty after midnight, however PC Stevens testified that he had seen Parsons at a quarter to one and denied that anything had been said about Parsons not doing his duty on the night of the murder. Kimpton then denied having made the statement about Parsons and swore that he had seen the sergeant on duty. Another constable, Isaac Hickton, also said he had seen Parsons on duty after midnight.

Mrs Page was not prepared to let the matter rest. At the next hearing, her daughter Priscilla, who had been present at the disputed conversation, testified that Kimpton had said not only that he had done Parsons' duty that night but it had not been the first time he had done so. Mrs Page and Kimpton were then brought into court, where there was a testy confrontation, each sticking to their testimony.

A neighbour, Mr Kettle, had been present at the time of the conversation, but asked to testify whether the disputed statement had been made, he said he couldn't remember. Mrs Page was heard to observe dryly that he had remembered it well enough last Saturday, and the jury expressed the strong opinion that the witness knew a great deal more than he was saying. James March, a labourer, who had assisted with transport of the body, testified that he had never heard Kimpton say he had done Parsons' duty. Unfortunately for March, his master was a member of the jury and immediately pointed out that he had heard March saying he had heard the statement not once but several times. A Dagenham grocer, Thomas Smith, supported Mrs Page by saying that Kimpton had also told him he had done Parsons' duty.

By now it was painfully apparent that several people in court had lied, the only problem being determining exactly which ones.

Julia Parsons, the sergeant's sister, had been staying with her brother on the night of the murder. She testified that she and Parsons' wife had met up with Clark and Parsons at about 9 p.m. Clark had been in a jocular mood, for when Mrs Parsons complained of feeling tired he had jokingly suggested he lift her onto the policeman's horse. The women returned home, and Clark and Parsons went on. Julia said her brother had returned to the station at midnight, had made out a report then gone out again. She had gone to bed and did not see him till 9 o'clock the next morning.

The coroner's opinion was that Parsons had been on duty the whole night, and the only question was whether or not Kimpton had made the damaging statement to Mrs Page. He believed that Kimpton had made it but why he had done so God only knew. In vain did Kimpton protest that he had not done so, for the jury said that they were satisfied that he did. The enquiry was adjourned for a month.

In August there was a hearing in Ilford concerning the potential involvement of three Irish itinerant agricultural labourers, who had been taken into custody after a drunken altercation in which words had been bandied about concerning the murder. Abia Butfoy gave evidence but when it was time for him to return to duty in Dagenham, he was nowhere to be found. Perhaps as a result of having to air the whole story again, Butfoy had suffered a crisis of conscience. He had gone to Scotland Yard and made a statement admitting that the policemen had lied at the inquest and that Kimpton had indeed done Parsons' duty for him. Officers were at once despatched to Dagenham, and Sergeant Parsons and the five constables, Hickton, Kimpton, Stevens, Butfoy and Farns, were relieved of their duties and placed under surveillance.

The news caused considerable excitement in Dagenham, and ripples of astonishment carried all the way to London. It was widely rumoured that the men had been arrested for the murder. Since Clark had been efficient, religious and popular, motives were hard to come by. Perhaps, it was hinted, his colleagues were jealous because he was just too efficient, religious and popular – perhaps he had discovered that they had been involved in smuggling or lectured them about their drinking habits, or maybe the incident with Mrs Parsons and the horse had aroused the sergeant to a frenzy of jealousy. Ultimately, no evidence was ever produced that the police were involved in the murder of Clark.

In August 1847 a memorial was placed on the grave of George Clark, the inscription reflecting the feelings of the community: 'His uniform good conduct gained him the respect of all who knew him, and his melancholy end was universally deplored.'

At the resumed inquest the constables, now in plain clothes, admitted that they had lied because Parsons had ordered them to, while Parsons was adamant that his original story was correct. When the inquest closed in September the jury returned a verdict of 'wilful murder against some person or persons unknown.'

Butfoy, Farns and Stevens had not been under oath when examined before the coroner so a charge of perjury could not be sustained and they were dismissed from the force. The others were suspended without pay which was especially hard for Kimpton, who was married with six children.

In the following March proceedings commenced against Kimpton, Hickton and Parsons on charges of wilful and corrupt perjury, but at the bail hearing, only Kimpton appeared, Parsons and Hickton having made their own arrangements by absconding. In London and Essex there was the unusual sight of placards being posted offering a reward of £50 for the apprehension of the two former policemen. Kimpton, lacking the £400 bail money, was taken to Ilford Gaol.

Hickton had gone to Liverpool, but seeing the wanted posters, his nerve failed him. In July he wrote to his father asking to send Sergeant Hardy of the Derbyshire police force to arrest him. Hardy was an old school friend and Hickton wanted him to get the reward.

Hickton and Kimpton were found guilty of perjury and the judge passed the maximum punishment, 'for if we cannot have truth from police officers what guarantee have we for the security of either our persons or property?' They were fined one shilling, and sentenced to prison for a week and then transportation for seven years. Hickton served his sentence in Portsmouth dockyard and Kimpton on board a convict ship at Woolwich. Both men were pardoned in 1849.

Parsons was apprehended in Lincolnshire, and stood trial in March 1848 for conspiracy to impede the course of justice. The judge commended the generally excellent behaviour of the Essex police, and pointed out that since the perjury was to avoid charges of neglect of duty and had nothing to do with the murder investigation, Parsons had not been indicted on the correct charge. Parsons was acquitted and walked from the court a free man.

£50 Reward.

WHEREAS

William Parsons,

a Police Serjeant, and

Isaac Hickton,

a Police Constable,

lately in the *K Division* of the Metropolitan Police, stand charged with Conspiracy and Perjury at the Inquest held at Dagenham, in the County of Essex, upon the body of GEORGE CLARK, a Police Constable, who was Murdered on the 29th June, 1846.

Her Majesty's Government

will give the above REWARD, to any Person who shall give such Information as will lead to the Apprehension of these Men, or a proportion of it for the Apprehension of either of them.

Description of Parsons,

Aged 30 Years, Height 5 feet 7½ inches, Fresh Complexion, small Grey Eyes, Sandy Hair and Whiskers, much freckled, walks upright, and is well proportioned, by Trade a Miller, Born in Saint Peter's, Norwich.

Description of Hickton,

Aged 33 Years, Height 5 feet 9½ inches, Fair Complexion, Grey Eyes, light Brown Hair, small Sandy Whiskers, round Shouldered, draws his Mouth on one side when talking, especially when excited, by Trade a Currier, and was employed at a Tanner's at Hales Owen, near Birmingham, about 3 Months since, Born in Saint Warbus, Derby.

Information to be given at the Police Office, Great Scotland Yard, to the Police Station, K Division, Arbour-square, Stepney, or any of the Police Stations.

Metropolitan Police Office,
   4, Whitehall Place.

Wanted notice for the two absconding policemen. (By kind permission of the London Borough of Barking and Dagenham)

SACRED

TO THE MEMORY OF
GEORGE CLARK
LATE A POLICE CONSTABLE
OF THE K DIVISION OF
METROPOLITAN POLICE
WHO WAS INHUMANLY AND
BARBAROUSLY MURDERED
IN A FIELD AT EASTBROOK
END, IN THIS PARISH,
WHILST ON DUTY, ON THE
NIGHT OF THE 29TH OR THE
MORNING OF THE 30TH JUNE
1846,
AGED 20 YEARS.

HIS UNIFORM GOOD
CONDUCT GAINED HIM
THE RESPECT OF ALL
WHO KNEW HIM, AND HIS
MELANCHOLY END WAS
UNIVERSALLY DEPLORED.

The monument to Clark. (By kind permission of the London Borough of Barking and Dagenham)

In June 1858 a Mrs Mary Ann Smith claimed that Clark had been murdered by a gang consisting of her husband, William, and four others: Ned Wood (in some accounts Wilcox), George Chalk, George Blewitt and a farmer called Page. She described how the men had been surprised by Clark while stealing corn from a barn. She had been standing lookout and had given the alarm when she saw Clark approach. William had died in an accident about a year later, Wood was said to have hanged himself, Page had poisoned himself six years ago, and Chalk was in Australia. That left 32-year-old hay carter George Blewitt, who was arrested. When he appeared at the Ilford petty sessions in July, it became apparent that there was a problem with Mrs Smith's story, and indeed, a problem with Mrs Smith. She had stated that Clark had been killed near the barn and the body carried to where it was found, however the evidence at the scene showed that the murder could only have taken place where the body lay. Mrs Smith, who believed – rightly or wrongly – that Blewitt or some member of his family had stolen money from her, revealed that she had supernatural visitations and dreams. She claimed that she had seen her dead husband, and heard the Devil tapping under her chair. Her neighbours, she said, whispered that she was 'not quite right', and by the end of her testimony, the court had come to much the same conclusion. 'The magistrates,' said Mr Atkinson for the defence, 'would not pull a feather out of a sparrow's wing upon such evidence as this.' At the summer assizes the jury found 'no bill' against Blewitt, who was freed.

Hope faded and memory faded. No one was ever convicted of the murder of PC George Clark. The solution to the murder must lie in the dreadful mutilation of the corpse, which can only have been carried out by those with a deep hatred either of the young man or, more probably, what he stood for.

But PC George Clark was not entirely forgotten. On Sunday 30 June 1996, the 150th anniversary of his death was commemorated in Dagenham by a service held at the church of St Peter and St Paul, and a tree-planting at Eastbrook End Country Park. Policemen visited local schools to talk about policing in Victorian times, restoration work was carried out on the monument, and a letter from Police Commissioner Sir Paul Condon was presented to Clark's great-great-niece.

2

BARNET

Double Jeopardy

O n 21 October 1949 Sidney Tiffin, a farm labourer of Tillingham, Essex
was out looking for wild fowl on the marshes when he saw a floating
bundle. He opened it to see if there was anything worth salvaging and found
instead the decomposing torso of a man. The head and legs had been cut off,
but the arms remained. Tiffin secured his find by pushing a stake into the mud,
and notified the police at nearby Bradwell-on-Sea. The torso was taken to
Chelmsford mortuary and Police Superintendent Totterdell arrived to see it,
having first notified pathologist Dr Francis Camps.

The cause of death, which had taken place in the previous three weeks, was a
number of stab wounds in the chest inflicted by a long, sharp, two-edged knife.
There were also extensive post-mortem fractures, suggesting that the torso had
fallen from a height. The skin colour indicated a non-European origin, and this
gave Totterdell a clue as to the identity of the victim. He hoped fingerprints
might settle the matter, but the soaked skin was peeling away from the fingers.
At his request, Camps made an incision around the wrists of the corpse and
removed the skin of both hands like a pair of gloves. 'I think we've got Setty's
torso here,' said Totterdell, as he prepared to leave with his trophies. At Scotland
Yard, Superintendent Cherrill of the fingerprint division donned a pair of
rubber gloves and put the skin of the hands over his own, thus enabling him
to get accurate prints and identify the dead man as London car dealer Stanley
Setty, who had been missing since 4 October.

Stanley Setty had been born Sulman Seti in Baghdad in 1903. His family had
come to England when he was a child, his father setting up a textile business in
Manchester. After a number of failed business attempts Setty achieved success
through shady cash-in-hand car deals, and the sale of forged petrol coupons
which centred around the cafés of London's Warren Street and his garage in

Stanley Setty. (© Metropolitan Police Authority, 2009)

Cambridge Terrace Mews. In 1947 he sold a cheap car to Brian Donald Hume, who ran a small electrical shop at 620 Finchley Road, Golders Green. Hume was 27 years old with a mop of dark hair and penetrating grey eyes, his stocky figure greatly outweighed by Setty's fleshy bulk. Hume later described his first impressions of Setty as having 'a voice like broken bottles and pockets stuffed with cash.'

Setty may never have realised it but the younger man was a ferment of resentment just waiting to boil over into violence. Hume was born in December 1919. He was initially cared for by a woman he was told to call Aunt Doodie, but at the age of 2 he was sent away to the grim and loveless environment of an orphanage. When he was 8 he was adopted by his grandmother, of whom he was very fond, but six months later he was sent to live with Aunt Doodie again. Shortly afterwards his grandmother died. He then learned that the woman who he had been told was his aunt was actually his mother, and that he was illegitimate. He felt angry and bitter towards his mother, and abandoned his education to run away from home. At the age of 15, working as an apprentice electrician in London, he wrote to his mother saying he never wanted to see her again.

In 1939 he enlisted in the RAF, but in the following year he was involved in a flying accident, and suffered head injuries which led to an attack of cerebro-spinal meningitis. Although he recovered his physical health he started to show signs of mental instability, declaring himself to be pro-Nazi and claiming to have had adventures which existed only in his imagination. He was examined by a medical board in 1941, which assessed him to be of a psychopathic personality, and he was discharged from the service.

In April 1942 he was arrested for posing as a flying officer of the RAF. He was again found to be suffering from a psychopathic disorder and was ordered to get medical treatment. Hume never obtained that treatment, but he was able to bring some stability to his life by qualifying as a radio engineer. In 1943 he opened his own business, and initially this did well. In 1948 he married attractive divorcee Cynthia Kahn.

The years of post-war austerity were bad for business and Hume decided to sell the lease of the shop, while continuing to live in the maisonette on the top two floors of the four-storey premises. A teacher and his wife occupied the lower maisonette. It was far from glamorous living. The rooms were small, and any noise made in Hume's apartment would have been clearly audible on the floor below and possibly also in the houses on either side. Hume bought a small factory in Hay-on-Wye where he manufactured electrical products, but his fortunes did not improve, and there was a baby on the way, a daughter who was born in July 1949. It was while Hume was on the lookout for easy money that he bumped into Stanley Setty again. They soon realised that they could be useful to each other. The younger, more active Hume stole the cars and Setty used his contacts to sell them on. Hume was able to qualify for a pilot's license, and this enabled him to get involved in Setty's other major business occupation – smuggling. He eventually earned himself the soubriquet of 'The Flying Smuggler'. Setty and Hume began to see each other socially, and Setty sometimes came to the maisonette to discuss business.

The incident which cemented Hume's dislike of Setty occurred in August 1949. Hume visited Setty at his garage, taking with him his dog, a German shepherd called Tony. The dog scratched the paintwork on one of Setty's cars, and Setty kicked him.

Setty was last seen alive by a friend in Great Portland Street, at ten to six on Tuesday 4 October. He had an appointment that evening but telephoned to cancel it. Setty shared a flat in Lancaster Gate with his married sister Mrs Eva Ouri and her husband, but that night he failed to return home. Under cover of darkness, someone parked Setty's Citroên car near his garage. Setty was usually scrupulous about putting his car away, and a concerned Mr Ouri contacted the police. When enquiries were made about the business deals in which Setty had recently been engaged, it was realised that he must have been carrying over

£1,000 in £5 notes in his pockets, most of which were new notes issued that day by a bank. The door and steering wheel of the Citroën yielded fingerprints for comparison, and it was these which identified the torso found in the Essex marshes as that of Stanley Setty. Despite extensive searches, the head and legs of the body were never found. On 7 October, the numbers of the £5 notes known to have been in Setty's possession were published in the newspapers.

The evidence that the torso had fallen from a height was an important lead, and Chief Detective John Jamieson thought of making enquiries at local airports. It was soon revealed that on 5 October Hume, a member of the United Services Flying Club, had hired a light aircraft at Elstree aerodrome, loaded two parcels on board and flown to Southend. When he arrived at Southend there were no parcels in the plane. He had also paid a debt of £20 in £5 notes. That night he returned to Golders Green by taxi, which he paid for with more £5 notes. On the following day he returned to Southend with another parcel, with the intention of flying back to Elstree, but due to adverse weather conditions he was forced to land at Gravesend and hire a car to get home. Once again, the parcel he had taken on board the plane was not with him on his return.

Hume had been going about his normal daily business hoping to avoid suspicion but on 27 October he was taken to Albany Street police station for questioning. Admitting that he was the Flying Smuggler, he was unable to deny hiring the plane and dropping off the parcels but said he had done so for three men called Mac (or Max), Greenie and The Boy, who paid him in £5 notes. He said he thought he had been getting rid of plates used for forging petrol coupons.

Despite the fact that over £1,000 in cash was missing, very little was found in Hume's possession. When the police examined Hume's bank account it was found to have been £70 overdrawn until £90 was paid in on 5 October.

On 29 October Dr Henry Smith Holden of the Metropolitan Police laboratory examined Hume's flat and took away a lounge carpet. There was a stain on the underside which appeared to be blood, but the carpet had been recently cleaned and it was impossible to test the stain for a blood group. Over the next few days Holden removed floorboards and discovered bloodstains which had seeped through, staining the plaster of the ceiling underneath. He also found traces of blood in the hall, on the stairs leading to the top floor bathroom and on the staircase wall. The evidence against Hume mounted up. Some £5 notes found in Hume's possession were proved to be part of the bundle known to have been in Setty's possession on 4 October, but the bulk of the money carried by Setty on 4 October was never found. A witness came forward to say he had sharpened a carving knife for Hume on 5 October.

Hume told the police he had been out drinking with a friend on the night of Setty's disappearance, but the friend would not support the alibi. Hume was charged with the murder of Stanley Setty.

The arrest of Brian Donald Hume. (© Metropolitan Police Authority, 2009)

The trial opened at the Old Bailey's number one court on 18 January 1950. Hume, who knew he could never convince the court that he was a law-abiding citizen, arrived casually dressed, exuding the charm of the wide-boy who might deal in dodgy cars but would never kill. Francis Camps said that in his opinion the amount of blood found in the flat could not have leaked from already wrapped parcels. He believed that both the murder and the dismemberment of the body must have happened in the flat. The Humes' charlady, Mrs Ethel Stride, said that on 5 October Hume had told her he was going to clean the kitchen cupboard and was not to be disturbed. Later she saw him with some bulky parcels. The prosecution, led by Mr Christmas Humphreys, was however unable to bring a single witness who had seen either Setty or his car near Hume's flat on 4 October.

The case for the defence, led by Mr R.F. Levy, was that Setty had been murdered and dismembered elsewhere by a gang. In the witness box Hume described himself as 'a semi-honest man . . . but . . . not a murderer'. The schoolmaster in the flat below said he had been at home on the nights of 4 and 5 October and had heard nothing suspicious and Cynthia Hume, who claimed never to have met Setty, said she had been in the flat on 4 October and had listened to a radio play. She had seen and heard nothing unusual.

Pathologist Dr Robert Teare was called for the defence and disagreed with Camps about the blood seepage. He also thought that if there had been a violent frontal attack by one man, it would have resulted in a noisy struggle, and Setty would have had defence wounds on his hands. The defence also suggested that it was impossible for a man of Hume's size to have carried out the murder and dismemberment of the tall, bulky Setty alone. Although none of the three men Hume had mentioned could be traced, witnesses were brought to suggest that they might exist. Mrs Stride admitted that apart from the carpet having been sent for cleaning, she had noticed nothing out of the ordinary.

The jury deliberated for two hours, but on their return said that they were unable to agree on a verdict. It was decided not to retry Hume on the murder charge and he was formally acquitted. He pleaded guilty to disposing of the body and was sentenced to twelve years in prison.

Hume served his time in Wakefield and Dartmoor, and was released on 1 February 1958. While he was in prison, Cynthia obtained a divorce. Hume had one saleable asset – his story, but when he approached the newspapers it became obvious that the only way he could make real money was to confess to the murder of Stanley Setty. Under the rules of double jeopardy he could not be tried again for the crime. In June 1958 the sensational tale appeared in the *Sunday Pictorial*. Claiming that he was 'getting the needle with Setty', partly because of the incident where Setty had kicked his dog but also because he suspected Setty of having secret assignations with Cynthia, he said that his rage

had finally boiled over when he came home and found Setty in his own living room. A quarrel erupted and he had gone into the hall and taken a German SS dagger which hung on the wall with the intention of frightening the other man. Setty had taken a swing at him and they had grappled, rolling on the floor, with Hume stabbing at Setty. The fight lasted only two minutes and the larger man suddenly slumped and coughed.

Hume had then dragged the body into the kitchen, pushed it into the coal cupboard and covered it with a piece of felt. After tidying up, he drove Setty's car to Cambridge Terrace Mews and left it there. During the night he formulated a plan. The next day, after his wife had gone out with the baby, he set to work with a hacksaw and knife. He had just an hour and a half to complete the task before Mrs Stride arrived. The head was placed in a box, the legs and most of the clothes were in another parcel, and the torso was wrapped in felt and blankets. The parcels were weighted with rubble and lead. It was only then, he claimed, that he saw how much cash Setty was carrying, but it was stained with blood and he had to burn most of it. Leaving the torso in the coal cupboard he took the other two packages to Elstree, where he hired the aircraft and ditched them. They sank rapidly. With the first part of the plan successfully carried out he intended to dispose of the torso in the same way, but here he encountered a problem. The large torso was hard to push out of the plane, and as he struggled, the outer wrapping, which included the lead weights, came away. The torso floated. In his confession Hume confirmed that Mac, Greenie and The Boy had never existed. He had based their descriptions on the three Scotland Yard officers who had questioned him.

Hume, calling himself John Bird, went to Switzerland, where, posing as a test pilot, he started a whirlwind romance with divorcee Trudi Sommer. He soon ran through his money and planned a series of bank robberies. His first was back in England in August, where he robbed the Midland Bank at Brentford, after shooting the cashier. After another small robbery in November he returned to Switzerland, where in January 1959 he tried to rob the Gewerbe Bank, Zurich, wounding one of the clerks and fatally shooting a taxi driver who tried to tackle him as he escaped. He was found guilty of murder and sentenced to life imprisonment with hard labour in the harsh environment of Regensdorf Jail. On 20 August 1976, calling himself Brian Donald Brown, he was deported to Britain, where he was immediately confined to Broadmoor.

3

BEXLEY

The Erith Mystery

Erith, on the banks of the Thames, was once a small village where ships paused to load and unload cargo and ballast on their way to and from the Port of London. A pier was opened in 1842, and in 1849 the arrival of the railway linked the fast growing little town with central London. By 1856 Erith was enjoying increasing popularity as a pleasant resort for day-trippers, and becoming an important centre of the engineering industry. Even so, in November 1856 the *Daily News* described Erith as 'this usually quiet village'. Previously notorious only as haunt of smugglers, Erith had become the scene of a remarkably brutal murder.

At a quarter past 11 on the morning of Saturday, 8 November 1856, a working man called Thomas Sewell was walking up the broad avenue skirted with ancient trees leading to Lesnes House, Lesnes Park, property of the Lord of the Manor, Captain (later Colonel) Wheatley. In an area known as Park Spring Copse, Sewell found the body of a short, powerfully built young man in some brushwood amongst a clump of trees about fifty yards from the road. The body, which was lying in a pool of drying blood, was quite cold, and the man was obviously dead. A carpenter's gouge, covered in blood, was in the hand of the deceased. A blue coat and grey cap lay a few yards away. Sewell went for help and the body was placed in a 'shell' (a kind of temporary coffin) and carried to the Erith dead-house where corpses dragged from the river were taken to await identification. News of the discovery spread through the village, and a great number of people came to the dead-house to view the body, but no one could identify the deceased. In his pockets were a week old railway ticket from Waterloo to Wandsworth, three halfpence in money and a catalogue of a sale in York Road, Battersea, dated September 27 1855. Clearly he was not a local man.

The avenue, Erith, 2009.

When it was known that a weapon had been found in the hand of the deceased, many people assumed that it was a case of suicide. Perhaps this was the reaction the desperate killer had hoped for, but as soon as the body was stripped it became apparent that murder had been committed.

Dr Parkinson Oates, a physician of Erith, examined the body and found sixteen stab wounds in the chest. Some were superficial, but eight had penetrated the heart. One wound, three inches deep, was so large that a portion of the left lung protruded. There was also an extensive fracture at the back of the head, the result of two violent blows. Part of the skull the size of an egg had been beaten into the brain.

The investigation was placed in the hands of Sergeant Ebbs and detective officer James William Crouch of the R division stationed at Erith.

When the inquest opened on Thursday 13 November the body had still not been identified, but later that day the family of the deceased man arrived to view the body and confirm his identity. He was 23-year-old George Carter, described by his friends as 'quiet and inoffensive', who had left his home in good health and spirits on 7 November, with at least £50 in gold on his person. His family were market gardeners of Wandsworth and on the death of his father in 1855 Carter had inherited some property. The fortune had proved his undoing. Carter had become a spendthrift, 'fond of resorting to taverns and the society of unfortunate women.' Since he had come into wealth he had not followed any occupation, and had been subsisting on money advanced to him by the executors of his father's will. Even the profligate Carter must have known that this life of ease would not last forever, and he had been planning to go to Australia to join Samuel Gardner, the husband of his cousin Eliza, who was seeking his fortune in the gold mines. In the days prior to his death he had been looking for a suitable ship.

Carter had been lodging with Eliza in Plough Lane Battersea. On the morning of Friday 7 November he had left the house in the company of a friend, 26-year-old Thomas Cartwright Worrell. Carter, perhaps with his forthcoming voyage in mind, was wearing a dark blue naval-style coat known as a pea-jacket, and a grey cap with black silk braid. Eliza thought that her cousin was only going out for a short time, but he did not return. It was not unusual for him to stay out overnight so she was neither worried nor surprised when he was not home that evening. She told the police that Worrell had called at her house at about five o'clock on the Saturday evening asking if George had come home. She said that he hadn't and asked where he had left George. Worrell said he had last seen him in York Road, Battersea, near the Builders' Arms, George having said he was going to Chelsea to see 'a pullet of his', meaning a woman of the town.

Worrell and Carter had been very much in each other's company for some time until Worrell's marriage in June. Worrell had then chosen to spend more of his time with his young bride, but a few weeks before Carter's death the two men had been seen together again. Eliza was not aware of any business Carter had in Erith.

Worrell had been brought up in Wandsworth. His father was a carpenter and it had been intended that the son should follow this trade, but Worrell had hoped for a faster route to wealth. He had visited the gold fields of both California and Australia, and after making a second trip to Australia he returned to England in 1855 with a small amount of money which he had since spent. He married Lydia Yexley, the daughter of a calico printer, in June 1856, and the couple lived in the upstairs apartments of 24 Clayton Place, Kennington. With his fortunes at a low ebb, Worrell had recently been thinking of returning to Australia.

On 15 November, Police Sergeant Underhill of the V division, Battersea, received orders from the Erith police to find Worrell, and visited him at his home the following morning. Worrell told him that on Thursday 6 November he had taken a cab to Battersea. Carter had afterwards engaged the same cab and they had both gone to the docks. Later that day, Carter had dined with him at his house and afterwards had accompanied him and his wife to the theatre. At 11 p.m. that night Carter said goodbye to them both at the White Horse, Kennington.

Worrell confirmed that at 10 a.m. on the morning of 7 November he had called for Carter at his Plough Lane lodgings. He added that Carter had told him that the previous night he had left his money for safekeeping at a public house. He said he had last seen Carter in York Road, but knew of someone who had seen Carter about two hours after they had parted company.

When the police checked Worrell's story, however, suspicions deepened. Carter had been in the Colville Tavern on Queens Road on the Thursday night and had left only part of his money – £8 10s – with one of the barmaids, but he had called for it the following morning and it had been returned to him. The person who Worrell said had seen Carter on the Friday denied that there had been any such sighting.

The police interviewed cab driver Abraham Jacobs, who said he was on the cab rank near the Horns Tavern at 10 a.m. on Friday 7 November when Worrell, whom he knew, engaged the cab to drive him to Battersea Fields. Jacobs had no doubt about the date, which contradicted Worrell's account, as he was about to apply for a summons that day against a man who had refused to pay a fare. After a number of stops for refreshment, Worrell asked Jacobs to stop at the Prince's Head, where they picked up another fare, a man Jacobs did not know but who he remembered was dressed in a cap and a pea-jacket. Shown Carter's coat and cap, Jacobs identified them as those worn by Worrell's companion. Worrell then told Jacobs to drive them to London Bridge station, where both men got out. It was then about midday. Henry Archer, a bricklayer's labourer of Battersea, knew both Worrell and Carter well, and had seen them both in the cab between 11 a.m. and midday on the Friday.

The London train arrived in Erith at about 1 p.m. Mrs Elizabeth Perkins, who lived at 3 Park Spring Terrace, had once lived in Battersea and knew both Worrell and Carter. From the back window of her house she could see the avenue leading to Lesnes Hall and the copse where the body was later found. Shortly after the arrival of the London train she looked out of the window and saw two men walking up to the avenue. Although she only saw their backs she thought one of them was George Carter, as he had a 'rather peculiar' walk. He was wearing a dark blue jacket.

Worrell was back home by 3 p.m. on 7 November and an hour later he engaged Jacobs again, this time to drive himself and his wife from his house to the City of London theatre that night.

The police now believed that Worrell and Carter had travelled together by train to Erith, a journey of forty minutes, and walked to the avenue no more than a mile away, where Worrell committed the murder, giving him ample time to be back in London to change or dispose of any bloodstained clothing and see his wife at 3 p.m. They had also identified the murder weapon. John Mayo, a Wandsworth carpenter, confirmed that the gouge found in Carter's hand was his property. Three months before he had lent it to a carpenter who was employed by Charles Worrell, Thomas' father, and it had not been returned. Charles Worrell confirmed that his son had visited him on 7 November and also that he had previously been to Erith.

On 20 November, Worrell was arrested by Sergeant Ebbs and delivered to Greenwich police station, where he was thoroughly searched. In his possession were three and a half sovereigns, a gold watch and chain, two gold rings, and two penknives. A sealed letter was found in Worrell's pocket book and this was opened and read. It was addressed to his parents, and included the words:

> ...the talk about Carter's affair has so preyed upon my mind that I scarcely know what I am about sometimes, but I write to inform you of my innocence in that affair. But there seems to have been a sort of web worked round me that I scarcely can get clear from, but God knows I am innocent of the crime they would make me guilty of, and so I can't think of walking about. When people have such an opinion of me as that, it is too much for me, so I mean to end my days by taking poison.

His apartments were searched and ten gold sovereigns were found in a locked drawer, along with two small bottles, one containing laudanum, the other powdered opium.

The charge of murder was read over to Worrell and he replied in a low voice, almost a whisper, that he was innocent. He was placed in a cell together with a 13-year-old boy. Worrell was an obvious suicide risk and the police watched him and spoke to him at regular intervals. He was very despondent, saying that he could not bear to live with the charge hanging over him and intended to kill himself. Inspector Wilson tried to reassure him that he was only charged on suspicion and if he was innocent he would be able to prove it. Worrell was not confident of being able to clear his name. He said that it was 'the mistake of a day' that had brought him there as two witnesses had said he had been in the cab with Carter on 7 November and not the day before as he had said, when he had gone to the docks with Carter to help him look for a ship. Wilson had the

THE MURDER AT ERITH.

Torchlight Interment of Worrell, the supposed Murderer of Mr. Carter.

On Thursday night, at 10 o'clock, a performance, in accordance with one of those remnants of the barbarous ages—viz., the interment of the corpse of a *felo de se*, by torchlight, in unconsecrated ground—took place at the Shooter's hill Cemetery, on the Dover road. The body was that of Thomas Cartwright Worrell, the supposed murderer of Mr. George Carter, of Battersea.

At the conclusion of the inquiry before Mr. Carttar, the coroner, on Wednesday evening, and when the jury returned their verdict of *felo de se*, the coroner at once issued his warrant for the interment of the deceased, it being imperative, in all such cases, that the burial should take place between the hours of nine and twelve o'clock at night.

In accordance with this warrant, Mr. Superintendent Mallalieu adopted the necessary means for carrying out the order of the coroner, and Mr. Burridge, of High street, Deptford, (the parish undertaker), was at once communicated with and ordered to make the necessary arrangements.

At a quarter past eight o'clock on Thursday evening, a hearse drove up to the dead house at Greenwich, accompanied by a body of police, under the command of Mr. Inspector Willson, and the shell containing the corpse having been placed therein, the cavalcade proceeded to Shooter's hill Cemetery. Upon arriving at the place of interment, Mr. Burridge ordered the hearse to be drawn up to a certain part of the cemetery which is unconsecrated ground. When the persons who unfortunately had to take part in this melancholy proceeding had arrived at that particular part of the Cemetery where the interment of the deceased was intended to take place, there was a very large concourse of persons, many of whom had been attracted by curiosity, and others out of friendship towards the deceased, they believing that he was innocent of the crime imputed to him.

In accordance with the instructions previously received, the pit in the unconsecrated part of the Cemetery (ten feet deep) had been prepared, and when the cavalcade arrived, the parochial authorities of the parish of Greenwich, who are bound to take part in the proceedings, were present, having previously arrived in carriages.

All preliminaries having been arranged, and a dead silence prevailing, the hearse was drawn up close to the spot where the hole had been dug, and the shell containing the corpse of the wretched suicide and supposed murderer, was hurled into the pit which had been dug for its reception, being deprived, in consequence of his own act and his supposed crime, of those religious services which every man, however base may be his acts, or vile his life, always looks forward to when called to his last account.

The corpse having been deposited in the hole, the grave-digger proceeded at once to fill up the place, and the concourse of people who had assembled dispersed quietly, evidently deeply impressed with the solemnity of the proceedings.

Report in the Borough of Greenwich Free Press of Worrell's burial, 29 November 1856.

prisoner searched again and gave orders that he was to be checked every few minutes.

Shortly after 1 a.m. Worrell was found stretched out on his bench, dead. Two small empty phials lay in the pan of the water closet. His cellmate was in the opposite corner, fast asleep. Dr Edward Downing examined the body and gave the cause of death as poisoning with prussic acid.

There were several theories as to how the phials had escaped discovery. One suggestion was that Worrell had concealed them in his boots, which had been felt externally but not removed; but the boots were close-fitting and it was thought that any bottle would have been crushed. Dr Downing thought that the phials were small enough for Worrall to have held them in his mouth, and it was recalled that the speech of the accused had been muffled when arrested. The police theory was that Worrell had hid the phials in his hair, 'of which he had an abundant crop, hanging thick and bushy about his ears.' Inspector Wilson tested this idea by asking a policeman with similar hair to place a phial behind each ear and walk about the cell, first slowly then rapidly. The policeman was then told to run, jump and finally to caper. None of this activity betrayed the presence of the phials.

Greenwich Cemetery (formerly Shooter's Hill), burial place of Thomas Cartwright Worrell.

At the inquest on Worrell, his grieving father tried to claim that Thomas had been with him at the time he was supposed to be in the cab with Carter, but close questioning revealed that he was uncertain whether the visit had been on the Thursday or the Friday. Lydia Worrell, 'a pretty ladylike young woman' was almost prostrate with grief, her appearance naturally exciting the sympathy of the court. She confirmed that they had been to the Standard Theatre with Carter on the evening of 6 November and her husband had left home at 9 a.m. the following day and had returned at 3 p.m. She described his manner afterwards as 'very strange'. The jury found that Worrell had committed suicide and that he had been sane at the time.

The inquest on George Carter was held at the Crown Hotel, Erith, and the verdict was that Carter had been murdered by Worrell. The members of the coroner's jury and seventy-six respectable householders of Erith sent a memorial to the commissioners of the Metropolitan Police commending the 'tact and extreme exertions' of PS Ebbs and PC Crouch 'in bringing to light the mysterious circumstances which originally enveloped the case and apprehending Worrell.'

On Tuesday 27 November, under the provisions of the act of parliament relating to the burial of suicides, the remains of Thomas Cartwright Worrell were interred at 10 p.m. by torchlight at Shooter's Hill Cemetery in unconsecrated ground.

4

BRENT

The Fatal Telegram

On Saturday, 28 January 1905, 65-year-old Mrs Ellen Gregory went shopping for food with her married daughter Beatrice Devereux. Thirty-one-year-old Beatrice lived at 60 Milton Avenue, Harlesden with her husband Arthur, 34, a chemist's assistant, their 5-year-old son Stanley, and twins Evelyn Lancelot and Lawrence Rowland, born in April 1903.

Beatrice was a talented pianist, a licentiate of the London College of Music. She had met Arthur in 1896 and they were married on 2 November 1898. Stanley was a sturdy little boy, but the twins, in Ellen's own words, were 'strong and healthy, only they had rickets, so they could not walk by themselves or feed themselves'. The wedding had been a love match, but by 1905 Ellen was anxious about her daughter's marriage. Although Arthur was fond of Stanley he was indifferent to the twins, something his wife found very distressing. Beatrice devoted herself to caring for the children, but money was tight and Arthur resented the extra expenditure on food necessitated by the twins' arrival.

Arthur had had a number of situations as a chemist's assistant, some of which he had obtained using forged testimonials. He did not keep these posts for long, usually being discharged for laziness. He had once served a nine-month prison sentence for fraud, and in 1903 he was again wanted by the police. He had been answering advertisements for domestic staff in the name of Annie Smith, asking to be sent the rail fare. When he received the money he would send another letter saying he couldn't come because of an accident.

Arthur's erratic employment record kept the family in permanent financial difficulties. Beatrice had once had to apply for parish relief, but Arthur had eaten the food provided for the children. Beatrice on the other hand had been known to go without food so that her children could eat. Ellen had lived with Arthur and Beatrice until June 1904, but subsequently she lived nearby and visited daily to help her daughter look after her three sons. Arthur may well have been aware that his mother-in-law thought him a poor husband and father, and he began to object to her constant presence in his home. He had once threatened to shoot her with a revolver, and had also struck Beatrice when she tried to prevent him from striking her mother. At the time of that incident Ellen had been holding one of the twins. Thereafter Ellen made sure to come to the house only when her son-in-law was out.

Since May 1904 Arthur had been working at a chemists' shop in Fernhead Road, Kilburn, earning £2 a week, but on 2 January he was given a month's notice. The manager told him that sales had not been up to expectation, but it was probably the quality or amount of Arthur's work that was at issue. Beatrice obviously knew about his duplicity in job applications, for she told her mother that she was afraid that he would not get another situation unless he made his own references. Arthur's last day at the shop was 27 January 1905, the day before Ellen and Beatrice's shopping trip.

Ellen was anxious to spend time with her daughter as she had found some work which required her to move away, and wasn't sure when she would be returning. On 28 January she said goodbye to Beatrice about two minutes walk from Milton Avenue, and never saw her alive again.

Ellen Gregory was no stranger to unhappiness. Born Ellen Fisher in 1839, she had married Charles Gregory, a solicitor six years her junior. Her twin sons, born prematurely in 1872, had died young. In 1896 Charles found himself in the bankruptcy court where it was revealed that he had been maintaining two homes, one with another woman twenty years Ellen's junior. The couple separated, and Ellen had had to live as best she could. Her son, Sydney, born in 1875, had had meningitis and although he had recovered he suffered from frequent headaches. In July 1903, after complaining of pains in the head, he disappeared, leaving a note to say he intended to drown himself. A bundle of his clothing was found on the foreshore at Plymouth Hoe. Despite this, his mother refused to believe that he was dead.

On the morning of 7 February 1905, William Garfath, the landlord's agent for 60 Milton Avenue, passed by the property and was very surprised to see boxes being loaded onto a van. He spoke to Arthur, pointing out that the rental period still had a week to run. Arthur explained that he was taking some items to a new apartment but would not be moving out of the property just yet. That evening Garfath was back in Milton Avenue and saw a second van, this time with furniture being loaded onto it. Suspecting that the family was about to abscond without paying the rent, he spoke to Arthur, who claimed that he had changed his mind since that morning and was moving out. There was a conversation about the expense of milk for the children – Arthur said they cost a lot of money and he spent half a sovereign a week on milk. He added that he did not want to be pestered by his mother-in-law, and that he had threatened to blow her brains out with a revolver if he saw her on his doorstep again. He wanted to clear out of the way so that she could not find him, and asked Garfath to tell her nothing if she came round asking after him. Arthur parted with 7s 6d for the final week's rent, and left without saying where he was going. That same evening Mrs Sarah Wells, who lived at No. 58, told Garfath that there was a fire in the back yard of No. 60, and he went to inspect it but found only smouldering remains. The next day he went all over the empty house and in the back bedroom found some sealing wax and screws, and in the front room a piece of board.

When Ellen returned to London in the middle of February she knocked on the door of 60 Milton Avenue but could get no answer. She spoke to Sarah Wells and was told that the family had gone away. Mrs Wells said that in the first few days of February she had heard sounds coming from No. 60 as if furniture was

Number 60 Milton Avenue, home of Arthur and Beatrice Devereux.

being moved around. On Saturday, 4 February, she had seen Arthur and Stanley making bonfires in the back yard. From that day onwards she had neither seen nor heard any sign of Beatrice or the twins. She had seen the vans being loaded on 7 February, and recalled that the first one had had a name on the side – Banister.

Ellen thought it strange that the family should move without leaving a forwarding address, as she and her daughter had always had a very affectionate relationship. She found Garfath and refused to be put off until he opened up the property and showed her over it. There was nothing there to suggest where the family could have gone.

Ellen had only one clue – the name Banister on the first removal van. Thomas Banister was a furniture remover at 591 Harrow Road, and Ellen went to see him but found him extremely unhelpful. He said he didn't know where the van had taken the boxes, as he had not gone out on the job himself or received any instructions in writing. Ellen suspected, as it later turned out quite correctly, that Arthur had asked Banister not to pass on a forwarding address if she made enquiries. She was convinced that Arthur had deliberately moved away in order to break off all contact between herself and her daughter. She was not, however, a lady who gave up easily. Concerned for the welfare of Beatrice and the children, Ellen made repeated return visits to Banister asking him for news. She also made local enquiries and found that Arthur had sold some of Beatrice's clothing before he left. Eventually her persistence paid off. Banister revealed that he was warehousing a tin trunk for Devereux, who would be getting in touch with him about it, and that when he did he would ask him to let his mother-in-law know where her daughter lived. This was the first that Ellen knew about the stored trunk, and a new and horrible suspicion arose. She told Banister that she thought her daughter's body must be in the trunk.

It was not, perhaps, too wild a conclusion. A trunk murder in Kensal Rise the previous year was still fresh in people's memories. George Albert Crossman had been living at 43 Ladysmith Road, occupying the upper flat, the lower one being let to a Mr and Mrs Dell. They had repeatedly complained to him of an unpleasant smell, which they had traced to a trunk in a cupboard under the stairs. Crossman had decided to remove the trunk from the premises but when Dell saw his landlord dragging the smelly box to the front door, he went and told the police he suspected that it contained human remains. When the police arrived, Crossman bolted, and they had just caught up with him in Hanover Road when he drew out a razor and cut this throat. He was dead in minutes. When the box was opened it was found to contain the decomposed remains of a woman embedded in cement.

Banister was alarmed at Ellen's suggestion, and told her he thought she was a wicked sort of woman to think such a thing. Even so, after Ellen had left he went to his warehouse at 2 Buller Road where the trunk was stored, and examined it, but could not detect any smell.

Ellen went to the police, and Banister finally supplied the address to which the boxes had been sent, 92 Harrow Road. It was found that Arthur and Stanley had taken lodgings there on Monday 6 February. On the 19th Arthur went away to a new job, asking the landlord and his wife to look after Stanley for a few weeks until the boy could be sent on to live with him. His new address was the chemist's shop of Mr Bird of Coventry. On 24 March Stanley was sent by train to join his father. The Coventry police made discreet enquiries about the suspect, but it was not until 13 April that Inspector Edward Pollard and Sergeant Cole went to Buller Road with Thomas Banister to examine the trunk. Arthur had told Banister that it contained books and chemicals, but on shaking it there was no vibration, so Pollard ordered it to be opened. A piece of wooden board formed an inner lid, which covered the whole of the contents of the box, and was fastened with screws and a layer of glue, hermetically sealing the interior. Pollard forced open this second lid, and saw some tablecloths and a quilt, covered with a thick layer of glue. He pulled them away, put his hand down and felt a child's head. He immediately sent an officer to wire the Coventry police and another to inform the coroner. The box was taken to Kilburn mortuary, where it was found to contain the bodies of Beatrice and her twin sons. They were sealed in so well that there had been very little decomposition. Alfred was arrested at the chemist's shop and on the following day Inspector Pollard and Sergeant Cole came to Coventry to collect him.

Pollard cautioned Arthur and told him that the bodies of his wife and children had been found in the trunk and that he was going to be charged with murder. Although the cause of death had not yet been ascertained it was thought to be poison. As they returned to London by train, Arthur asked Pollard if he had opened the trunk and when Pollard replied that he had, Arthur said, 'On opening it you did not smell anything?' Pollard said, 'No.'

'No, you would not,' replied Arthur, 'because I prepared the glue with boric acid to prevent the fungi growing, otherwise they would have decomposed and smelt . . . I had in my mind at the time a recent case, but the cement in that case was bound to give way, but I thought of a better plan.'

The prisoner was unusually cheerful for a man in his position. Pollard got a luncheon basket for him and Arthur also enjoyed a cigar and chatted amiably with the officers. At Harlesden police court he made a statement:

I, Arthur Devereux, hereby declare that one evening towards the end of January or beginning of February last, after having been out for a few hours with my child Stanley, I returned to find my wife and twins lying dead in their beds, evidently, to my mind, having died from poison taken or administered. Rather

Beatrice Devereux and her twin sons.

The warehouse in Buller Road where the trunk was stored.

than face an inquest I decided (with a recent trial fresh in my mind) to conceal the bodies in a trunk which I had had in my possession for about two years. This I proceeded to do at once. I missed some poisons (chloroform and morphia) which I always kept in my writing desk after leaving my last situation, in the event of my wishing to end my own life rather than face starvation. The room smelled strongly of chloroform, so I concluded that my wife had administered it to herself and children, probably also the morphia. I had had a violent quarrel with her previously to going out; also many times quite recently and during the past twelve months. I make this statement quite voluntarily, without any threats having been made or promises held out to me.

The post-mortem examination found morphine in all three bodies and it was concluded that this was the cause of death. Morphine has a bitter taste but could have been given to Beatrice in stout, which she was known to drink.

Arthur awaited his trial in Brixton Prison, where he was cheerfully confident of being able to clear himself. Five days before the trial commenced he began to behave erratically, grimacing and mumbling during interviews, making nonsense scrawls and claiming that he had helped God create the world. The prison

Arthur Devereux.

ARTHUR DEVEREUX. THE ACCUSED

medical officer concluded that Arthur was feigning insanity and certified him as sane. The trial opened at the Central Criminal Court, the Old Bailey on 26 July. Arthur stuck to the story he had given the police, and evidence was provided of a history of insanity in his family. Sydney's disappearance and Beatrice's money worries were also cited to support the idea that there was instability in the Gregory family which might have led to Beatrice taking her own life and those of the twins. The most telling evidence against Arthur was a telegram he had sent on 13 January, more than two weeks before the death of his wife and twin sons, applying for a job in Hull, in which he had described himself as a widower with one child. It took the jury just ten minutes to return a verdict of guilty.

Arthur Devereux was calm and composed as sentence of death was read out. He wrote to Ellen from prison asking that she bring up Stanley in ignorance of his father's fate, and this she promised to do. On Tuesday 15 August he was executed at Pentonville Prison. Mrs Gregory took sole charge of little Stanley and made a piteous plea before the magistrates at Willesden. She had spent all her remaining funds to ensure that Beatrice and her children did not have a pauper's funeral, and was now reduced to absolute poverty. A fund was set up for the assistance of Stanley Devereux, and all Arthur's property was directed to be used for the benefit of the boy. This included the tin trunk in which his mother and brothers had been sealed.

5

BROMLEY

A Scream in the Night

In January 1868 the weather in the small rural town of Bromley was unusually severe, with heavy rain and gusting winds, and Saturday the 18th was the coldest and bleakest day of the month. At 11 p.m. that night in Masons Hill, a broad thoroughfare connecting Bromley Common to the High Street, police constable John Sims was called to the house of Thomas Partridge, a beershop keeper, to deal with a complaint. He found Partridge standing on the landing together with special constable Samuel Deadman. Also present were Partridge's wife, their tenant 27-year-old Jane Jackson, and a labourer called John Williams with whom she had been living. Mrs Partridge, saying that she was owed three weeks rent, wanted Sims to turn Jane out of the house. She also accused Jane of threatening to stab her. Jane, who had been drinking but was not incapably drunk, threw herself to her knees in great distress and begged Mrs Partridge's pardon, asking to be allowed to stay until Monday.

'I cannot,' said Mrs Partridge, 'you have made such threats against me.'

'How can you tell such lies about me?' demanded Jane.

Sims decided not to interfere, deeming it to be a civil rather than a criminal matter, and left the premises, but remained outside to watch. Eventually Jane left the house followed by Deadman. Williams seemed unconcerned, except that as Jane left he asked her what she had done with a half sovereign she had had. 'I have lost it,' she replied.

From across the road, Sarah Head, a gardener's wife, saw Jane standing on the steps of Partridge's house and Deadman pushing her down them and into the street. Jane protested that she had lodged there for some time and Partridge said he didn't care, she would not lodge there that night. Sarah saw both Partridge and Deadman follow Jane as she walked down the street and when Jane exclaimed, 'Don't follow me; I don't want you to follow me

The Tigers Head, Masons Hill, Bromley. (By kind permission of the proprietor)

about!' Deadman said, 'I shall.' Jane made a desperate attempt to return to the beershop, insisting that she would stay in the house that night, but the two men prevented her from entering.

At about twenty-five minutes to midnight Jane arrived at the Tigers Head public house, Masons Hill, where the publicans were Ann and William Cook. Crying, she told Ann that she had been turned out of her lodgings and had lost half a sovereign. She drank half a pint of porter and two pennyworth of rum. Jane seemed to have little with her except the clothes she wore and a bag over her arm. Her only jewellery was some cheap earrings and brass rings.

Ann noticed a bruise on Jane's lip and asked who had hurt her. She said that her husband (presumably John Williams) had done it. Ann saw Deadman standing outside the Tigers Head peering through the window at Jane but he did not come in. Jane begged to be allowed to sleep there that night but Ann said she could not allow it. About a quarter of an hour later Jane left.

At a quarter past midnight, Sarah Head was at home when she heard a noise outside, and went to her gate. Jane was in the street, talking to Deadman, Partridge and a mounted police sergeant. They were standing only fifty yards from Partridge's house. 'There they are again,' Sarah said to her husband. Jane was complaining bitterly to the sergeant, saying that she had been turned out of her lodgings, and then, when she had taken shelter in the closet in Partridge's yard, she had been expelled from that too. 'I did it by the orders of Partridge,' said Deadman. The sergeant, who may have felt sympathy for the woman out in the cold street with nowhere to stay, told the men they were wrong in so doing. The little group went on down the street together, the sergeant walking his horse, and Partridge said, 'What am I to do in the event of the woman coming back and doing damage?' 'Give her into custody,' said the sergeant.

The policeman left, and Sarah saw Jane trying to get back into Partridge's yard and being pushed away by Deadman. 'Don't push me, keep your hands off,' she said.

'Don't be too hard on that poor woman,' said Sarah, 'You have a wife and children of your own and don't know what they may come to.'

Sarah went indoors but at about twenty-five minutes to one, Jane came to her door and asked for lodgings. Despite her concern Sarah said she couldn't do this, and advised Jane to go across to a nearby barn where she might get shelter.

Labourer Charles Marshall, who lived next door but one to the Tigers Head, was awake that night because his wife was ill. His clock, which he knew to be a quarter of an hour fast, was just striking the hour of one, when he heard a scrambling noise in the road, with screams followed by cries of 'Murder!' in a woman's voice. The sounds continued for about five minutes. About a quarter of an hour later, he heard the noises again, and another cry of 'Murder!', which seemed this time to come from the back of his house, near a well which was in the garden of the house next door. Although he later stated that such noises were not a common occurrence, he did not trouble to see what was going on. Ann Cook also heard shrieks after 1 a.m. which came from the direction of the well. She thought the voice was Jane Jackson's. She and her husband also did nothing.

Martha Sparks, who lived at Sandfield Cottage next door to the Marshalls, and in whose garden the well was situated, heard the latch of her door rattle, and some cries of 'Murder!' at about a quarter to one. Her husband, William, was deaf and she quickly shook him awake and told him to see what was going on. He got out of bed and had a look around, and saw both Partridge and Deadman at Partridge's house. It was then about 1 a.m. At about the same time another neighbour, William Ashdown, heard a woman's voice crying out, 'You did, you villain! You did!' and then soon afterwards there were screams, and cries of 'Murder!' followed by more screams.

Edward Moss, a painter, was on his way home from Bromley station at 1 a.m. It was five or ten minutes' walk from the Tigers Head, and as he passed by he saw two men at the corner, only thirty yards from the well. One he could not identify, but the other, he was sure, was Deadman. He did not see Jane.

Ten days later the contents of a woman's bundle floated to the top of the well in the garden of Sandfield Cottage. The well was used by all the neighbours. It was circular, open at the top, 4ft in diameter, with a windlass 3ft high, and the water was 9ft deep. A grapnel was let down and caught on something heavy which initially could not be pulled up. Eventually the grapnel was shifted to one side and this time a body was brought up, the grapnel having fastened about the chest. It was Jane Jackson, and she had clearly been dead for some days.

Before leaving her lodgings, Jane had taken with her some money and a few things she valued, including a portrait of her mother, which, along with her bonnet, were missing when her body was found, though the well was specially dragged for them.

Local doctor Walter Thomas Beeby made a post-mortem examination, and found nothing which led him to conclude that Jane was the victim of a crime. He gave the cause of death as drowning. There was a great deal of mud and sand in the hair but little on the boots, from which he inferred that she had gone into the well head first. The body had been so long in the water it was hard to make out marks of violence, although there was an injury to the head which could have been the result of a blow.

The inquest jury considered three possible theories of Jane's death: accident, suicide or murder. If it had been an accident or suicide it was thought that she would have gone down feet first, but the screams clearly refuted any suggestion of suicide. The jury remained undecided, and returned a verdict of 'found drowned', which prompted a suggestion in the newspapers that the proceedings had been poorly conducted. Inspector Tanner was sent down from the commissioners of police, and as a result of his enquiries Partridge and Deadman were arrested on a charge of murder. When the Partridges' house was searched, one of Jane's earrings was found in the possession of Mrs Partridge. Mrs Partridge claimed that Jane had left the earrings behind, but according to Ann Cook, Jane had been wearing them after she left, and Jane's sister was adamant that Jane only owned one pair of earrings.

The police took statements from both Partridge and Deadman, whose claim that they had not seen Jane since turning her out of the closet shortly after midnight contradicted the evidence of other witnesses. A young woman who lodged in Partridge's house told the police that when the two men returned to the house they told her they had left Jane talking to the mounted policeman, whereas the policeman stated that when he had departed he left Jane with the two men. On the fatal night, asked where Jane was, Deadman said, 'Oh she won't come back here no more.' The next day he had claimed that Jane had slept in the barn all night.

Little was known about the dead woman other than that she had been in domestic service before going to live with Williams some two years previously, and was shortly expecting to receive a legacy. The *Bromley Record* published an article on 1 March said to be the results of the paper's own efforts in collecting information. The source of this information was undoubtedly Mrs Partridge, who, it transpired, did not hesitate to put words into other people's mouths when it suited her. The article stated that Jane had made her living as a prostitute for the last seven years, while, 'None could be much worse than she for foul and abusive language.' It was also claimed that Jane had threatened suicide on many occasions, and as soon as she went missing her sisters had said they expected to find she had drowned herself. The legacy story was dismissed as 'a fabrication to fill the newspapers.'

On the following day the case was heard by the county justices of Kent, and Jane's sister, Susannah, gave an entirely different picture of the deceased. She confirmed that Jane had been in domestic service until two years ago, after which she had cohabited with John Williams. Asked if she had told Mrs Partridge that her sister had threatened suicide, Susannah denied that she had ever done so. She said that Jane had never used foul language, and it was true that the family would have some money coming to them in nine months when her brother came of age.

Mrs Partridge had also claimed that Henry Bennett of Mason's Hill, who had witnessed Jane being turned out of her lodgings, had commented as he passed by that it was a disgrace to have such a woman in the house. Bennett denied that he had ever spoken to Mrs Partridge on that occasion. Mr Allsop, who appeared for the prisoners, said that Jane, who 'had nowhere to lay her head', had doubtless been hunted about by the prisoners, and goaded on into a state of desperation, which, coupled with drink, was the means of her getting into the well either by accident or suicide. Despite this plea the prisoners were committed for trial. The case excited such considerable local interest that the *Record* published a special supplement on 5 March.

The trial was held on 12 and 13 March at Maidstone Crown Court before Mr Justice Byles. The prosecution stated that it was clear that all the witnesses who described the screams and cries of murder were talking of one and the same incident. Only one witness had recognised Jane's voice, but in any case

SUPPLEMENT TO
THE
BROMLEY RECORD

No. 118.   MARCH 5, 1868.   PRICE ONE PENNY.

CHARGE OF MURDER
AGAINST
PARTRIDGE AND DEADMAN.

THE great excitement which this mysterious affair is causing, has induced us to perform our promise, made a long time ago, to issue a Supplement to our Journal should it be at any time be required. It would not assist the due course of justice were we to express our opinion as to the evidence against the prisoners. Indeed, we have been advised it would be unwise to do so. Therefore we have given the depositions without comment, leaving the public to form their own opinion. We may, however, state that the trial will take place during the present month at Maidstone, and that the result will appear in our next.

The two prisoners were brought up at the Town Hall on Wednesday morning, before C. F. Devas, Esq., and from the serious nature of the charge, and the position of the accused, the Hall was nearly filled by the inhabitants.

Charles Marshall of Mason's hill, said—I remember the morning of the 19th January last. I was in bed about a quarter to one. I could not say exactly. I heard squeaks as if a woman was squeaking, and then I heard cries of murder. My house is next door but one to Cook's, the Tiger's Head. The cries of murder appeared to proceed from the middle of the turnpike road, right opposite to my window. I heard the cry twice, and then there was sounds of scuffling. About a quarter of an hour afterwards I heard the voice at the back of the house; she holloa'd once there. The cry was "murder" plain. I did not get out of bed. I was present when the body of deceased, Maria Jackson, was got out of the well. The well from which we took the body was at the back of my house, at or near the place from which the last cry proceeded. The well is about thirty feet from my house, and is in the adjoining garden.

By Mr. Alsop—I was examined before the coroner, and I stated to him all I have stated to-day. I have been residing at Mason's hill about five months, before that at Mooreland's road for four or five years; but I have been about here for fifteen or sixteen years. I left my work on Saturday and went home between five and six o'clock in the evening, and afterwards came to Bromley shopping. I went to the Rising Sun about eight o'clock and played skittles, but drank nothing, and left there between ten and eleven, and went home, and got there a little after eleven; I am not sure to half an hour. It was about half-past eleven, but I will not swear at all to the time, as I do not know exactly.

I went to bed about a quarter or twenty minutes to twelve; I could not say for a little while, but it was pretty near twelve o'clock. I lay awake, as my wife was unwell. I heard the cries first when my clock struck one, but that being a quarter of an hour fast is the reason for my saying it was a quarter to one. I first heard squeaks as if there was a row, and directly after the squeaks I heard the cries of murder. I said to my wife there is a row outside, and she said I would not get up if I were you. The noise at a quarter to one did not last more than five minutes. I am quite sure it was a woman's voice I heard; I did not hear any other voices; but I heard scrambling on the road as if there were two or three persons. She called out murder twice in the front and once in the back, and there was an interval of about a quarter of an hour between the cries.

Susannah Sophia Jackson, of 22, Tottenham street, Tottenham Court road, said—The deceased was my sister. I saw her body and identified it; her age was twenty-seven. I knew that she cohabited with John Williams, and that they lodged at the beer house kept by Partridge. I had seen her there, as I had been down there two or three times, and I was there on the Wednesday previous to her death. My sister (the deceased) appeared to live happily with Williams, and, as far as I know, she was a very steady young woman, and had been in several situations. It is about two years since she left service. The ear-ring now produced I gave to my sister, when she was in London about a fortnight before her death. She was wearing the same rings when I saw her on the previous Wednesday, and she had no other ear-rings then. The ear-rings were odd ones, one belonged to me and one to my sister. I think that I gave 1s. 6d. for the ear-rings.

By Mr. Alsop—My sister never complained to me of Williams striking her, and I never heard them have any words; she told me they never had except about the landlady. Since the death of my sister I have never said to Mrs. Partridge that she had threatened to commit suicide, and that I knew she was treated very kindly there. From the way in which I saw her living with Williams I should be astonished to know that he had given her a black eye.

Mr. Alsop here questioned the witness as to her places of residence, &c., with a view to her respectability, and Mr. Devas interfered and said that no insinuations should be made, but Mr. Alsop denied having done so purposely, and the previous line of cross-examination was continued.

The witness added that her sister had been living with Williams from eighteen months to two years, and I believe that they became acquainted by her being down at his home. I never heard my sister make use of bad language, and she was very steady. I spent the whole of the Wednesday with my sister, and she was very comfortable with Williams. We are supposed to have some money coming to us, but not until my brother is of age, which is in about nine months hence. The property is the largest windmill in Sheerness.

Walter Thomas Beeby, a surgeon practising at Bromley, said—I was called in to make a *post mortem* it was known that she was near the spot at the time and no other woman was. These sounds pointed clearly to a murder, at or near the well, and the prisoners were near the spot at the time. The contradictions in the stories of the accused as well as the presence of the earring in Partridge's house were strong evidence against the pair.

There were no witnesses for the defence, which consisted solely of the speech made by defence counsel Mr Pearce. He suggested that Jane, intending to seek shelter in the barn, had accidentally fallen into the well, and that because the body had been found there, the witnesses had persuaded themselves that this was where the screams came from. Pearce urged the jury to disbelieve the evidence of Edward Moss, who had seen Partridge and Deadman together shortly after 1 a.m., and Ann Cook, who had testified that Jane was wearing her earrings when she called at the Tigers Head, in fact Pearce's entire defence was that the jury should disbelieve all the prosecution witnesses but believe the story of Mrs Partridge. He submitted that the prisoners had no motive to commit murder.

Men have been hanged on far flimsier evidence than that offered against Partridge and Deadman, however there was still Mr Justice Byles' summing-up to come. He advised the jury that 'nothing was more dangerous than evidence as to place and time', especially with regard to sounds heard at night. 'It was a very dark and boisterous night, and it was a harsh thing to turn the poor woman out. . .', but there was no evidence of any knowledge or ill will which could lead the prisoners to put the woman to death. There was no evidence to show when she had got into the well. He placed some weight on the statement of Sarah Head, who had told Jane to go to the barn, for he thought the deceased might have fallen into the well on the way there. He failed to mention that Sarah had also heard screams, thus attributing importance to the one part of her evidence that favoured the defence, but ignoring the rest on the grounds of unreliability. After the judge had alluded to the possibility of suicide or of murder by a complete stranger, and commented that he saw no inconsistency in the statements of the accused, the jurors can hardly have known what to believe. After a considerable absence the jury acquitted both prisoners. What became of Partridge and Deadman thereafter is unknown.

6
CAMDEN

Diminished Responsibility

Ruth Neilson wanted to make something of her life. Instead she made history.

Born in Rhyl in 1926, Ruth was a small, slender girl with auburn hair, who loved clothes and soon learned to make the most of her appearance. Her father, Arthur, who changed the family name from Hornby to Neilson, was a professional musician whose career had dwindled, and took out his frustrations by abusing Ruth and her sister, Muriel. When the family moved to London, Ruth discovered the world of dance halls and night clubs and was attracted to a lifestyle that must have seemed both exciting and sophisticated. She was working as a photographer's assistant at the Lyceum ballroom in the Strand when she met a Canadian soldier who took her to restaurants, bought her gifts, and talked of marriage. In September 1944 Ruth gave birth to a son, but by then she had found out that her lover had a wife and two children in Canada.

Ruth found evening work posing as a photographer's model. Sometimes she had to pose in the nude, but at £1 an hour, it was good money. Afterwards, the cameramen took her out for drinks which was how, in 1946, Ruth first went to the Court Club at 58 Duke Street and met the owner, Morris (known as 'Morrie') Conley. In post-war Britain the nightclub business was booming and Conley was always looking for attractive hostesses. Conley offered Ruth a salary of £5 a week, plus commission on the food and drink she could persuade his customers to buy. It was no secret that men who slept with the hostesses usually spent more in the club. For Ruth, who had once worked in cafés and an Oxo factory, the club was an escape from poverty, and a place in the glamorous world that had dazzled her, but there was a sordid reality beneath the glossy façade and the long hours and late nights were exhausting. In 1950 Ruth became pregnant again and had an abortion, but she had no choice but to return to work soon afterwards.

Number 58 Duke Street, site of the Court Club.

One of the club's regular customers was 41-year-old dentist George Ellis. He spent extravagantly on drink, told wild stories that no one believed and took a liking to Ruth. One night George was razor slashed across the cheek while waiting for Ruth outside a club. Ruth felt guilty as she had stood him up, and was sorry for him when he told her that his wife had left him, taking their two children. Ruth and George began to spend time together, but often argued about his excessive drinking. George eventually checked himself into Warlingham Park mental hospital for a few weeks, where he was treated for alcoholism. Ruth was not in love with George but he was a professional man who could offer her a good home and she had her son's future to consider. In November 1950, Ruth and George were married.

They moved to Southampton but the happy married life both had hoped for did not last. George started drinking again and there were frequent rows which exploded into fights and beatings, after which Ruth would go back to her mother, bruised and with bare and bloody patches on her scalp where her hair had been torn out. A few days later, driven by a desperate insecurity, she would return to George. She became obsessed with the idea that George was being unfaithful, and began checking up on his female patients.

The couple parted again, and George, who had been fired from his Southampton job because of his heavy drinking, found work in Cornwall. They were reconciled when Ruth discovered that she was pregnant. The drinking, the rows and Ruth's jealousy continued, and George booked himself back into Warlingham Park. Ruth became so convinced that her husband was having an affair that she created a scene at the hospital, and had to be forcibly sedated. Their daughter, Georgina, was born in October 1951, but after less than a year of marriage, George filed for divorce.

Ruth, now with two children to support, went back to working for Morrie Conley. She was popular, earned good money and made new friends, a younger more exciting set than the jaded businessmen she had previously entertained. They were motor racing drivers, amongst them Mike Hawthorn and David Blakely, and racing enthusiasts, one of whom was businessman Desmond Cussen. Blakely, three years younger than Ruth, made a bad first impression. She thought him pompous and arrogant.

Blakely's parents had divorced in 1940, and in the following year his mother married Humphrey Cook, who had been a well known racing driver before the war. Cook arranged for David to train as a hotel manager, but the young man's great passion was for racing cars. He had good looks and charm, but he was also fickle and immature. In 1951 he met Anthony and Carole Findlater. Anthony was an engineer and racing enthusiast, Carole a journalist. David and Anthony agreed to share the cost of racing a sports car, and David started an affair with Carole. The affair ended when Carole told Anthony, but the two men remained united by their racing project.

When David's father died leaving each of his children £7,000, David started cultivating the life he had always wanted, that of a playboy. His absences from the hotel job led to his dismissal in October 1952.

By then, Ruth had become the manageress of Conley's Little Club. She was happy, always smartly dressed, and for a touch of extra glamour she bleached her auburn hair to peroxide blonde. David Blakely had recently announced his engagement to the daughter of a wealthy businessman, but when he met Ruth again at the Little Club, they started an affair. Ruth lived in a flat above the club, and after evenings of heavy drinking, David stayed with her overnight. Ruth became pregnant again and had an abortion in February 1954.

By the spring of that year David was taking Ruth out, to the cinema, the theatre and race meetings, and she was introduced to the Findlaters. It was a hectic lifestyle, and in May she arranged for her daughter to be adopted.

Ruth soon tired of David's capricious behaviour and while he was away racing at Le Mans, she decided to end the relationship. Desmond Cussen was in love with her and although she didn't return his feelings, he seemed like a more stable prospect, and the two were soon sharing a bed. When David returned, however, he broke off his engagement, was more attentive to Ruth than ever, and proposed marriage. It was only then that Ruth's emotions were engaged, and with those, her jealousy.

Both Ruth and David were having money problems, David because he had spent most of his inheritance and Ruth because she wanted to send her son to boarding school. The ever devoted Desmond helped Ruth with the fees and Ruth helped David to pay his way at the club. Ruth needed to improve her commissions which meant flirting with customers, and David found this hard to tolerate. There were frequent drunken rows, and Ruth was often covered in bruises.

In the spring of 1955, Ruth's parents were living in two rooms in a house where Mrs Neilson was a cook and domestic while Arthur was working as an animal attendant in a laboratory. David Blakely, the arrogant playboy, public-school educated, with a well-connected family and the prospect of making a fashionable marriage, must have been well aware of the social gulf between his family and Ruth's and never seriously meant to marry her. Ruth, however, believed that David's offer of marriage was genuine, thinking that she only needed to break away from the world of nightclubs to become an acceptable match. Desmond suggested she move out of the club and into his flat and she was able to square this with David by agreeing that they could sleep at a nearby hotel.

By Christmas 1954 David was confiding to friends that he wanted to end the relationship with Ruth and she was telling her friends that she was sure David was being unfaithful to her. David had a flat at Penn, Buckinghamshire, and when Ruth got Desmond to drive her there to watch him, she found that he often spent his lunchtimes in the company of an attractive married woman. There were more fights and more bruises.

Early in February 1955, Ruth and David had another serious fight in Desmond's flat and Anthony Findlater and his friend Clive Gunnell, in a response to a telephoned appeal from David, drove there to find the couple drunk, bruised and scarred. When David tried to leave, Ruth, convinced that he was ending the relationship, created a hysterical scene in the street and was only calmed down with some difficulty. Ruth was taken to the Middlesex Hospital for her injuries to be treated.

On the following day Ruth ordered Desmond to take her to look for David. At the Findlaters home, 29 Tanza Road, they saw David, Clive and the Findlaters driving off to the Magdala public house. They waited outside until the party emerged and when David drove off on his own, Ruth first tried to find him at the flat of a woman in London she was convinced he was sleeping with and then at Penn, where he was able to avoid her. Eventually they caught up with him and Desmond forced David to apologise to Ruth.

The couple were reconciled, David explaining that he was unable to cope with Ruth living at Desmond's flat. Ruth borrowed money from Desmond for the rent of a flat at 44 Egerton Gardens and she and David moved in, calling themselves Mr and Mrs Ellis. Despite this apparent resolution, David told his friends that he was afraid of Ruth. He said she had once tried to use a carving knife during a row and he was convinced she was getting gangster friends to follow him. Ruth continued to get Desmond to help her shadow David's movements, and fresh rows erupted over the woman at Penn.

At the end of February there was an argument over a dance for the British Racing Drivers Club at the Hyde Park Hotel. David did not want to take Ruth because his group included his mother and stepfather and he did not want them to meet the peroxide blonde hostess with whom he was having an affair. He told Ruth he wasn't going. When Ruth got Desmond to take her, David had to admit that he would be there. Things seemed amicable that evening but when Ruth drank a toast to her divorce she may well have sensed from David's reaction that he did not want to marry her.

In the middle of March Ruth was pregnant again. When she discovered that David was still seeing the woman at Penn, there was a fight, during which he took her by the throat and hit her in the stomach. On 28 March Ruth miscarried. In the days that followed she looked depressed and ill, and friends who saw her believed she was on the edge of a nervous breakdown. She was also drinking a great deal.

David entered his car for a race on 2 April, but it broke down during a practice run. He didn't have the money to repair it, and accused Ruth of bringing him bad luck. On 3 April, Ruth was confined to bed, running a high fever, but four days later she had recovered enough to go to the cinema with David. On 8 April David was drinking with the Findlaters at the Magdala, saying, 'I can't stand it any longer. I want to get away from her.' He dared not go to Penn in case Ruth followed him, so the Findlaters agreed that he could stay the weekend with them. When he failed to appear at Egerton Gardens Ruth, who had convinced herself that David was sleeping with the Findlaters' 19-year-old nanny, made repeated phone calls to Tanza Road. Sometimes a voice answered, but then the person on the other end would hang up. Sometimes Ruth heard giggling and thought that they were laughing at her. Eventually the Findlaters took the phone off the hook. At 2 a.m. Ruth got Desmond to drive her to Tanza Road, where she saw David's car outside. She called from a phone box and someone hung up. She rang the doorbell again and again, and when she didn't get a reply, her anger and frustration boiled over and she pushed in the car windows with a torch. The police were summoned, and told Ruth to go home. On Saturday morning Ruth, again chauffeured by Desmond, was back at Tanza Road, keeping watch and remained there until after midnight.

On the Sunday Ruth continued to phone, but David did not contact her. She sat drinking Pernod with Desmond, saying how badly David had treated her, and eventually she got Desmond to take her to Hampstead, where he left her at the top of Tanza Road.

David had been enjoying some drinks at the Findlaters' that evening, and at about 9 p.m. he and Clive drove to the Magdala to get some more beer and cigarettes. When Ruth arrived at Tanza Road the car had already gone, but she guessed where David might be and found his car outside the Magdala. As David and Clive emerged Ruth approached them. She called out 'David' but he took no notice and she drew a heavy black revolver from her bag. She shot him twice but he was still able to run around the car to escape, and she chased him and shot him again. One shot went wide and hit a passer-by, Mrs Gladys Yule, on the thumb. David collapsed on the footpath near the door of the saloon bar. Clive was briefly frozen with amazement and disbelief. When he was able to move he found David lying face down on the pavement with Ruth standing over him, still firing. The revolver clicked. It was empty. Ruth was pale, but calm, almost emotionless. 'Now go and call the police,' she said. Alan Thompson, an off-duty constable who was at the Magdala that night, took charge of the gun and placed Ruth under arrest. David Blakely was taken to New End Hospital, where he was found to be dead.

At 11 p.m. on Monday 11 April Ruth Ellis was charged with murder at Hampstead police station. She awaited her trial in Holloway Prison, where she maintained her cool demeanour, saying that she was perfectly sane and that her intention had been to kill. The case, involving as it did a blonde model and a racing driver, became a press sensation.

Ruth claimed that the gun had been given to her three years previously by a man whose name she could not remember, but she was obviously protecting someone. She knew nothing about guns, but the weapon had been recently oiled and cleaned.

At her trial, which opened on 20 June, Mr Melford Stevenson for the defence submitted that the provocation Ruth had received had affected her mind to such an extent that it justified a verdict of manslaughter. A psychologist was

The Magdala public house. (By kind permisison of the proprietor)

called to testify that when Ruth killed Blakely she was 'very disturbed', but he also stated that she was sane and mentally capable of forming the intent to kill. Ruth showed little emotion under questioning, except when she was shown a photograph of David, when she shed tears but quickly recovered her composure.

Mr Christmas Humphreys for the Crown approached to cross-examine.

'Mrs Ellis, when you fired that revolver at close range into the body of David Blakely, what did you intend to do?'

She replied, 'It was obvious that when I shot him I intended to kill him.'

Humphreys sat down.

If the jurors had wavered towards a verdict of manslaughter this feeling was quickly disposed of by Mr Justice Havers, who directed them that the evidence did not support that verdict. If they were satisfied that Ruth had fired the shots intentionally then they should find her guilty of murder. It was, he advised them, no defence to say that she was jealous or had been ill-treated. As the law then stood, this was correct. The jury deliberated for only fourteen minutes before finding Ruth guilty of murder. Ruth accepted her death sentence calmly, and made it clear that she did not want to petition for a reprieve.

Ruth later admitted that the gun had been given to her by Desmond Cussen, who had also driven her to Tanza Road, but Cussen always denied this. Ruth's son recalled that on 10 April, Desmond had taken a gun out of a drawer, oiled it and put it in Ruth's handbag.

Public opinion was in favour of a reprieve. Some of the letters which flooded into the newspapers were against the death penalty on principle, others stated that women should not be hanged, and many had sympathy for what Ruth had suffered at Blakely's hands. A few, swayed by the revelations about Ruth's lifestyle, were less sympathetic. At 9 a.m. on 13 July 1955, Ruth was hanged by Albert Pierrepoint.

The Findlaters divorced in 1956. George Ellis committed suicide in 1958. In 1971 when the old Holloway Prison was demolished, and later rebuilt, Ruth's remains were exhumed and re-buried at St Mary's parish church in Amersham. Her headstone reads 'Ruth Hornby'. Ruth's son, who was just 10 when she died, never recovered from his unsettled early upbringing. He committed suicide in 1982. Desmond Cussen emigrated to Australia and died in 1991.

In 2003 Ruth's daughter, Georgina, took the case to the court of appeal asking for the conviction to be reduced to manslaughter on the grounds of provocation, but the verdict was upheld on the grounds that Ruth had been correctly convicted on the laws as they stood at the time.

Ruth Ellis made history not only because she was the last woman to be hanged in Britain. The case was instrumental in the changes made to the Homicide Act of 1957, in which it became possible to make a plea of diminished responsibility.

7

CITY

Faithful unto Death

The ancient thoroughfare of Houndsditch lies just inside the City of London, where it joins Bishopsgate Street and Aldgate High Street. In 1910 it was a busy commercial centre, cutting through a crowded network of smaller byways, the living and working spaces of both dealers and manufacturers. Many of the area's inhabitants were families from Eastern Europe. In some of the narrow lanes and alleys of the old city, the English language was almost unknown. Conversations were in German, Russian, Lettish, Yiddish or French. Although for the most part this new population was hardworking and honest, it was inevitable that some Londoners should view the recent arrivals with concern, and claim that government immigration policies were too lax. Many believed that the crowded tenements had become swarming nests of criminals, revolutionaries and anarchists. The events of December 1910 and January 1911 would confirm the worst fears of the anti-immigration lobby and lead to a hysteria that was not to evaporate for several months.

At 44 Gold Street just off the Mile End Road, a quiet young man calling himself George Gardstein was lodging with the family of Jacob Kempler and storing supplies of chemicals and equipment in his room. Gardstein was a career criminal with anarchist leanings who always carried a gun, and had no qualms about using it. Handsome and well-dressed with a neat moustache and a confident air, Gardstein told the Kemplers that he was a student of chemistry, his studies being funded by his wealthy family. The real purpose of his experiments was to devise methods of attacking metal with acid, as a means of safe-breaking. Gardstein's mistress was attractive 23-year-old Nina Vassileva, who worked in a local cigarette factory. Nina knew how her lover made his money and the violence of which he was capable. She herself was wanted in Russia, probably for revolutionary activities.

Houndsditch. London.
The famous centre
of the
Novelties Trade.

Houndsditch.

On the evening of 30 November 1910 a 22-year-old clerk, George Richardson, was working late at 16 Houndsditch when he was approached by two men and a woman who started a casual conversation about local jewellers' shops. He later identified Gardstein as one of the men and Vassileva as the woman. The second man may well have been a young associate of Gardstein's, a Russian watchmaker and burglar, Josef Sokoloff. Gardstein was especially interested in the shop of H.S. Harris at No. 119, and wondered if Harris lived on the premises.

Number 119 Houndsditch was, as Gardstein must later have discovered, a lock-up shop. The business occupied only the front half of the ground floor, while the rear portion and upper floors were rented to another business. Neither Harris nor the other lessee lived there. To the left of No. 119, No. 118, was a dairy, and No. 117 was a shop. Number 120, on the right, was both the home and business premises of Max Weill, a fancy-goods importer, who lived with his sister and employed a maidservant. All the buildings in that section of Houndsditch backed onto a row of tenements which faced into an alley called Exchange Buildings. Each tenement had one room on each of three floors, connected by a staircase. Numbers 118 to 120 Houndsditch were back-to-back with 11 to 9 Exchange Buildings. The two sets of premises were separated by a narrow yard, except where the walls of the tenement privies backed directly onto the rear walls of the Houndsditch buildings.

Gardstein, determining to rob Harris' safe which was reputed to contain diamonds valued at £20,000, established a base of operations by bringing in an associate, jewel-robber Max Smoller, who rented tenement No. 11. Nina, Max and Josef moved in. Fritz Svaars, a young Lettish revolutionary and bank-robber, rented No. 9, where a workshop was established for the purpose of breaking through the wall and cutting open the safe. Sokoloff and Svaars acted as lookouts. Number 10 was already let, but was unoccupied after 12 December.

At 10 p.m. on the night of Friday 16 December, Max Weill returned home from visiting a friend to find his sister and maid in a state of terror. For the last forty-five minutes the sound of 'drilling and sawing and the breaking away of brickwork', as he later described it, could clearly be heard at the rear of the property. Weill decided to investigate. He peered through the front window of Harris's shop but all seemed in order. Convinced that someone was trying to break in from the rear, he reported the noise to a nearby policeman, Walter Piper, a young probationer constable. After listening to the noise Piper decided to make his own enquiries. He knew that while most of the tenements of Exchange Buildings were lock-ups, there were a few with tenants who had lived there for some time. Piper learned that No. 11 had been occupied for only three weeks by some foreigners who acted in a very secretive manner and only came out at night. The young constable boldly went and knocked on the door of No. 11, which was opened immediately by a man. Playing it cool he asked if 'the missus' was at home. The man replied in what sounded like a Russian accent, that she had gone out. Piper decided he needed back-up and, returning to Houndsditch, he met Constables Ernest Woodhams and Walter Choate. Choate and Woodhams kept watch on the premises while Piper went to Bishopsgate Street police station, where he notified Sergeant Robert Bentley and Constable Smoothey of what he had discovered. All three returned to the scene, where they were later joined by two plain clothes officers, Constables Martin and Strongman, and two more sergeants, Charles Tucker and Thomas Bryant. It was now 11.30 p.m., and the work had stopped. All was quiet.

Bentley decided to try and gain entry to No. 11. Closely followed by Bryant and Tucker and with the other men on watch, Bentley knocked on the door. The policemen were armed only with truncheons, and were therefore completely helpless in the face of what happened next, a scene of such turmoil that to this day there is disagreement about exactly who was there. A man opened the door, and, after a pause, Bentley stepped into the passage. Bryant was able to see the lower half of a man (possibly Sokoloff) standing on the staircase. Bentley asked if anyone was making a noise, which the man denied. Bentley then asked to look inside and made for the parlour door, which was open. As Bryant followed him into the passage, another man (later identified as Gardstein) rushed from the parlour firing a gun. Bentley was hit in the neck and right shoulder and fell. Bryant was also hit, but managed to get to his feet and stagger away. He was later found leaning for support against the wall of No. 10. Strongman and Tucker, despite the desperate situation, approached No. 11, and as they did so a hand holding a pistol protruded from the doorway, and more shots were fired. Woodhams ran to help Bentley, but was hit in the thigh and collapsed, then the man holding the pistol emerged from the building firing at Tucker and Strongman, who retreated. Tucker was hit and Strongman helped him away as bullets flew all around them.

Sokoloff had fled the scene, but Gardstein was out in the street with his gun, while Svaars and Smoller charged out of No. 9. Choate grappled with one of the men, was shot several times and collapsed, while Smoller fired off a wild shot which hit Gardstein in the back. Smoller and Svaars, accompanied by Vassileva, helped their wounded associate away.

Once the shooting had stopped, the scene in the little alley was one of terror and confusion as people rushed from their homes to find the bodies of fallen policemen lying in the street. Piper, who did sterling and largely unacclaimed work managing the emergency, sounded the ambulance alarm, and, stopping a passing cab, persuaded the occupants to give it up so that Tucker could be taken to the London Hospital. A motor ambulance took the unconscious Bentley to St Bartholomew's.

Choate had been hit eight times, five in the legs and three in the body. He and Woodhams were taken to the London Hospital. Bryant, wounded in the arm, was able to walk to a nearby doctor's surgery but was later taken to hospital, where it was discovered that he also had a chest wound.

When the police searched the tenements they found oxygen cylinders, rubber tubing, tools and debris. A hole had been made in the privy wall of No. 9, which had almost broken through to the rear of the 119 Houndsditch premises. In No. 11 a fire burned in the hearth and there was food on the table. Boards and ladders had been placed so that it was possible to pass between the yards of No. 9 and No. 11.

Forty-seven-year-old Tucker, who was married with two teenage children, died on the way to hospital. He had been about to retire some weeks before, but had signed on for another year due to the demands on the police service made by the coronation of King George V. Choate, who was 34 and unmarried, died the following morning. Thirty-seven-year-old Bentley, whose wife was due to give birth to their second child in a few days, died on the Saturday evening. The post-mortem reports showed that the policemen had been shot with automatic weapons, Mauser or Dreyse pistols.

The Houndsditch murders.

Smoller and Svaars had taken the stricken Gardstein to the nearest place of safety, 59 Grove Street (now called Golding Street) the home of baker Mark Katz, who let rooms to a number of lodgers including Svaars and his mistress, Luba Milstein, and painter Peter Piatkow. Sara Trassjonksy, a near neighbour, was a frequent visitor, as were mechanic Josef Fedoroff and artist Yourka Duboff.

Gardstein was laid on a bed in the front room, and Sara and Luba did what they could, but he was grievously injured and it was decided to summon a doctor. At 3.30 a.m., Dr Joseph Scanlon of 55 Commercial Street was brought to the house, where he found the patient in great pain and vomiting blood. He said the man should be taken to hospital but both the patient and his friends refused to consider the idea. All the doctor could do was supply a bottle of medicine to relieve the pain and promise to call again. It was not until Scanlon saw the account of the Houndsditch murders in the morning newspapers that he thought to notify the police of a suspicious shooting. The police suggested he make his morning visit as promised, and when he returned to Grove Street at 11.15 a.m. the patient was dead. Scanlon reported his findings to the police, and forty policemen led by two Inspectors were sent to the house. They found

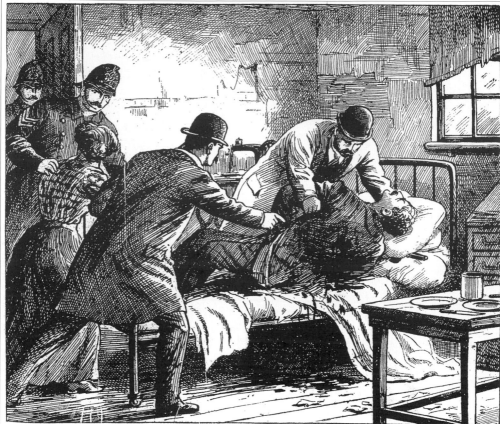

HUNT FOR THE HOUNDSDITCH ASSASSINS.
ONE OF THE GANG FOUND DYING BY THE POLICE IN AN EAST-END GARRET.

The police discover the body of George Gardstein.

Gardstein lying dead on a blood-soaked bed, and Sara burning papers and photographs. On the table beside the bed were cartridges for Mauser pistols and rifles, and a loaded Dreyse pistol. Two clips of ammunition were under the mattress, and in Gardstein's pocket was a key to 9 Exchange Buildings.

Detectives, hampered by having no knowledge of the languages spoken by the inhabitants of what the *Daily Mail* called 'this great foreign city east of Aldgate', searched almost without rest for the escaped criminals, but Smoller, Svaars and Sokoloff had disappeared. Public agitation continued, and there were blanket denouncements of the foreign immigrant population and the 'Radical cranks' who had let them into the country. 'A savage delight in taking life is the mark of the modern Continental anarchist criminal', observed *The Times*, with the strong implication that the police should be armed.

The only arrests that could be made were of those associates of the criminals who had not run away. Sara and Luba were arrested on suspicion of being accessories to the crimes, and Duboff, Fedoroff and Jacob Peters, a cousin of Fritz Svaars, were arrested for both murder and conspiracy. It was thought that Duboff and Peters had been present at the tragedy in Exchange Buildings, but the evidence against them was weak. A description of Nina giving her hair colour as brown, was circulated, but the day after the murders the distraught girl had dyed her hair black. She was soon identified however and the police decided to watch her in case she led them to the missing men.

The inquests concluded that Tucker and Bentley had been killed by Gardstein, and Gardstein and Choate by person or persons unknown. On 23 December the funeral of the three murdered policemen was held at St Paul's Cathedral, attended by the Home Secretary Winston Churchill and the Lord Mayor, Sir Thomas Strong.

On New Year's Day the police received information that Fritz Svaars and Josef Sokoloff were lodging at 100 Sidney Street, Stepney. Detectives were sent to watch the house, but, concerned that the men might slip away, it was decided to take action. In the early hours of the morning of 3 January 1911 the police quietly blockaded the house, hoping to arrest the fugitives without further loss of life. With great difficulty the other occupants of the building were evacuated, and when the police were sure that only the wanted men remained in the house, they threw pebbles at the window to attract their attention and give them the opportunity to surrender. Instead they were greeted by a stream of bullets. This time the police were armed, and returned fire. Later they were joined by volunteers from the Scots Guards, and this additional firepower placed the besieged men in an impossible situation. The battle, which attracted Winston Churchill to the scene, had raged for almost six hours and drawn thousands of onlookers, when wisps of smoke were seen rising from the back of the building. Gradually the fire took hold, the upper rooms were seen to be full of thick, dark smoke, and flames began to pour from the roof. At 2 p.m. all firing ceased, and firemen began to pour water on the blaze. Two charred bodies found in the debris were later identified as Svaars and Sokoloff.

The elusive figure of Peter Piatkow, known as 'Peter the Painter', had by now achieved legendary status. Many suspected him to have been in Sidney Street, and some suggested he was the mastermind behind the robbery. He was able to slip across the Channel and disappear. Max Smoller was never traced. It was believed that he escaped to France.

Early in February there were more arrests; Vassileva and two of Gardstein's friends, John Rosen, a barber, and sailor Karl Hofmann. The legal proceedings continued for several months but by May 1911 all those arrested had been acquitted of all charges apart from Vassileva, who was found guilty of conspiracy to break and enter. Her conviction was quashed in the following month. She had undoubtedly lived at 11 Exchange Buildings for her fingerprints had been found there, but whether she was an accomplice to crime or was there simply as Gardstein's mistress could not be determined.

The 'Siege of Sidney Street' is a part of British history, but it should never be allowed to overshadow the tragedy that preceded it. In the City of London Cemetery is a monument to the three policemen killed in the execution of their duty. It is inscribed 'Faithful unto death'.

8

CROYDON

Justice

The short life of Derek Bentley was marked from the beginning by disadvantage and tragedy. He was born on 30 June 1933, his twin brother dying at birth. There were two older sisters and the family lived in a two room flat in the slums of Blackfriars. At the age of 4, he was playing on a parked lorry with friends when he fell 15ft to the pavement, hitting his head. He suffered a fit and was rushed to hospital. His parents were advised that the blow had triggered a major epileptic fit and that they should expect them to recur. At the age of 6 he was again rushed to hospital with a fit, during which his face turned blue. When he was seven his grandmother, aunt and sister were killed in a bombing raid, a loss which affected him deeply. Although he did not have any major epileptic fits during this period, he continued to suffer severe headaches and sickness, during which his lips and fingertips turned blue. In September 1944, his home was hit by a flying bomb and he was buried under a fallen ceiling. He was treated for shock, and the headaches worsened. A doctor who had attended him from 1945 later stated her belief that his headaches were a symptom of *petit mal*, a form of epilepsy.

The frequent illnesses and several changes of address meant that Derek missed a great deal of schooling. When he started secondary school at the age of 11 it was found that he was illiterate, and he remained so for the rest of his life. In 1945 the Bentleys moved to Croydon, where Derek was enrolled in Norbury Manor School. Unable to cope with the demands of a normal education, and taunted by other boys for his ignorance, he truanted. His headmaster described him as 'extremely retarded, work-shy, but not necessarily mentally retarded' and suspected the boy of petty thieving. In March 1948, Bentley appeared at a juvenile court for attempted shop breaking. He left school later that year aged 15 and was soon before the juvenile court again accused of stealing some tools from a building site. He was sent to an approved school where he was given an IQ test and scored 66, which officially graded him as feeble-minded.

In 1951 he started work for a firm of furniture removers, but in March 1952 he was obliged to leave after straining his back. In May 1952 he started a new job as a dustman, but his performance was considered unsatisfactory and after a month he was re-employed as a road sweeper at a lower wage. His attendance was poor and in July he was dismissed. Thereafter he was unemployed. He was examined by the National Service medical board in February 1952, which found he had poor vision in his right eye, and was of subnormal intelligence.

Bentley's parents were particularly concerned about his friendship with Christopher Craig, who was three years his junior. Where Bentley was dull, Craig was lively. His great passion was guns, of which he owned many, and from the age of 11 he carried one with him all the time, even to school, where he sometimes displayed it in the classroom. His teachers seemed to think it was a harmless hobby. Craig later stated that from an early age he had had the ambition to be 'a villain'. He liked to pretend to be an American 'tough guy'. His first brush with the law was at the age of 15, when he ran away with another boy and was found with a gun and ammunition. He hated the police and fantasised about dying in a gun battle, which would end with him diving out of his bedroom window. On 30 October 1952 his older brother, Niven, was sentenced to twelve years in prison for armed robbery.

Bentley's parents tried in vain to keep the boys apart, but in the summer of 1952 Craig and Bentley carried out a number of burglaries. It was a sensitive time. In the post-war years of rationing and the black market, petty crime was rife, and guns of all kinds were readily available. In 1947 the number of convictions of adolescents between the ages of 17 and 21 had increased by 250 per cent since 1939. In the early 1950s several murders of policemen had touched a nerve with the public.

On 2 November 1952, Craig and Bentley were out looking for property to burgle. Craig was carrying a knife and a loaded Eley 0.455 revolver. Bentley had a knife he used to pick locks, and Craig had a homemade knuckleduster he gave to Bentley. Bentley must have known of Craig's obsession with guns, but as Craig later observed, Bentley never wanted anything to do with an enterprise that involved using a gun. If he had thought that Craig might use one, he would not have gone out with him. In Tamworth Road they tried a butcher's shop, but it was occupied. Their next target was an electrical shop but there was a courting couple in the alley. Their third attempt was Barlow and Parker's, a wholesaler's warehouse. They scrambled over a 6ft spiked gate which led into an alleyway beside the building, but all doors were securely locked. They were just about to give up and go home when Craig noticed a drainpipe leading up to the roof. The two boys climbed up. They didn't know it but they had already been spotted from across the road by Mrs Edith Alice Wren, who had been looking out of her daughter's bedroom window. Edith told her husband, who hurried out to a telephone box and informed the police. It was about 9.15 p.m. By the time Craig and Bentley were on the roof, where they found that the door leading downstairs to the warehouse was securely locked, a police van had arrived with Detective Constable Frederick Fairfax, and PCs Norman Harrison, Allen Beecher-Brigden and Claude Pain. Moments later patrol car 7Z drew up, driven by Constable Sidney Miles with wireless operator PC James McDonald. The lights and voices below told Craig and Bentley that they were trapped. The roof was flat, 90ft in length and 54ft wide, and offered little hiding space. In the centre were four roof lights 4ft 6in at their highest point. At the side nearest the alley was the entrance to the warehouse. The only structure to hide behind was the lift head, 11ft 6in high, at the end of the building furthest from Tamworth Road, so they crouched behind it. Fairfax had climbed the drainpipe onto the roof and, realising where the boys must be hiding, called out that he was a police officer, and demanded that they come out. According to Fairfax's later deposition, Craig shouted, 'If you want us fucking well come and get us!' Craig was later to deny this. Bentley decided to give himself up, and emerged from behind the stack. Fairfax grabbed him and pursued Craig.

McDonald had been struggling to climb the drainpipe. A far heavier man than Fairfax he was unable to get to the top, and started on his way down. Harrison had climbed onto the roof of No. 25 and from there reached a sloping roof of Barlow and Parker's adjoining the main property.

Fairfax's account of what happened next, later to be disputed, was that Bentley broke away from him shouting, 'Let 'em have it, Chris!' (This is as per his original deposition dated 3 November. The better known 'Let him have it, Chris' comes from Harrison and McDonald's accounts, although by the time of the trial all three had agreed that 'him' was the correct word. As Fairfax was the only policeman on the roof at the time, the singular makes more sense.)

Craig fired and Fairfax was hit in the right shoulder, spun around and fell to the ground, but finding that he was not badly wounded, he got up and lashed out at Bentley, knocking him over. Craig fired again, missing Fairfax, who pulled Bentley in front of himself as a shield. The detective went through Bentley's pockets and found the knife and knuckleduster. Fairfax, wounded, unarmed, still with no back-up, and knowing he faced a man with a loaded gun, began to retreat, taking his unresisting prisoner and moving around the four central roof lights towards the wall of the locked roof entrance.

McDonald made another attempt to climb the drainpipe and, with Fairfax's assistance, he finally reached the roof. Harrison was edging closer, but when Craig fired on him and missed, he realised that his position was too exposed, so retraced his steps and returned to ground level. By now the street was crowded with onlookers, and more police cars, fire engines and ambulances had arrived. At Croydon police station all available guns were being despatched to the scene.

It was clear to Fairfax that the important task was to get the roof door open and get more men on the roof. He called out to Craig to surrender his gun but Craig refused. Eventually the standoff was resolved. Miles had located the warehouse manager and collected the keys. The door to the roof flew open and PC Miles stepped out with Harrison close behind him. Almost immediately Miles was hit between the eyes by a bullet, and fell to the ground, dead. Harrison threw any missiles that came to hand, a milk bottle, a brick, and his truncheon. Craig responded with bullets. 'I am Craig!' he cried, 'You've just given my brother twelve years. Come on, you coppers, I'm only sixteen.'

Fairfax asked Bentley to try and get Craig to give himself up. Bentley walked closer to his friend, saying, 'For Christ's sake, Chris, what's got into you?' and tried to get around behind him to get at the gun but Craig realised what he was up to and said, 'Get back or I'll shoot you.' Bentley gave up and walked back to the police. The policemen were joined on the roof by Constable Jaggs, who had climbed up the drainpipe.

Fairfax took Bentley downstairs, where two constables had arrived bringing firearms, and he was given a revolver. Returning to the roof he ordered Craig to drop his gun, but the 16 year old was determined to have a shooting match. After an exchange of shots, all of which missed, Craig tried to shoot himself, but the gun misfired. He ran to the edge of the building and dived off the roof, hitting the edge of a greenhouse on his way down. He broke his spine, breastbone and forearm.

Fairfax believed that Craig had fired the gun directly at him, but when he was examined at Croydon General Hospital it was found that the bullet had not penetrated his skin, it had simply passed over the surface of his shoulder, and lodged under his braces at the back. It appeared to have come from below, suggesting a ricochet. This supported Craig's claim that he had fired at the ground.

The bullet which killed Miles was never found. While Craig never disputed that he had shot Miles, he remained puzzled as to how this could have happened, as he had not aimed his shots at the roof door area because he knew Bentley was there. He had, however, been firing wildly in the dark with a highly inaccurate gun.

While Craig lay in hospital, Bentley was charged with the murder of PC Miles. The charge was based on the supposition that he and Craig had been engaged in a joint enterprise and were therefore both liable to answer for the outcome. There was an outpouring of public sympathy for the widow of PC Miles, expressions of support for the police, and outraged horror at this latest example of teenage crime. The possibility of reintroducing whipping and birching was again debated.

Police on the roof of Barlow and Parker after the shooting. (© Metropolitan Police Authority, 2009)

Tests on Bentley at the Maudsley hospital in November 1952 gave his IQ as 77 – officially 'dull and backward' and not therefore certifiable as feeble-minded. In non-scholastic tests he had a mental age of 11 or 12. The examination found no evidence of epilepsy. He was declared fit to plead and stand trial.

The trial commenced at the Central Criminal Court, the Old Bailey on 9 December, presided over by Lord Chief Justice Goddard. Seventy-five-year-old Goddard was a hard-liner who believed that in the face of the new breed of teenage gangsters and cosh-boys, a return to the days of flogging and birching criminals was long overdue.

Bentley insisted that he had never dictated the statement attributed to him, which was compiled from replies he had given during questioning. He had not been able to read the statement but it had been read over to him before he signed it. One remark in the statement stands out as vitally important – '. . . after the plain clothes policeman got up the drainpipe and arrested me, another policeman in uniform followed . . .' At the time of the shooting, therefore, Bentley considered himself to be under arrest. The idea that he had been acting in concert with Craig after he had given himself up was fundamental to the charge against him and was unsupported by any evidence apart from the damaging 'let him have it Chris.' To Goddard these words could only mean that Bentley had been encouraging Craig to shoot, although another interpretation is that he was telling his friend to give up the gun, something far more in keeping with Bentley's known character. Another point central to the prosecution's case was whether Bentley knew when the two set out that Craig was carrying a gun. If he did that would make him legally complicit in its use. Bentley always denied that he knew Craig had the gun in his pocket, but according to McDonald's statement, shortly after Bentley was arrested, he said, 'I told the silly bugger not to use it.'

Goddard's summing-up, during which he put on the knuckleduster and brandished it, describing it as a 'shocking weapon', was hostile and emotive. Bentley had denied saying 'let him have it Chris' and Craig had also said that the words were never spoken, but Goddard invited the jury to compare the statements of the accused with the evidence of the three police officers who had faced death on the roof. As the jury filed out, Goddard asked if they wanted to see any of the exhibits. To his consternation the foreman asked to see Fairfax's waistcoat, presumably to test which of Fairfax's and Craig's statements about the wounding was supported by the evidence. Goddard retorted angrily that they were not trying the wounding of Fairfax but the death of Miles. Both the prisoners were found guilty of murder with a recommendation to mercy for Bentley. Craig, who was still only sixteen, was sentenced to be detained. Bentley was sentenced to death.

Most people did not believe that Bentley would hang, even after the appeal was dismissed, but despite a campaign which included debates in parliament, sentence was carried out by Albert Pierrepoint on 28 January 1953. Bentley's last words as he stood on the trapdoor were, 'I didn't tell Chris to shoot that policeman.'

Fairfax was promoted to detective sergeant and awarded the George Cross. Harrison and McDonald received the George Medal and Jaggs the British Empire Medal. Miles was posthumously awarded the Queen's Police medal for gallantly. Fairfax was still a sergeant when he retired in 1962. He died in 1998.

Craig was released in 1963 and put his days as a teenage tearaway behind him. He became a plumber, married and raised two children. In 1966 Derek Bentley's family was given permission to rebury his remains in Croydon cemetery.

In the 1970s there was a new sensation – an allegation that Miles had been shot not by Craig, but by a police marksman. Phillip Lee, a man with a string of petty convictions to his name, had made a series of statements alleging that he had been at the scene in 1952 and viewed events from a vantage point nearby. The original witnesses were re-interviewed and all were certain that Lee had not been present. It was also shown that Lee could not have seen what he claimed to have observed from the position where he said he had been standing.

The funeral of Constable Miles. (© Metropolitan Police Authority 2009)

In his 1988 book *To Encourage the Others*, David Yallop also suggested that Miles may have been accidentally killed by a shot from a police marksman, although M. J. Trow in *Let Him Have It Chris* believes there is no evidence for this. Not only was Miles' wound made by a large calibre bullet, more in keeping with Craig's weapon than the far smaller police issue revolvers of 1952, but contemporary records show that no policeman at the scene had a weapon until after Miles had been shot.

But Trow's book dropped a new bombshell. He had interviewed 80-year-old Claude Pain, who retired from the police force two years after the shooting of PC Miles. Pain claimed that he too had been on the rooftop, having shinned up a rickety ladder provided by a helpful neighbour. He said he had ducked down and made it across to the roof lights, and was therefore easily close enough to hear anything Bentley said. Pain was adamant that the fatal words were never spoken.

From left to right: Fairfax, McDonald, Harrison and Jaggs being congratulated on their awards.
(© Metropolitan Police Authority, 2009)

Pain was not asked to give evidence at the trial, which naturally gave rise to
the uncomfortable suspicion that his evidence had been suppressed because
it did not fit with that of the other policemen. At the time of writing, Trow, to
his understandable frustration, was told that the National Archive files which
would have allowed him to see Pain's original deposition, would not be open for
examination until 2047. Claude Pain died in 1992, and, a year later, the National
Archives made its files available.

It is worth quoting in full the relevant part of Pain's deposition made at
Croydon police station on 3 November:

> . . . there is a small passage-way at the back of Barlow and Parker's and I covered
> the new entrance in this passage-way. Det. Constable Fairfax climbed over a wall,
> and went towards the factory premises. Several minutes afterwards P.C. 550 'Z' Sid
> Miles, who I knew was driving the wireless car, came up to me, and informed me
> that there were two chaps hiding behind a stack on the roof and they were firing
> a gun. He told me to stay where I was while he went round to the front of the
> building. I had heard a couple of reports before this, but I wasn't sure what they
> were. PC Miles then came back and asked me to phone for assistance as the men

on the roof were armed. I went to a nearby public house and phoned the station asking for further assistance and then returned to the passage-way. Whilst standing there I heard revolver shots, about 7 or 8 at intervals. On hearing this I went round to the front of the premises and was informed by P.C. 5128 'Z' McDonald R/T operator on the car 7 'Z' that P.C. Miles had been shot in the head.

Claude Pain, who had claimed that he was on the roof during the shoot-out, crouching only yards from where the stricken Miles had fallen, had, according to his original statement, never been on the roof at all, but was in the passage-way at the side of the building at the time of the shooting.

After a lengthy campaign by the Bentley family, led by Derek's sister Iris, Bentley was granted a royal pardon in respect of the death sentence in July 1993. The conviction was finally set aside by the court of appeal on 30 July 1998. Bentley's gravestone in Croydon cemetery reads: 'Here lies Derek William Bentley. A Victim of British Justice.'

9

EALING

Free to Kill Again

The morning of 11 February 1954 dawned peacefully at 22 Montpelier Road, Ealing. The property, a large detached double fronted house of fourteen rooms, was a residential home for elderly people. The business was run by 73-year-old Mary Menzies and her married daughter, Vera Chesney, 43, with the assistance of a maidservant, 18-year-old Eileen Thorpe. That morning Mrs Menzies did not wake Eileen at her usual hour of 6.30 a.m., and when the maid awoke at 7.45 she quickly busied herself preparing breakfast for the nineteen residents, assuming that her employer was elsewhere in the house. Later that morning an ambulance arrived with a new patient, and when there was still no sign of Mrs Menzies or her daughter, Eileen started to worry, and the driver notified the police. Both the front and back doors of the property had been secured before the three women retired for the night, but Eileen told the police that that morning she had found the back door unlocked. There was no sign of her employers in their respective bedrooms and Eileen said that they would never normally go out of the house without informing her.

An inspection of the premises soon revealed that the bathroom door was locked, and the key missing. The key was eventually discovered downstairs, and when the door was opened Vera Chesney, wearing a nightdress and a cardigan, was found lying dead in the bath. She appeared to have drowned. The bath and her hair were still wet but the water had drained away. Her wristwatch had stopped at 2.30 a.m.

The CID was informed and Superintendent Wilfred Daws arrived to take charge of the scene. As the elderly residents of the home gathered anxiously in the hallway, the house was subjected to a careful room by room search. The body of Mary Menzies was found behind some curtains in an unused back room. She had been strangled with a scarf, one of her own stockings and a belt.

Montpelier Road, Ealing.

She had also been beaten over the head and the scarf was saturated in blood. Nearby was a badly dented brass coffee pot. It was thought that the attack must have begun in her bedroom for when the furniture was moved, blood splashes were found on the walls and there were pools of dried blood underneath the carpet.

The residents were told there had been a burglary and were removed to another location. Every room in the house was then photographed and dusted for fingerprints. There was, however, no evidence that a burglary had taken place. Nothing appeared to be missing.

The case was now being supervised by chief superintendent Tom Barratt, whose experienced eyes soon noticed some vital clues. A stone was holding the door of the French windows closed from the outside, because the lock was faulty, and a small screw from the lock was found on the carpet. He realised that this was where the intruder, who must have known about the faulty lock, had gained entry. Mary Menzies owned two dogs, chows, and he asked the neighbours if they had heard them barking in the night, but even though they had heard water running and some bumps, the dogs, who usually barked at strangers, had not made a noise. Mrs Chesney always slept with the light on, but the light in her room, which was connected to an electric clock, had been switched off at ten past one.

The killer had been careful not to leave any fingerprints, for all smooth surfaces had been wiped clean, but there were some black hairs on the women's clothing and traces of blood and skin underneath Mary Menzies' fingernails. The murderer would undoubtedly have some nasty scratches. The analysis of Mrs Chesney's stomach contents showed that at the time of her death she had recently consumed an amount of alcohol equivalent to six and a half ounces of spirits. While there were a great many dusty drink bottles in the house, suggesting that she was a regular drinker, two gin bottles were clean and new, and Barratt wondered if these had been brought by the killer, suggesting that he was well acquainted with Mrs Chesney's habits.

Many letters were discovered in the house addressed to Mrs Chesney and signed 'Don'. The police soon established that this was Mrs Chesney's estranged husband, Ronald, usually known as 'Don', who was known to visit her from time to time. He had been living in Germany, but on 3 February he had been in London to see his wife, returning abroad on the same day. Although he somewhat resembled a man seen in Ealing by the neighbours on the night of 10 February there was no evidence that he was in the country on that date. The letters revealed that for many years Chesney had been seeking a divorce which Vera, a Roman Catholic, had refused to allow. There were also references to a marriage settlement, made in 1929, in the sum of £8,400, which would revert to Chesney if his wife died. Relatives of Mrs Chesney told the police that Vera had been afraid that he would harm her, and Eileen recalled that when Chesney had visited his wife the dogs had not barked, but fussed around him.

Chesney was now the prime suspect, and when his details were sent to Scotland Yard, it was discovered that he was a smuggler who had served many short prison sentences both in Britain and abroad, and that twenty-seven years previously, he been tried for the murder of his mother.

Ronald Chesney was born John Donald Merrett in New Zealand in 1908. He was a naturally clever boy, and his mother, Bertha, had high hopes for his future, but unknown to her, he had determined on a life of extravagant pleasure funded by crime. In 1926 Merrett and his mother were living in Edinburgh, where he was supposed to be attending university. Instead the tall, strong seventeen year old, who looked older than his years, was spending time with dance hostesses, financing his jaunts by forging his mother's signature to cheques. He was able to conceal his thefts from her bank account by intercepting her post. On the morning of 17 March, Mrs Merrett and her son both seemed calm and on good terms. The maid, Mrs Sutherland, had just gone to make up the fire in the kitchen while her employer sat at a table writing a letter, when she heard a loud bang, and Donald came in and told her that his mother had just shot herself. Mrs Merrett was unconscious but alive, and since attempted suicide was then a crime, she was taken to the royal infirmary and treated as a prisoner.

The young John Merrett.

When Mrs Merrett regained consciousness she stated that she had been writing letters and Donald had been standing beside her. She had told him to go away and not annoy her, and 'the next thing I heard was a kind of explosion and I do not remember any more.' Despite this, when Mrs Merrett died on 27 March, the inquest concluded that it was a case of suicide. Donald may have thought he was safe, but the police had been gradually gathering evidence of the forgeries which gave him a motive for murder. On 29 November Donald was arrested, and the trial opened in Edinburgh on 1 February 1927. He was found guilty of uttering forged cheques but the experts disagreed over the evidence relating to the shooting. The prosecution claimed that lack of blackening around the wound meant that it could not have been inflicted at close quarters, while the defence brought out the respected and authoritative figure of Sir Bernard Spilsbury to state that the wound was consistent with either suicide or accident. The jury brought in the Scottish verdict of 'Not proven' by a majority of ten to five. Merrett was sentenced to twelve months in prison, of which he served eight.

While serving his sentence he had been corresponding with Mrs Mary Bonar, a friend of his mother's who had always believed him innocent of murder. Mary was living in Hastings with her attractive 17-year-old daughter, Vera. Mary invited Merrett, now 19, to stay with her. Under his new name of Ronald Chesney he quickly established a reputation in the town as a scoundrel with whom no respectable woman was safe. He was easily able to charm Vera into eloping with him to Scotland, where he paid his way with worthless cheques. He was soon arrested and sentenced to six months in prison, which he served in Durham Gaol. In 1930 Mrs Bonar married a typewriter salesman named Thomas Chalmers Menzies, whose claim to a baronetcy was later shown to be false, nevertheless she continued to style herself 'Lady' Menzies. The couple were separated after a year of marriage and Menzies died a few years later.

On reaching the age of 21, Chesney was finally able to take possession of the fortune left to him by his grandfather. He was now a wealthy man, and enjoyed driving about in large cars, visiting London, going to sporting events and having affairs with numerous women. He made the marriage settlement on Vera because he was advised it would be a sound investment.

After Vera suffered a number of miscarriages, the couple adopted two children. They took a twenty-room house in Weybridge staffed by servants, where they entertained lavishly. Chesney's fortune could not last forever and he took to smuggling, an ideal occupation for a man who had developed a fascination for the sea. Six feet tall, powerfully built with blue eyes and a slightly hooked nose, Chesney cultivated a piratical air by growing a beard and wearing an earring in his left ear, a rakish appearance which enhanced his success with women. In 1935 he sold the house, and bought a cutter, the *Gladys May*. He found gun-running both easy and lucrative and he also carried cigarettes, liquor, diamonds and gold. His family, who lived with him on the cutter, was able to live a life of luxury. Vera had long become resigned to her husband's many infidelities, and consoled herself with drink, but her mother often expressed her disapproval, especially as the children were now old enough to notice what was going on. The money that had come so easily to Chesney began to slip through his fingers. He had developed a gambling habit, and made heavy losses. He borrowed money on the security of the boat, and when he was unable to repay, it was impounded. The family returned to England, occupying No. 2 St Mary's Road, Ealing, which Vera and her mother turned into a home for the elderly.

On the outbreak of war, Chesney, now with valuable seafaring experience, joined the Royal Navy. His tales of adventure on the high seas, and generosity in buying drinks, made him popular with his shipmates, but when he saw Vera there were frequent quarrels over money. Vera and her mother moved to Montpelier Road, while her husband, stationed in Germany shortly after the end of the war, began dealing in black market goods, a business which soon became immensely

John Merrett (aka Ronald Chesney).

profitable. In November 1945 he was introduced to attractive 18-year-old Gerda Schaller. Gerda, dazzled by the older man's experience and self assurance, fell in love, and remained devoted to him, even though he did not conceal the fact that he was married. Their passionate closeness was such that one night Chesney confessed to Gerda that he had murdered his mother.

Chesney and Gerda were together for six years, during which he made huge amounts of money from smuggling and dealing in black market goods, and spent it on a champagne lifestyle, but his days of easy profits were numbered. Always cutting a distinctive figure, he was often recognised, and was increasingly being kept under close observation by the authorities. He had some narrow escapes from detection, but on several occasions he was caught with smuggled goods and served terms in prison. He wanted to marry Gerda but Vera would not give him a divorce, and he often spoke of wanting to be rid of her. He also tried, unsuccessfully, to get a share of Vera's settlement money. He and Gerda went through a marriage ceremony which he managed to persuade her was genuine, but this did not stop his compulsive womanising, and ultimately she left him.

In 1950, Chesney, now 42, began courting a beautiful 24-year-old German blonde called Sonia. During a spell in Wandsworth Prison, obsessed with the money he would get if Vera died, he approached several men, offering them £1,000 if they would run his wife down in a car as she went shopping, but none of them would agree. By 1953 it was almost impossible for him to make a good income as a smuggler. Everywhere he went he was followed or searched, and there were too many of his old contacts who had once been useful but had since learned to distrust him. He was desperate for money.

The CID investigating the murders at Montpelier Road were now sure that the killer had crept into the house at night bringing gin, plied Vera with drink and then drowned her in the bath. Hoping to leave undetected, he had unexpectedly encountered Mary Menzies, and murdered her too. The hunt was on for Ronald Chesney, and a description of him was circulated both in Britain and abroad, while the murder was a leading story in every newspaper. Someone who knew him told the police that the wanted man was '. . . a most entertaining personality. He spoke of women and drink and fun, and of people he knew whom he thought were smugglers.'

There was no record of Chesney having escaped by air, and the police, convinced that their quarry had got away to the continent by sea, interviewed coastguards and private motor-launch owners, and checked the identity of departing boats with customs officials, all without result.

On 15 February, Chesney's startled solicitor received a phone call from the fugitive asserting his innocence and asking for the trust fund money to be released. Chesney promised to come over to England to straighten things out, but instead he went to Cologne to see Sonia, but was told that she had gone away. The wanted man was finally done with running. He wrote a letter of farewell to Sonia and one to his solicitor, saying he wanted Sonia to have his property. He walked alone into a wood and shot himself.

The body found in the wood was soon identified as Chesney. Even days after the murders, the hands and wrists of the dead man were covered with scratches and bruises. A post-mortem was carried out in Germany, at which Superintendent Daws was present. Although photographs were taken of the scratches, he decided that it would be necessary for the purposes of the inquest on Mary and Vera for the actual injuries to be examined in England, and on 20 February he obtained permission from the German authorities for the forearms to be severed. He brought them to England on the same day and handed them to pathologist Dr Robert Teare. Chesney was buried in Germany. The only mourner at his funeral was Gerda.

The police investigation finally revealed how Chesney had entered England and returned undetected. In 1953 he had obtained a copy of the birth certificate of a photographer he knew, Leslie Chown, to whom he bore a superficial resemblance, although Chown was clean shaven and bespectacled. Chesney shaved off his piratical moustache and beard and removed his earring, donned spectacles and had his passport photo taken. After re-growing his hair and beard, he took a short visit to England to see Vera, making sure that he was noticed both on the way there and on his return. He then flew back to England, changing his appearance to resemble Chown and using the false passport.

On 24 March 1954, Dr Teare told the inquest on Mrs Menzies and her daughter that he had examined Chesney's hands and forearms and found extensive scratches and bruising, consistent with him having been in a fight. Dr Nickolls, director of the Metropolitan Police laboratory, said that he had taken scrapings from underneath the fingernails and found wool fibres similar to those of Mrs Chesney's cardigan. The dark hairs on the victims' clothing matched Chesney's. The inquest jury brought in a verdict of murder against Ronald Chesney.

ENFIELD

Abandoned Characters

Long before the formation of the London Borough of Enfield, Enfield Chase was a wooded area well stocked with deer. It was used as a royal hunting park until 1777, when it was largely deforested and the land divided into allotments. In 1832 Enfield, its royal glory days gone, was a small, attractive market town, and an unlikely place to be the scene of a bloody and senseless murder.

Early on the morning of Thursday, 20 December 1832, a small boy called Ellis was walking up to Enfield Town from Enfield Chase when, reaching a spot called Batcham Road, he saw a figure lying by the side of the roadway. He called out to a passing farm labourer called Wheeler, who went with him to inspect the body. A man was lying face down with his head in the ditch and his feet in the road. Wheeler alerted another passer-by, James Ashby. Not sure if the man was drunk or dead, they turned him over and received a terrible shock. The face had been slashed in five places, so deeply that the right whisker was almost completely cut away, and there was a stab wound through the throat, in which the knife had been cruelly twisted. He had been killed as one might slaughter a sheep. Despite the mutilations, they recognised the dead man as 24-year-old Benjamin Danby, the son of Benjamin Couch Danby, a hairdresser and perfumer. Young Danby was likeable but irredeemably dissolute. He had never shown any inclination to take up a profession, preferring instead to spend his time in public houses and his money on drink. His father had eventually despaired of him, and sent him abroad. When Danby senior died, he left a handsome legacy to his three daughters but just a guinea a week allowance to his prodigal son. This allowance had been increased to two guineas by a sympathetic sister. Benjamin had not long returned from his travels and since 12 December had been staying with a relative, Peter Addington, a master baker

*Police constable in 1829,
from a contemporary print.*

of Enfield. According to the *Observer* he 'met with a very kind reception, and his joyous spirits and free sailor-like manner attracted the notice of the inhabitants.' Put another way, young Danby spent freely on drink and gave the impression of being much wealthier than he was. It was perhaps not too surprising that his brief life had ended in a ditch.

Wheeler fetched a light and saw some items lying near the body: some shot, a small penknife, closed up and unstained, some coins and a pair of gloves. The body was placed on a board and carried to the Old Sergeant public house on Parsonage Lane, which was about a quarter of a mile away, and Constable John Mead was called to inspect the remains. Addington was brought to identify the body, and wept copiously. He said that Danby had left his house at twenty minutes to six on the Wednesday evening, promising to be back by 10 p.m., but he had not reappeared. The baker had not been alarmed, assuming that the young man had fallen in with some convivial company. He didn't say so, but it must have been a regular occurrence for Danby to return home late and the worse for drink.

Constable Mead next visited the spot where the body had lain, finding a great deal of blood and the marks of trampling feet. It was obvious from the number and variety of footprints that more than one person had been involved in Danby's death.

On the previous morning, Danby had been out shooting birds with a borrowed gun and had called at the White Horse public house, but in the evening he had been drinking and playing dominoes at the Crown and Horseshoes. He could not have had more than £2 in his purse. His companions that night had been four local men, Richard Wagstaff, a baker; John Cooper, who worked for a brewer; Samuel Fare (also known as Sleith) an unemployed labourer; and William Johnson, the son of a gardener. Danby had been seen leaving the public house in their company, and they at once became prime suspects in his murder. The Enfield constables were sent out to apprehend them.

Both Johnson and Fare were calm when asked to go with the constables, but when Johnson was locked up in the Enfield watchhouse on Thursday night, he became so agitated that it was felt necessary to have someone with him to watch him night and day in case he harmed himself. Fare, on the other hand, seemed unaffected by his experience. When searched, Fare's pockets contained four knives, some shot corresponding to that found near the body, and the bowl of a pipe which was later identified by Mr Addington as one which Danby had carried, using it to charge his gun. Eleven shillings were found in a box in Fare's house, a sum he was unable to account for. Later, some blood spots were seen on Johnson's trousers and a bloodstained glove was found in his coat pocket. A strip of fabric found near the scene of the murder matched Johnson's trousers, from which a strip had been torn.

Between 9 and 10 a.m. on the Thursday morning, Patrol Constable Watkins spotted John Cooper proceeding along the road with a horse and dray, and noticed that there was blood on Cooper's cap. Watkins asked Cooper how the blood came to be there, to which Cooper replied that he had used it to carry dog's meat for his master on the previous Saturday. The astute Watkins pointed out that if the meat had been carried several days ago the stains would not be so wet, also the blood was on the outside. 'You could not have carried it on that side of your cap: that story won't do for us,' he said, and conveyed Cooper to the watchhouse. At first, Cooper said he knew nothing about the murder of Danby, but after an hour in the lockup he sent for Watkins and Mead and said he wished to make a statement.

Cooper was taken before a magistrate, Dr Cresswell, where he gave a full account of Danby's death. He said that he had left the Crown and Horseshoes

The Crown and Horseshoes, Enfield. (By kind permission of the proprietor)

with Danby, Wagstaff, Fare and Johnson at 11 p.m. on Wednesday night. Wagstaff, on reaching his own door, suggested to Cooper that he too should go home, but Cooper said he wanted to see Danby safely home. Wagstaff went into his house and the others walked with Danby to Mr Addington's door. They asked him if he wanted to get some more beer, something he was keen to do, but on going to the nearest shop at the top of the hill they found that it was closed, and returned. Johnson then tripped Danby, who fell on top of Cooper in the ditch. There was a struggle, during which Johnson cut at Danby with a knife. Cooper scrambled out of the ditch and retrieved his cap – which was lying under Danby – and found it stained with blood.

'What are you doing to him? Don't hurt him!' he exclaimed.

Johnson offered him the knife, saying, 'Go and finish him, or we shall be found out.'

Cooper refused, and Danby lifted his head and pleaded, 'For God's sake, don't murder me, I'll give you anything,' but Johnson stabbed him in the neck.

'I should have run away,' Cooper told the magistrate, 'but was afraid that Johnson would follow me and serve me the same.'

The two men went down the lane to the New River, where Johnson washed his hands and knife and threw Danby's handkerchief into the river. 'Jack, don't you split,' he said. Cooper then went home to bed.

Having got this off his chest, Cooper said he felt very much relieved. If he was hopeful of being released, he was to be disappointed for he was obliged to remain caged up until the inquest was over. As if to make a point, Cooper requested a Bible, which he perused with great attention. Soon afterwards Danby's handkerchief was found caught in brambles by the riverside about 200 yards from the spot where it was said to have been thrown away.

Richard Wagstaff was questioned, but there was no evidence that he was involved and he was not detained.

The inquest opened on Thursday 20 December at the Old Sergeant public house, and was not to be concluded until the 27th. Joseph Perry, landlord of the Crown and Horseshoes, said that Danby had been drinking freely of both beer and gin in his public house on the Wednesday evening. At 8 p.m. Perry had seen Fare and Johnson lying asleep on the benches in the tap-room, while Danby was playing dominoes with Wagstaff and two other men named John Taylor and Charles Jackson. He woke Fare and Johnson which led to some grumbling, Fare threatening to knock Perry down and Perry forbidding him to come there again. The altercations simmered down and at 11 p.m. the men were still there, Danby and Fare having got through two more pots of beer each and half a pint of gin. Jackson and Taylor had by now left the house and Cooper had arrived. Perry told his wife not to draw any more drink, but Cooper, Fare, Johnson,

The Old Sergeant, Enfield. (By kind permission of the proprietor)

The bridge (rebuilt in 1841) outside the Crown and Horseshoes, Enfield.

Wagstaff and Danby said that if they would be allowed another half pint of gin they would go away. They were given the gin and left the house together. As they left Mrs Perry, knowing that Danby was a relative stranger to the area, told the pot-boy, Joseph Matthews, to accompany Danby over the bridge that crossed the river near the house, in case he should mistake his way and fall in. Matthews obeyed, and saw Danby stagger drunkenly over the bridge, Fare having hold of his left arm and Cooper his right.

Wagstaff told the inquest that he had suspected that Fare, whom he knew was out of work, and Johnson, who was 'almost starving', intended to rob Danby, which was why he had suggested to Cooper that he go home. When Cooper wouldn't take the warning, Wagstaff, afraid that he would be blamed for anything that happened, decided to have nothing to do with the planned crime, went into his house and shut the door. The jury admonished Wagstaff, saying that as an honest man if he thought a crime was about to be committed he should have tried to prevent it.

An acquaintance of Fare told the court that a few days before the murder, Fare had been heard to say that Danby had a well filled purse which he would like to lighten, and would be prepared to cut his throat if he met him in the dark.

The inquest was adjourned, and Danby's remains were transferred to the home of Mr Addington. On 22 December Benjamin Danby was buried in Enfield churchyard, where the funeral was attended by considerable crowds. Feelings in Enfield ran high, since the townsfolk were appalled not only by the barbarity of the murder, but that it should have been perpetrated by people living in the neighbourhood. William Johnson, who was aged about 29, was said to have led a very dissipated life. Four years previously he had made a good marriage, to the daughter of Mr Smith, the Enfield carrier, her marriage portion being a tidy £100. This he soon spent, and thereafter he treated his unfortunate wife with great cruelty. His parents were decent industrious people, his father being a gardener and also the owner of a small nursery where he reared plants and seeds for sale. Johnson had once had a comfortable position as head gardener to a wealthy man, and had then been considered of good character. He had the reputation of being the best cricketer in the area, and local teams often employed him to play for them, paying handsomely if they won. For the last three years, however, he had been deemed 'the most abandoned character in Enfield.' The reasons for his decline in fortunes were never revealed, though one might reasonably suspect that drunkenness had played its part.

Fare was 22 years old and single, the son of a poor but industrious woman. A jobbing labourer, he had recently found work in short supply and had had to apply for parish relief. Cooper was only eighteen, employed in a brewery at Enfield, and had never previously been in custody.

On 26 December, Cooper was brought before the coroner's court to read over and sign his deposition. The press representative, who must already have been disposed in his favour, reported that he was youthful and slimly built, 'evidently not possessed of much strength.' On the following day Johnson and Fare were brought into court, both described as strongly built and about 5ft 10 inches tall. Both were in a state of agitation and trembled visibly.

The jury, after consulting a short time, returned the verdict that Benjamin Danby had been murdered by William Johnson and John Cooper and that Samuel Fare had abetted them in the crime. *The Times* observed that the crime had arisen from '. . . the free and imprudent conduct of the deceased in associating with almost every abandoned vagabond with whom he met at the public houses . . .'.

The prisoners were transferred to the New Prison, Clerkenwell, where Johnson, his manner continuing to be sullen and dejected, was kept under constant watch.

Despite the jury's verdict, when the trial opened at the Central Criminal Court, the Old Bailey on 4 January 1833, there were just two prisoners, Johnson and Fare. Cooper had turned King's Evidence and was to be the star witness. Cooper described how he, Fare and Johnson had accompanied the drunken

Danby up Chase Side to the crossroads with Holtwhite's Lane, where Johnson
tripped Danby and stabbed him. Both he and Danby had pleaded with Johnson
to show mercy. As he described how Johnson offered him the knife and told
him to finish the man off, a thrill of horror ran throughout the courtroom,
to be followed by a shudder as Cooper described how Johnson had cut the
victim's throat.

Once the prosecution evidence was in, Fare's counsel submitted that there
was no case against his client. The court concurred and Fare was discharged.
Johnson's defence was that the bloodstains found on his clothing came from a
stag hunt, and several witnesses confirmed that Johnson had been present at a
hunt on 19 December and had been nearby when the stag was gutted with a
knife. The jury retired and took just over an hour to return a verdict of guilty,
after which Johnson was sentenced to death.

Fare was later tried for robbing Danby and was found guilty and transported
to Tasmania for a term of fourteen years.

Thus far, Johnson had been silent about the events of 19 December except to
deny any involvement, but he made a final statement to Mr Sherriff Humphrey
on 6 January. He claimed that Danby had accused Cooper of robbing him and
had flown at him like a tiger, and in the scuffle all three had fallen to the ground.
The knife was Cooper's and not his, and it was Cooper who had first cut Danby
as he lay on the ground, though Johnson admitted that he had also cut the
man. He believed that Cooper had only confessed because he thought Johnson
would accuse him first. Humphrey felt that Johnson was telling the truth, and
went to ask Cooper what had become of his knife. Cooper denied owning a
knife, but when Humphrey asked what had happened to the knife he used to
borrow from his master, Cooper reddened, looked agitated, and hesitated a long
time before saying he knew nothing about it. Johnson, who maintained to the
last that his statement was true, seemed resigned to dying for his participation in
the crime, and was hanged the following morning.

11

GREENWICH

The Straws of Evidence

At 4.15 a.m. on Wednesday, 26 April 1871, police constable Donald Gunn was on duty in Kidbrooke Lane, Eltham, when he saw a young woman on her hands and knees, moaning piteously. He asked her what was wrong and she said, 'Oh my poor head: oh my poor head!' He then saw that her face was covered in blood, and her clothes were dirty and pulled about as if she had been in a struggle. He asked her how she had come to be injured but all she could do was ask faintly for him to take her hand, which he did. He tried to help her up, but she fell forward onto the ground, murmuring, 'Let me die.' Gunn arranged for the young woman to be taken to Guy's Hospital. By the time she was seen by house surgeon Michael Harris she was unconscious. Harris found that the girl had about a dozen incised wounds on her head and face, of which two on the left side had depressed the skull and lacerated the brain beneath. The bone above her right eye was broken into fragments, allowing the brain to protrude, and there were further fractures to her face and jaw and defence injuries to her arms. Harris thought that she had been attacked with a sharp, heavy instrument such as a hammer.

Although the roads in the town were dry, the ground in Kidbrooke Lane was soft and muddy, and when the police searched the spot where the girl had been found, they saw the marks of a scuffle and a man's footprints, spaced far apart as if he had run away. The footprints were heading in the direction of Morden College, a residential care home, and when the police followed the trail, they found a small metal whistle half buried in the mud. Between the lane and the college was a small running brook, on the far side of which were some spots of blood. In the grounds of the college, a slater's hammer was discovered with blood and hair clinging to it.

The victim was identified as Jane Maria Clousen, the 17-year-old daughter of a night-watchman. Until recently Jane had been working as a servant at the home of Ebenezer Whitcher Pook, a printer, of 3 London Street, Greenwich. Jane had told her aunt, Elizabeth Trott, and her cousin Charlotte that she was 'keeping company' with Pook's son, twenty-year-old Edmund, although neither had seen them together. On the Sunday before the attack, Jane told Charlotte that she was meeting Edmund on the following day at Crooms Hill near his home, 'to know for certain whether it will be on Tuesday or Wednesday that I am to go into the country with him to some of his friends for a christening,' adding that she would be away for some time with Edmund as they were going to be married. On 13 April, Jane was abruptly dismissed from her employment, and since then she had been living in rented accommodation at 12 Ashburnham Road, Deptford. Her landlady, Mrs Hamilton, had noticed that the girl was in low spirits but was not able to discover the reason. On Tuesday night, a few hours before she was found, Jane and Mrs Hamilton were out walking and Jane said that she was going to Crooms Hill to see Edmund. The two parted company at about twenty to 7. Crooms Hill is over two miles from Kidbrooke Lane, but it was never discovered how and in whose company Jane arrived at the location where she was attacked.

Jane never rallied from her terrible injuries and on the evening of Sunday 30 April, she died without revealing the identity of her assailant. The post-mortem revealed that she was two months pregnant.

On 1 May, Superintendent Griffin and Inspector Mulvaney of Scotland Yard went to London Street and interviewed Edmund, who said he had been at home on the night of the murder. Mulvaney had learned from Mrs Hamilton that Jane had received a letter which she had burnt, and asked Edmund if he had written a letter to Jane, but he denied it, adding, 'I know nothing of her. She was a dirty young woman, and left in consequence.' Mulvaney asked for the clothes Edmund had been wearing on Tuesday night. A shirt was produced, and Mulvaney noticed stains that looked like blood on the right wristband and asked for an explanation. Edmund said they had come from a scratch, but when Mulvaney pointed out that the scratch was on Edmund's left wrist he fell silent. Edmund said he had only seen Jane once since she left his father's service, when he had noticed her in the street talking to a young gentleman. The police took Edmund into custody, his father protesting that Edmund was 'a different sort of boy altogether' and nothing could have gone on between his son and Jane without the family being aware of it.

At the inquest Mrs Plane, who kept a confectioner's shop on Royal Hill, not far from the Pooks' home, said that between half past eight and nine on the night of the attack, Edmund had rushed into her shop in a state of great agitation and looking as if he had run a long way, and asked to borrow a clothes brush, which he used to brush mud from his trousers.

On 2 May, Edmund was charged with murder at Greenwich police court and remanded to Maidstone Gaol. During the rail journey to Maidstone, the

Scenes from the Eltham murder.

opinion of the public became very clear, as hostile crowds gathered at each station on the way to hiss at him. As the inquest and police court hearings continued during the month of May, it became apparent, however, that the case for the prosecution was far from cut and dried.

Although witnesses had seen a young man and a young woman together near the scene of the attack on the night in question, the evidence of the man's identity was sketchy and easily shaken. Two witnesses had heard a woman scream just after half past eight, but thought it sounded more like 'lovers' play' than anyone in pain. Shortly afterwards, they saw a man running towards Morden College. The running man wore a dark coat, and was clean shaven, like the suspect, but neither witness could be positive it was he.

Dr Henry Letheby, professor of chemistry at the London Hospital, was given Edmund's clothing and the hammer for analysis. Letheby had considerable experience of examining evidence in medical and legal enquiries, and had written about the method of identifying bloodstains by use of the microscope. A hair seven and a half inches in length had been found on Edmund's trousers and this corresponded precisely in appearance with hair taken from the head of the deceased. Letheby was able to confirm that stains on Edmund's trousers and shirt cuff and clots on the hammer were blood. It was not possible to say for

Scenes from the Eltham murder.

certain that the blood was human, but to his experienced eye, the stains 'bore all the characteristics of human blood'. The hair sticking to the hammer was the same colour as that of the deceased.

Edmund's solicitor was Henry Pook who, despite the coincidence of surname, was not related to his client. He introduced many points which were intended to cast doubts on the medical evidence. He suggested that there might have been contamination of the samples during the time they had been in the possession of the police, and also established that it was not possible for Letheby to tell the difference between blood from a wound and blood from someone biting their tongue during a fit. This was very material as Edmund was known to suffer from fits. The murder weapon had been purchased from a shop in Deptford High Street on 24 April, but Mrs Thomas, who had sold it, was unable to describe the customer. Ironmonger William Sparshott recalled that a man whom he later identified as Edmund had entered his shop that day and asked for a hammer, but not having what the customer wanted Sparshott had directed him to the Thomas's shop.

Alice Durnford, the 18-year-old daughter of a Lewisham plasterer, had been 'keeping company' with Edmund for a year. The relationship had been kept secret from her parents and so, when Edmund passed her house, he used to signal to her with a whistle. Alice thought the whistle found near the scene of the murder was like the one Edmund had used. John Thomas Barr, a pawnbroker, knew Edmund by sight. He had seen Edmund walking rapidly in the direction of Royal Hill, Greenwich, on the night of the murder, and had heard the church clock strike nine about ten minutes later. The timings were now looking critical. If the witnesses who had heard the screams were correct, then Jane had been attacked between half past eight and nine. The distance from the murder scene to Royal Hill was just over a mile and a half. It was certainly possible for Edmund to run the distance in twenty minutes. There were other witnesses however who said that they had seen a couple walking towards Eltham shortly before 7 p.m. Edmund's account of his movements on the night of the murder was that he had gone to Lewisham to see Miss Durnford, but after waiting for her on the bridge near her house, had not seen her and gone home.

The inquest jury eventually returned a majority verdict of murder, naming Edmund Pook as the killer of Jane Clousen. When Edmund next appeared at the police court it was decided because of the hostile crowds that had gathered outside the front of the courthouse, to transport him there in a cab from an outlying railway station and then have him enter the building via a ladder placed against the stable. On 30 May he was committed to take his trial at the Old Bailey and was taken to Newgate Gaol. While the prisoner waited to know his fate, Ebenezer Pook, his family and friends had to endure being hooted and yelled at in the streets of Greenwich.

At the trial, which opened on 12 July, a new witness appeared. Walter Perrin, who knew Edmund, said he was coming out of the Thomas's shop on 24 April and had seen and spoken to Edmund outside. He had then seen Edmund go into the shop and, shortly afterwards, observed Mrs Thomas taking a hammer from the window. There was also a fresh complication – a blue duster, stained with blood, had been found on the morning after the murder not far from the scene, and handed to the police. It had been assumed by them at the time that this had no connection with the case and had never been given to Dr Letheby or introduced into evidence.

For the defence it was pointed out that the work of a printer often resulted in small scratches, and Edmund sometimes had fits and bit his tongue, getting blood on his clothes. His elder brother, Thomas, provided Edmund with an alibi for the time when the hammer had been purchased, saying he had been out in Edmund's company that evening. Moreover several witnesses supported Edmund's alibi for the night of the murder by testifying that they had seen him alone near Lewisham Bridge at 8 o'clock, and that he appeared to be waiting for someone. The time of the murder was also called into question. PC Gunn had patrolled the lane at a quarter to 2 but had seen and heard nothing untoward.

Harris, who had seen Jane at 7 a.m., had estimated that the wounds had been inflicted from two to twelve hours previously.

It was greatly in Edmund's favour that there was no independent evidence that he had been courting Jane. Indeed the only suggestion that there had ever been a relationship was the statement made by the deceased girl. Jane had claimed that a locket she wore was a gift from Edmund, but a man called Humphreys had come forward saying he had given it to her, and the jeweller remembered selling it to him. This inevitably raised the possibility that Jane's stories about a relationship with Edmund may have been wishful thinking.

In his summing–up, Chief Justice Bovill pointed out that the case against Edmund Pook relied a great deal on the identification of witnesses, some of whom, including Perrin, he felt were unreliable, or even opening themselves to a charge of perjury. The evidence of sightings was contradictory. He was scathing about the failure of the police to connect the blue duster with the crime. He felt that the police, while being an important body of men to whom the public was greatly indebted, sometimes came to a conclusion about a case and then followed up only the evidence that supported that conclusion. Mulvaney had suggested that Edmund had written a letter to the deceased, yet there was no evidence that he had ever done so. Several witnesses who identified Edmund as the man in Sparshott's shop had said he wore light trousers, but he did not own any light trousers.

Under the circumstances it was inevitable that the jury returned a verdict of not guilty. The newspapers accepted the verdict as correct and there was heavy criticism of the police, *The Times* describing the behaviour of Mulvaney and Griffin as 'stupid' and 'reprehensible'.

This however was a case which was never going to go away. Edmund had supporters who opened a subscription to defray the costs of his defence and a committee was formed which offered £200 for information leading to the discovery of the murderer. There were also many 'stump orators' in the neighbourhood who denounced the trial as a disgrace, and named Edmund as the murderer. The charge of dirtiness against Jane was said to be a lie as those who knew her could attest that the girl had been of cleanly habits. For days after the trial, large crowds stood outside the Pooks' house, yelling, hooting and whistling, and effigies of a woman with a man attacking her with a hammer were paraded through the town, stopping all business in the streets. Ebenezer Pook was obliged to demand police protection. He later took out a summons against the police for perjury, but it had never been suggested that they had given false evidence, and this was not granted. Questions were asked in Parliament but Home Secretary Henry Bruce declined to take any action. A pamphlet, *The Eltham Tragedy Revisited*, was issued based on letters published in the *Kentish Mercury*. 'I hope never again to be a spectator of a trial in which the judge was so unjudicial, and sensational, the witnesses so random, the counsel so insulting and the police so simple,' stated the writer, who went on to list ten points in favour of a conviction, adding ' . . . the straws of evidence all blow in one direction'. In August Ebenezer and Edmund Pook took out an action for libel against the author, Mr Newton Crosland, and the publisher of the *Kentish Mercury*.

It was not then permitted for the accused to give evidence in a murder trial, and this meant that when the libel action was heard it was the first time Edmund had been questioned in court about the case. Edmund explained that he had run home from Lewisham because he felt a fit might be coming on, and had used the clothes brush at the shop so his mother would not worry, thinking he had fallen down in a fit. In both the libel trials the verdict was for the Pooks with damages of £50 and 40s respectively. They also received damages of 25s for an article in the *Weekly Dispatch*.

Edmund Pook continued to live in Greenwich and work as a printer. In 1881 he married 20-year-old Alice Maria Swabey, the daughter of a label maker. He died in 1920 aged 70. The murder of Jane Maria Clousen remains unsolved.

12

HACKNEY

The Lady in Black

Manfred Louis Masset was born in Islington on 24 April 1896. His mother, Louise Josephine Jemima Masset, was an unmarried governess, who never revealed, even to her family, the identity of Manfred's father. Although Louise, then 32, liked to pretend that she was born in Paris, she was actually the English-born daughter of a Frenchman and his English wife. When Manfred was three weeks old Louise took him to be cared for by a nurse, Helena (referred to as Helen in the trial papers) Eliza Gentle, who lived with her mother and stepfather at 210 Clyde Road, Tottenham. Louise paid Miss Gentle £1 17s a month to care for Manfred. At first she visited the child only once a fortnight, although when he was two she began to see him once a week, and sometimes used to take him out. Miss Gentle became very fond of the little boy, and believed that Louise was a kind and loving mother.

From August 1898, Louise had been living with her elder married sister Leonie Cadisch and her family at 29 Bethune Road, Stoke Newington. Louise's father had died in 1877 and her mother, who had remarried in 1883, was living next door at No. 31. On 27 September 1899 Louise's stepfather died, and she, her mother and sisters adopted the traditional black mourning costume.

On 18 October 1899 Miss Gentle's mother, Mrs Norris, received a letter from Louise, saying that she had seen the boy's father who wished him to be brought up in his cousin's family so he could learn French. She was sorry to have to remove him from their care, but thought that not to do so would be 'in the way of his future prospects'. Nothing had been said about this at earlier meetings, but Miss Gentle, though upset to part with the child, knew that she had to accept the inevitable. On the same day, Louise also told Leonie of her decision, saying that on Friday 27 October she and Manfred would be travelling on the 2.30 p.m. train from London Bridge station to Newhaven, where they would

Louise Masset, Manfred and Miss Gentle.

take the boat to France. On the appointed day, Miss Gentle dressed the child in a blue serge sailor suit, and parcelled up a change of clothing as well as Manfred's favourite toy, a little pair of scales he used to weigh out sugar and currants. As instructed by Louise, Miss Gentle took the boy by tram to the Birdcage public house on Stamford Hill, where she handed him over to his mother. Louise was carrying a Gladstone bag. Both Miss Gentle and the child were very upset at parting, and when Louise and Manfred boarded an omnibus and rode away, the child cried for his nurse. The bus reached London Bridge at 1.35 and there Louise and Manfred alighted. Mrs Georgina Worley, the attendant of number 2 waiting room at the railway station, later remembered the little boy in the sailor suit and the lady dressed in black sitting there between 1.45 and 2.30 p.m. She had spoken to the lady, who had explained that she was waiting for someone. Mrs Worley left the room at 2.30 and when she returned ten minutes later, the pair had gone. They were next seen at about 2.40 in another waiting room, where the attendant, a Mrs Ellen Rees, spoke to them and saw them leave shortly after 3 p.m.

Later that same day, Mary Teahan, a governess, and her friend Miss Briggs travelled by train from Richmond to Dalston Junction, arriving at 6.19 p.m. Leaving Miss Briggs in the waiting room, Mary headed for the water closets. As she was closing the door of the cubicle, she saw an object on the floor, and was able, in the dim light, to make out the features of a small, pale face. Believing that she had found someone lying ill, she ran out and told Miss Briggs, who spoke to Joseph Standing, a porter. He went to look, and found the body of a male child, naked and covered only by a black shawl. Standing fetched a lamp, and was able to see clearly that the child was dead. There were two wounds on the boy's face, which was smeared with blood. Near the body was a clinker brick, a kind of hard, darkened brick used decoratively, and of a kind not seen near the station. The police were called, followed by a doctor who examined the body and found it to be still warm. The child appeared to have been stunned by blows to the head, and then suffocated. Based on body temperature it was estimated that death had taken place between one and three hours before the body was found.

At London Bridge station, shortly before seven o'clock, Mrs Rees saw a lady enter the waiting room to wash her hands, and recognised her as the same lady she had seen earlier with the little boy. The boy was not with her and she carried a small brown paper parcel. The lady asked about the time of the next train to Brighton, and on being told it departed at twenty past seven, hurried out to get the train.

Louise Masset did not and never had had any intention of going to France that day. She was meeting a man. Eudore Lucas was a 19-year-old student who had arrived in England from his native France in August 1898 and lodged with Louise's mother and stepfather at 31 Bethune Road, next door to where Louise lived with her sister. He and Louise had met, and a friendship developed, based on a strong mutual attraction. In May 1899 Lucas, Louise and another lady and gentleman took a holiday together at Brighton, staying at a Mr Findlay's hotel in the Queen's Road. On that occasion they had occupied separate rooms. About a month later Louise and her young man began to 'walk out' together, and became friendlier, writing affectionate letters to each other. The relationship

Above & below: *Two views of Dalston Junction station.*

was kept a secret from Louise's family. In September Louise told Lucas that she had an illegitimate child. In a later statement he claimed that he was pleased to know that as it was fair of her to tell him. On either the 24 or 25 October Lucas met Louise at Liverpool Street station by appointment. She told him she was going to Brighton on the following Friday by the 4 o'clock train from London Bridge, and would be staying at Mr Findlay's. It was agreed that they would meet on Saturday and book into the hotel under the name of Brooks, posing as brother and sister, taking adjoining rooms. On the Saturday, Louise met Lucas as arranged at Brighton station. Any emotion she might have felt following the events of the previous day must have been under careful control, for he noticed nothing unusual in her manner and behaviour. At the hotel Lucas occupied room 10, and Louise room 11, but that night the young Frenchman crept into Louise's room and they slept together for the first time. Was Louise hoping to marry her youthful lover? Was his reaction when he heard about Manfred really as generous as he claimed? Although Lucas came from a comfortably off family, he was then earning only £3 a month as a correspondence clerk, his object in coming to England being to learn the language. He was not in a good position to offer marriage, especially when there was a child to keep, and what his family might have thought of a 36-year-old bride with an illegitimate child can only be guessed at. Louise Masset, seeing in young Lucas the hope of marriage and thus an entry into respectable society, may well have believed that without Manfred her chances would be greatly enhanced.

Louise was back home by the Sunday evening, looking tired but calm, and had a conversation with her sister the following morning describing the rough sea crossing from France. She went out to her regular post as daily governess that afternoon, and her employer thought her to be cheerful and in her usual spirits.

On Monday 30 October, Miss Gentle received an envelope with two letters from Louise. One was a reference, and the other said that she had just returned from her journey and Manfred had been ill on the boat, but sent his love.

On that same morning however, Miss Gentle read a description of a murdered boy in the *Daily Mail* that disturbed her so much that she went to her family doctor for advice. From there she went to Hackney Mortuary, where she saw the body of a child. It was Manfred. Miss Gentle later made a statement to the police listing the clothes Manfred had been wearing and the items she had parcelled up for him.

The police decided to keep watch on 29 Bethune Road, and Sergeant William Burch and Sergeant Nursey, with other officers, arrived at 3.30 in the afternoon, but Louise did not return home that night, for by then she had learned that she was a wanted woman. She fled to the Croydon home of her younger sister, Mathilde, who was married to auctioneer George Simes. At about 11 p.m. Simes opened the door to find Louise standing there in a state of some distress.

'Can I speak to you?' she asked.

'Yes; what is it?' he replied.

'I am being hunted for murder, but I have not done it,' she told him.

'The child found at Dalston was not yours, was it?' he asked.

'Yes, I am sure that it is,' she said. Louise told him that she had seen the placard of an evening newspaper saying that the child's body had been identified, and when she bought a paper and read the description she felt sure it was Manfred. She was almost too hysterical to talk, and Simes calmed her agitation as best he could, saying that if she would tell him the truth whatever it might be, he would do his best for her. His suspicions must have been obvious for she exclaimed, 'Oh! How do you think I could kill my own child!' He asked her to describe her movements on the Friday, and Louise said that she had handed Manfred over to two women at London Bridge station and had then gone to Brighton. After dining at a restaurant she had engaged a room at Mr Findlay's hotel and on the following day Lucas had joined her. The story about taking the boy to France was, she admitted, an invention so that she could go away with Lucas for a few days.

Louise told Simes that one day when she had taken the boy out she had met two women at Tottenham, and when they found out that he was a nurse-child they said that they were forming a home at King's Road, Chelsea, and would take the child for £12 a year and he would be well-educated. She had arranged to meet them in the waiting room at London Bridge station, where she had handed over the boy and £12. The women had taken Manfred to the refreshment room and she had waited for a receipt for her money but they had not returned.

Although it was by now midnight, Simes knew he must take immediate action. Leaving Louise in the care of his wife, he went to 29 Bethune Road to speak to his brother-in-law, arriving there at 2.30 am. After discussing the situation with Richard Cadisch and his wife, it was too late for him to return home and he stayed overnight. The next morning he and Richard left to go to Croydon, walking to London Bridge station. On the way they realised that they were being followed, and on discovering that the two men shadowing them were policemen, Simes made a statement to them. The result was that Simes, Cadisch, Sergeant Burch and Detective Allen all went to Croydon, where Louise was asked to make a formal statement. Louise repeated what she had told Simes, giving the address of the children's home as 45 King's Road. Louise was taken to Dalston police station, where she was charged with the murder of her son.

On 1 November, the proprietor of Findlay's hotel found in the drawer of room 11 a pair of toy scales, one of which had in it some grains of sugar. He handed them to the police. On the same day Police Sergeant Richard Nursey opened a parcel wrapped in brown paper, which had been passed to the lost

Manfred Masset; a sketch from a photograph produced in court.

MISS GENTLE.   LOUISE MASSET.

Miss Gentle and Louise Masset in court, with a sketch of Manfred.

property office at London Bridge station after being found at Brighton railway station. The parcel contained a child's blue serge suit. The suit and scales were shown to Miss Gentle, who identified them as Manfred's. She was also able to identify the brown paper as that in which she had wrapped the extra clothes for Manfred, as it was part of a piece she had received from a draper. She had cut it in half to wrap the parcel, cutting through the draper's name as she did so, and kept the other piece. Put together, they fitted.

Louise had asked to see Manfred's body but it was not until 2 November, after the coroner's court hearing, that permission was given. The body had been coffined, and Louise leaned over the side, placed her hand on the child's head and sobbed, 'Oh, my child, my poor boy!'

The shawl in which the body had been found was taken to local drapers' shops, and at McIlroy's of 161 High Street, Stoke Newington, the assistant, Maud Clifford, identified it as one she had sold on 24 October. On 4 November at Dalston police court, she picked out Louise as the lady to whom she had sold the shawl. The shop had stocked three shawls of that pattern, only one of which had been sold, although it was not an uncommon design. Mrs Rees, the attendant at London Bridge station, was also able to pick out Louise at an identification parade on 24 November. Inspector Frederick Forth visited 29 Bethune Road and found in the back garden a rockery formed of clinker bricks. There were also some in the front garden, forming a border, and a few loose ones on the ground. He took three away and compared them with the one found near the body. It was of the same kind. He also made the journey from Dalston Junction to London Bridge, changing from the train to a bus at Broad Street. The journey took half an hour, showing that Louise could have been at Dalston Junction at the time of Manfred's death.

The proprietor of 45 King's Road, the address of the supposed children's home, was a dairyman, who stated that none of his female assistants were away on 27 October. At the trial, which opened at the Central Criminal Court, the Old Bailey on 13 December, Louise made a detailed statement describing her meetings with the two ladies. She said she had first waited for them in one waiting room, then thinking there had been a mistake went to the second one, and had finally met up with them on the platform. She had given them £12 and the parcel of clothes. They had gone to the refreshment room to get paper and pen to write out a receipt and after waiting for them, she had gone there to find them, but they had gone. She said she had never been in the lavatory at Dalston Junction station or in Mrs Rees' waiting room, or purchased a black shawl.

The jury, after considering the evidence for only half an hour, found Louise Masset guilty of murder and she was sentenced to death. Petitions for a reprieve were sent to the Home Secretary and the Queen. Many people believed that Louise was innocent and tried to prove that the two ladies who had taken Manfred really existed, or that Louise had been in Brighton at the time of the murder, but no convincing evidence was found. On 9 January Louise was hanged at Newgate Gaol, the first murderer to be executed in England in the 1900s. She went to her death calmly, and just before the end, admitted, 'What I suffer is just.'

13

HAMMERSMITH AND FULHAM

Femme Fatale

At about 9.30 p.m. on 26 May 1882 police constable Arthur Flawn was called by charlady Susan Pape to 6 Moor Park Road, Fulham, where there had been a violent altercation. He was met at the door by 32-year-old John Carlisle, and Lina Sykes, a lady who, though probably in her forties, claimed to be 29. They took the constable up to the top back bedroom, where he found 48-year-old Richard George Wells lying sulkily on the bed. Lina said she wanted Wells removed from the house, and Carlisle said that Wells had hit him on the hand with a poker. Carlisle's hand was swollen and bruised, but Wells, who had a black eye, said he had been kicked in the ribs, which he thought were broken. He refused to leave, claiming that he paid the rent of the house, something Mrs Sykes hotly disputed. PC Flawn thought that both men had been drinking, although the lady was sober. Since he had not seen the incident he decided not to interfere.

Flawn left, and Susan Pape departed at 10 p.m., but an hour later Sergeant George Bartle was called to the house, probably by a neighbour. The front door was open and Carlisle stood on the top step, bleeding from a wound on the right side of his head. 'Oh, policeman, come on, he has stabbed me this time,' he said, then staggered down the steps into Bartle's arms. Carlisle was tall and well-built, and his weight brought both men crashing to the ground. 'I am dying,' murmured Carlisle, and drifted into unconsciousness. Bartle looked up and saw Wells standing in the hallway. Instead of coming to assist, Wells simply slammed the door shut. Bartle sent for a doctor, and four minutes later Dr Francis Egan, a police surgeon of nearby Walham Green station, arrived. Leaving the injured man in his care, Bartle knocked on the door, which was opened by Lina Sykes.

In the hallway Bartle saw that the globe of a gas bracket had been recently smashed, and a bent poker lay on the floor. Upstairs he found Wells, who made a statement. Wells said that he and Mrs Sykes had been at the races that day to see the running of the Oaks, and there he had met up with Carlisle, a man already known to him. He introduced Carlisle to Mrs Sykes and the three had a few bets together and drank champagne, then returned to Fulham in a cab. The men had enjoyed some whisky, but then a quarrel had arisen between them. They had been in the back garden when Wells had snatched a glass of whisky and water from Carlisle's hand and dashed it against the wall. The two men had fought, rolling on the ground, punching and kicking.

Things eventually calmed down, and they decided to be friends again. Wells had thought that Carlisle was leaving, but on entering the drawing room a little later on, he was angered to find the younger man still in the house. Wells admitted to Bartle that he had picked up a bottle of whisky from the table, and hit Carlisle over the head, saying, 'I don't want you here, why don't you go?' Wells added unrepentantly, 'If I have killed him I don't care.' Bartle placed Wells under arrest. As they returned downstairs, Bartle looked into the drawing room and saw furniture in disarray, some of it tipped over, and the broken whisky bottle on the floor.

Meanwhile, Dr Egan was examining the injury to Carlisle's temple, but there was a large pool of blood on the ground and its source was not immediately obvious. Carlisle died minutes later without regaining consciousness. The body was removed to the Fulham Union workhouse mortuary, where Egan found that the blow on the head had fractured the skull, and there were two stab wounds in the back, one of which had been deflected by a rib. The other, seven inches deep, had penetrated the chest cavity, damaging the liver and lungs, and would have been fatal in minutes.

At the police station, Wells made a statement describing the struggle in the garden, and hitting Carlisle with the whisky bottle, but denied that he had ever stabbed him. That, he said, had been done by Lina Sykes. When the police searched the house for a possible murder weapon they found a long white handled poultry knife, on one side of which were stains that looked like blood. It appeared to have been wiped, then thrown into a basket in the kitchen with some ordinary dinner knives.

The inquest opened on 20 May, where the court was told that John Carlisle was born near Skipton, in Yorkshire, and was a man of private means who had no regular employment but liked to attend race meetings. One newspaper speculated that he was a bookmaker. Dr Egan told the court that Carlisle could not have walked far after receiving the fatal wound. Had he been stabbed in the drawing room, he could not have reached the doorway. It followed that the fatal blow had been delivered while Carlisle was in the hall. Egan confirmed that

Sergeant Bartle.

neither the blow on the head nor the shallower stab wound were sufficient to cause death. He identified the poultry knife as the kind of weapon that would have caused the stab wounds.

Mr John Haynes, a solicitor acting for Wells, said he would be cross-examining Lina Sykes, since his client had told him that her account of the night's events was untrue. Indeed, as the facts of the case unfolded, it emerged that Lina Sykes was no stranger to violence, was a brazen and prolific liar, and had a murky past in which she had previously been present at a very suspicious death.

It is not known exactly when or where Lina was born or indeed her real name. In the 1861 census she was calling herself Lina Braham and gave her age as 21, and her place of birth as St James, London. She claimed to be married but there was no sign of a husband. In 1866 Lina was to claim that for the last eight or nine years she had been the mistress of Sir Gilbert East, baronet. Sir Gilbert, born in 1823, had married in 1845 and was the father of four children. A keen yachtsman, he had been at the Royal Victoria yacht club, Ryde, in August 1866. Early on the morning of Sunday the 12th he had been seen in a rather intoxicated state arm-in-arm with a young woman, going through the tollgate to the pier to join his yacht. Five minutes later there was a loud scream. People ran to help and his lady companion said that Sir Gilbert had fallen into the water. He did not reappear and some days later his body was found floating in the sea. Miss Lina Braham, described as fashionably dressed and between 26 and 28 years of age, was the principal witness at the inquest, and attracted a great deal of attention, not only because of her relationship with the deceased but for her highly excitable manner, speaking loudly and sharply when giving evidence. Showing 'an air of perfect indifference to the nature of the inquiry', she announced snappily, 'Well here I am. What do you want with me?' She stated that at the time Sir Gilbert had fallen, she had not been holding onto his arm. She had heard him slip, and found him clinging to the side of the pier. She had tried to save him but was unable to do so. Asked how he fell, she said, 'Why, the same as any other person of course.' When asked why she had not helped Sir George as he walked down the pier, she replied, 'Lord bless the man, how can I tell?' Her gloves, which were dirty and torn, were offered in evidence.

The jurors found that the cause of death was drowning but were unable to express an opinion on how Sir Gilbert had come to fall in the water.

Lina's activities over the next few years are unknown, but in 1870, calling herself Lina Keyzor Braham, and stating her age as 23, she married Henry Cecil Sykes. Sykes, a gentleman with £600 a year to his name, had been studying for holy orders, and was fully aware that Lina had been living what he later called 'an immoral life'. On her marriage certificate she refused to give either the first name or profession of her father but one of the witnesses was 23-year-old Fanny Julia Schiller, the daughter of a German tailor. Could the two women have been related?

In the 1871 census, Lina, conveniently forgetting that she had given her age as 21 ten years previously, claimed to be 23, and gave her place of birth as England. Her husband was 'temporarily absent'. By the 1881 census Lina was admitting only to 28 and stating that she had been born at sea.

While living in Woking Lina met Richard George Wells, a solicitors' clerk. Wells was a married man, with two grown-up daughters. Initially their association had been purely professional, but before long, their relationship was

Number 6 Moor Park Road, Fulham, 1882.

a matter of scandalous rumour in the neighbourhood. Wells left his wife, and he and Lina lived together in London hotels under the name of Wallace before taking the house at Fulham.

On the morning of 26 May 1882 Wells had engaged Elias Carter, a cab driver, to take himself and Lina to Epsom for the Oaks. A picnic basket was packed, well stocked with beer, whisky, champagne and sandwiches.

They had returned in the same cab accompanied by John Carlisle, and paused on the way several times for further refreshment. All had seemed friendly until they reached the house, but trouble was already brewing. A certain amount of drunken flirting may have been going on, and Lina might already have singled out Carlisle as a more entertaining and attractive prospect than the man she was with. Whether Carlisle would have felt flirtatious about Lina when he sobered up will never be known. Shortly before they arrived home, with Wells temporarily absent from the cab, Carlisle confided to Carter, 'he is jealous of me, and says I put my arm round her waist.' As they reached the house Wells held his hand out to Carlisle and said, 'If we part now, we part as friends, but if you enter my house we shall be enemies.' Lina simply pushed Wells aside and rang the bell, asking Carlisle to come in and have a glass of wine. The cabman heard the two men talking loudly indoors, and Mrs Sykes called Wells a 'dirty old beast', threatening to have him locked up or turned out of the house.

At the inquest and police court hearings Lina, cutting a stylish figure in a silk gown with a long train, and flashing a diamond ring, contradicted the evidence given by the cabman as to what he had overheard, and denied positively that Carlisle had put his arm around her waist. She said that after Wells had hit Carlisle on the head with the whisky bottle she had been frightened, ran into the water closet and bolted herself in. While there she had heard Wells say, 'I'll kill you,' and Carlisle reply, 'You won't.' She then heard someone running up and down the stairs to the kitchen. After Carlisle said, 'He has stabbed me this time', followed by the slamming of the front door, Wells came and pulled on the closet door and said, 'You are in here. I will give it to you now,' but she didn't reply. Eventually she returned downstairs and found Wells peering through the Venetian blind. She denied that she lived with Wells as his wife. Asked by Mr Haynes if Wells had said that Carlisle had seized him by the throat and he had acted in self-defence, she denied this too. As Wells, committed for trial, was being taken away, he declared that the evidence of Mrs Sykes was 'wholly untrue'.

The trial of Richard Wells opened at the Central Criminal Court, the Old Bailey on 1 August 1882, and Lina was the principal witness. She denied any immoral relationship between herself and Wells, describing him as an 'agent or handyman' who occasionally visited the house or came there for his letters, and sometimes slept there but not with her. Confronted with a hotelier, Mr Seizman, she said that she had never stayed at his hotel with Wells. She could not account for the fact that her medicine bottles were made out in the name of Mrs Wells, and said it was a mistake that bills were made out in the name of Wallace. The claim that she and Wells had stayed at the Charing Cross Hotel under the name of Wallace was 'pure imagination'.

The defence then questioned Lina about her past. She confirmed that she had been a witness to the death of Sir Gilbert East sixteen years previously but since she was claiming to be only 29 years old, this line of questioning put her in a spot. She told the court that in 1866 she had been only thirteen years of age,

Mrs Sykes in court.

and even though her evidence at the inquest was a matter of record, she denied that she had ever said she had lived with Sir Gilbert as his wife for eight or nine years. Despite being warned that she might be indicted for perjury if she did not tell the truth she stuck to this story.

It was probably the element of provocation that led the jury to find Wells guilty of manslaughter and he was sentenced to penal servitude for life.

When Henry Cecil Sykes read in the newspapers about the murder of John Carlisle he was astonished to see that his wife, whom he had not seen for several years, had been a witness to events. Not only did the case give him ample grounds for divorce, he now had her address. Armed with this information, Sykes brought a suit for divorce naming Wells as co-respondent, adding for good measure that from 1877 to 1881 Lina had also committed adultery with 'diverse other persons unknown'. The action was heard in May 1883. The court heard that after their marriage, Lina's career had been 'one of drinking, driving about in cabs and running her husband into debt.' Sykes had eventually been forced to make an arrangement with his creditors, and in August 1873 a deed was drawn up under an order of the court of chancery handing control of his income to his wife. After that her behaviour worsened, and 'her violence to her husband was sometimes carried so far that she shut him out of the house.' Eventually they separated, with Lina agreeing to pay her husband £2 a week out of his own property. These payments were made for only one or two weeks, and he then lost touch with her and had had to earn a living as best he could, as a tutor and press writer and sometimes as an omnibus or tramcar conductor.

Wells was brought to the court guarded by two warders. The former clerk was in convict's uniform, his head closely cropped. He confirmed that he and Lina had been living together as husband and wife, and Sykes was granted a *decree nisi*. In 1884 Sykes remarried, but in the following year he died, aged 40.

Richard Wells was later released from prison. He remarried in 1898, and died in 1914, aged 80. Lina probably changed her name again, as her fate thereafter is unknown.

Who stabbed John Carlisle? If Dr Egan was correct, the stabbing can only have taken place in the hallway. Since Carlisle was stabbed from behind, how much he knew about the identity of his attacker is in question, but Bartle saw Wells in the hallway only moments after the attack. He did not see Lina. Wells's motives are not hard to deduce, but if Lina was attracted to Carlisle and wanted Wells to leave she had no motive at all to kill the younger man.

14

HARINGEY

Hue and Cry

On the bitterly cold morning of 23 January 1909, two men, 21-year-old Paul Hefeld and his 30-year-old associate, known only as 'Jacob', were seen lurking near the gates of Schnurmann's rubber factory in Chesnut Road, Tottenham. Hefeld had worked there for a fortnight in December 1908, during which time he had learned that every Saturday morning a messenger was sent by car to the London and South Western bank, Hackney for cash to pay the wages.

At 9.30 two employees, a 17-year-old clerk, Arthur Keyworth, and driver Joseph Wilson returned to the factory with £80 in gold silver and bronze. They may have felt particularly secure in carrying out this duty as the factory was directly opposite Tottenham police station. Keyworth was carrying the money into the factory when Jacob, who was tall and powerfully built, seized him from behind and tried to snatch the bag. Both men fell to the ground and there was a struggle. Wilson had been driving away, but stopped the car and ran up to help. Jacob's hands were around Keyworth's throat but as Wilson pulled the attacker away Hefeld took a pistol from his pocket and fired at him several times. Wilson, dressed in layers of warm clothing topped by a heavy driving coat, was uninjured, though his garments, right down to his vest, were riddled with bullets. Jacob jumped up, grabbed the money bag, took out his own pistol and fired at Keyworth but missed. The robbers then ran away while Keyworth and Wilson rushed into the factory to give the alarm.

George Smith, a 17-year-old gas stoker, was passing by and tackled Jacob, bringing him down, the money bag falling to the ground. Hefeld came up and stood over Smith, callously shooting. Bullets whipped through Smith's cap, grazing his scalp, and one struck him in the shoulder. At this moment police constables William Tyler and Charles Newman rounded the corner.

More policemen, including Constable Bond, who had been in the middle of shaving and was not wearing a shirt, and night duty officers roused from their beds, emerged from the station, and the robbers grabbed the money and ran, heading towards the marshes on the banks of the river Lea, every so often turning and firing at the unarmed pursuers. Meanwhile, at the factory, Wilson had jumped back into the car accompanied by Keyworth, Mr Schnurmann and Paul Casewitz, the factory manager, and set off in pursuit. As the car rounded the corner Newman jumped onto the running board, and Tyler and Bond ran alongside. The car chased the men into Mitchley Road. Believing that the robbers had run out of ammunition, the driver tried to run them down, but they stopped, turned and fired at the car, breaking the windscreen, flying glass grazing Newman's cheek and Wilson's neck. Another shot pierced the radiator, immediately disabling the car. Newman, Tyler and Bond pursued the men across wasteland into Dowsett Road.

'Come on, give in; the game's up!' shouted Tyler. One of the men raised his revolver and shot Tyler through the neck.

At that moment, a 10-year-old boy, Ralph Joscelyne, who had rushed out into the street to see what was happening, ran into the line of fire and was shot in the chest. Mrs Elizabeth Andrews was at her front gate holding her baby in her arms, when she saw the running men firing, and the boy fall to the ground. She thrust the baby into the arms of a neighbour and took Ralph to the car but on finding it could not move she stopped a passing cyclist, who carried the child to the main road and got a van to take him to hospital.

The robbers hurried on in the direction of Epping Forest, over fences, though fields, and across brooks, but they had reckoned without the rapid communication available to the Metropolitan Police by telegraph and telephone. Superintendent Jenkins took charge of the operation and arranged for the roads around the area to be closed, for police from surrounding stations to converge on the scene, and for revolvers and cartridges to be issued to police officers. The firearms at Tottenham police station were kept in a locked cupboard, but had never previously been called for, and the key was missing. Sub-Divisional Police Inspector Large arrived on horseback, and solved the problem by giving orders for the cupboard to be broken open.

Cars and a Vanguard omnibus were pressed into service, and the police closed in on the fugitives, assisted by a large crowd of excited volunteers. Jacob and Hefeld made their way over the marshes looking for a crossing over the river Lea. They encountered some footballers and workmen and fired on them, wounding several. A group of duck shooters were out on the marshes and joined in the chase. Many of the police pursuers were unarmed, including Constable Nicod, who borrowed a revolver and approached the men to get a better shot at them, only to find that the weapon was defective. He was shot in the hip and leg.

After crossing the Lea the men skirted Banbury Reservoir and ran on, wounding one of the impromptu hunting party on the way, and encountering a Gypsy encampment, where they fired on both people and horses but missing their targets. Still their pursuers gained ground, on foot, on bicycles, in cars and on horseback. The robbers ran through Salisbury Hall Farm, where they rested for a while behind a haystack, then onto the Chingford Road. They needed a vehicle, and seized the first one they could get, an electric tram. Driver Joseph Slow had already seen the chase and heard cries of 'Stop! Murder!' He pulled up and looking round saw Jacob at the back of the tram pointing a revolver at both himself and the conductor, Charles Wyatt. At that moment Slow felt more in danger from the crowd, some of whom had guns and were firing at the fugitives. With bullets whistling past his ears, Slow scrambled up the steps to the top of the tram, and crouched down. He risked a look downstairs and saw Wyatt being held prisoner by Hefeld, a gun to his head, being ordered to drive on. Wyatt protested that he couldn't drive, but under threat of death was obliged to comply as best he could. Some of the pursuers took up positions behind hedges and fired repeatedly on the tram, the bullets shattering windows and showering the interior with glass. Slow decided to stay put. There were three passengers on board, a woman with a child, who cowered on the floor and miraculously escaped injury, and 63-year-old Edward Loveday, who demanded to be allowed to leave but was ignored. Wyatt drove on, feeling the heat of the gun barrel against his cheek. He noticed that there was no lack of ammunition, as the men frequently and expertly reloaded their guns from fresh supplies in their pockets. Wyatt knew that Slow, from his position, was able to cut the circuit and bring the tram to a standstill, and fervently hoped that this would not happen in case he was blamed and shot in retaliation.

The trams ran on a single track with loops to enable others to pass, and as Wyatt slowed at the next loop for another tram, the woman and child managed to scramble to safety. The second tram was promptly commandeered by the police who piled aboard, ordered the driver to reverse, and set off in pursuit. A more immediate threat was Constable Hawkins, who was giving chase on an advertising cart. It drew level, but as Hawkins was about to fire, Hefeld shot the pony and the occupants of the cart were hurled into the road, a can of paste landing on top of them.

As Wyatt approached a turn in the road, he said, 'You had better get off here, as there is a police station just round the bend.' 'There is not,' said Hefeld, gruffly. 'All right, we will go on,' said Wyatt. At Kite's Corner, Loveday tried to overpower Hefeld, but was shot through the neck. The fugitives decided to change vehicles and, seeing a milk cart standing at the kerb, they left the tram and jumped into the cart, shooting the driver George Conyard when he tried to resist them. Jacob took the reins and, lashing the horse, drove off at a gallop with Hefeld sitting in the back, a pistol in each hand, firing at pursuers. The cart was not built for speed, and Jacob managed to turn it over when taking a bend. Abandoning it, they seized another horse and cart and took it to Forest Road, but it was heavy going and the horse struggled, especially uphill. It was not until later that it was found that the chain brake was still on one wheel.

Crossing Wadham and Winchester Roads, the two men finally came to a standstill at a railway bridge over the Ching brook, where they abandoned the cart and paused to reload. Unable to shake off their armed pursuers, they were exhausted and almost out of cartridges. Unexpectedly they found their way blocked by a 6ft boundary fence. The taller Jacob was able to scramble over, but Hefeld tried and failed. Hefeld told Jacob to save himself, then, as the men closed in he fired at them until he was down to his last cartridge and finally turned the gun on himself.

Jacob ran on in the direction of Hale End, looking for a suitable hideout. Oak Cottage was a four-room dwelling with a lean-to scullery, occupied by Charles Rolstone, a coalman, who was at work that morning, and his wife Eliza and their children. Hearing police whistles, Eliza went to the front gate, but a policeman ordered her to go inside and shut the door as there was a murderer about. Returning to the cottage, she was surprised to find the front door closed.

The railway arch where Hefeld shot himself (inset Paul Hefeld). (© Metropolitan Police Authority, 2009)

Alarmed, because her two sons aged 5 and 3 were in the kitchen, she went around
the back to find the door of the lean-to also closed. Peering through a hole in
the door she was terrified to see a wild-eyed stranger, his face covered in blood,
who told her to keep quiet. She ran for the police, screaming that her children
were inside the house. Constable Dewhurst and a civilian broke in through the
back door and brought the children to safety, by which time Jacob, having tried
but failed to escape though the chimney, had fled upstairs. The house was soon
surrounded by armed police. Jacob was seen through a bedroom window and
shots were fired and a great deal of damage was done, but he was not hit.

It was looking as if there would be a lengthy siege but Constables Eagles
and Dixon, arriving on their bicycles, had other ideas. Eagles borrowed a
double barreled shotgun from a bystander, and entered the cottage. The two
downstairs rooms were unoccupied, but hearing a noise upstairs Eagles went
into the yard, and got a ladder from the garden of the next house. Scaling the
ladder he reached the level of the back bedroom window, which he opened.
An onlooker suggested a collie dog be sent into the house, and the dog ran up
the stairs. Eagles peered through the window, and saw the dog on the landing,
and a man standing in the doorway of the front bedroom pointing a gun
at him. Eagles then discovered that the shotgun would not fire. He quickly
descended the ladder and borrowed a revolver, then, breaking in through a front
window, Eagles, followed by Constables Dixon and Cater, entered the house,
cautiously ascending the staircase. They called on Jacob to surrender, but there
was no answer and Eagles and Cater fired some shots through the panels of the
bedroom door. They heard a shot inside the room, and bursting in, found Jacob
lying dead. The chase, which had lasted over two hours, was over.

There were two more deaths that day. Schoolboy Ralph Joscelyne was found
to be dead when he reached hospital. Thirty-one-year-old Constable Tyler was
admitted to Tottenham Hospital but died soon afterwards. All the wounded
pursuers eventually recovered. Hefeld, with a serious head wound, was found to
be alive and taken to hospital where he was expected to survive.

Tyler and Joscelyne were buried at Abney Park Cemetery, Stoke Newington,
on 29 January. Three thousand officers and men of the police force took part
in the joint funerals and from Tyler's home in Arnold Street and Josceleyne's in
Colsterworth Road, to the cemetery two and half miles away, the streets were
lined by crowds, standing in respectful silence, with many more watching from
windows, roofs and balconies.

On the same day, the murderer was buried quietly at Walthamstow Cemetery,
his coffin marked only with the name 'Jacob'. He was later identified as Jacob
Lepidus, although this was not thought to be his real name. He was said to be
a member of a Russian revolutionary family whose terrorist brother had been
killed when a bomb he was carrying exploded in Paris. A Pole called Stryga

Oak Cottage.

was killed in such an incident in May 1906, but whether or not there was any connection with Lepidus is unknown. Hefeld had also been wanted by the Russian police and was rumoured to have been involved in a raid on a Scottish bank two years previously. Constable Eagles believed that he had killed Jacob, but when the body was examined, death was found to be due to a single bullet which matched the murderer's own gun. The inquest brought in a verdict of suicide.

A souvenir of the 'Tottenham Outrage'. (© Metropolitan Police Authority, 2009)

When it was learned that Mrs Tyler was entitled only to a widow's pension of £15 a year, a fund was set up to support her, and she eventually received over £1,200.

The stolen money was never found. It was thought that the robbers had dropped it into the Lea during their flight. Paul Hefeld refused to give any information to the police. His condition deteriorated and he died on 12 February.

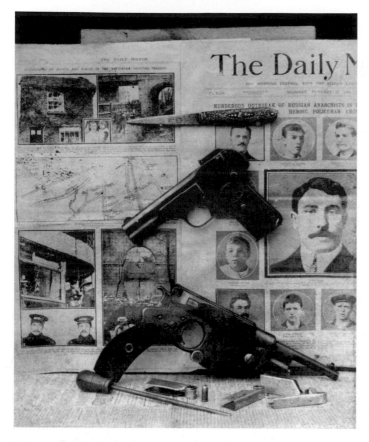

Weapons used in the
'Tottenham Outrage'.
(© Metropolitan Police
Authority, 2009)

At the inquest the coroner commented that Tottenham had obtained a 'very unenviable and undeserved notoriety' as it was being said that it was 'full of Anarchists', which he believed to be 'far from the case'. It was true that the 'Tottenham Outrage', as it came to be known, added fuel to the existing distrust of foreign immigrants, and greatly influenced police actions at the 'Siege of Sydney Street', which took place two years later.

Constables Cater, Dewhurst, Dixon, Eagles and Nicod were all promoted to the rank of sergeant. Dixon, Eagles and Cater were also awarded the King's Police Medal, specially created in the wake of the Outrage to reward exceptional courage in the line of duty. Tyler's bravery could not be recognised, as the medal was not given posthumously.

Ralph Joscelyne's mother, Louisa, grieved for another forty-three years, and it was said that she polished her dead son's boots every day. When she died in 1952, they were buried with her at her request.

15

HARROW

The Prerogative of Mercy

The London Borough of Harrow and Wealdstone is not one which has achieved any great notoriety in the annals of true crime. Murders which hit the headlines and grab the attention of the nation tend to happen outside its boundaries. Harrow murders are usually domestic, often impetuous and frequently inexplicable. All three descriptions may be applied to a murder which occurred in 1948.

Christopher Brendan McCormack was a 49-year-old painter who lived at 21 Wolseley Road, Wealdstone, a two-storey family house which he shared with his wife, 47-year-old Annie Mary McCormack, their married daughter, Mary Frances Robinson, her husband Matthew, the Robinsons' infant son, and eight male lodgers. The Robinsons' occupation of the house may have been unplanned, since Mary's marriage had taken place less than six months before the birth of her son. Annie McCormack must have been hard pressed to keep up with the work required by a household of thirteen people, although it is not known how much help Mary was able to give, or what the landlady was expected to provide in the way of meals apart from breakfast. As if this was not enough, Annie, who was known locally as 'the kind neighbour', was always on hand to help others. 'Whenever anything went wrong it was always send for Mrs MacCormack [sic],' said a friend. When local housewives were taken ill Annie would go and sit with them and also did their shopping and housework. If neighbours were short of rations she helped them out even if she herself was short. The children of Wolseley Road knew her as 'Aunty Annie' and all her sweet rations went to them.

Whatever disagreements there were between the McCormacks were confined to their time alone, as the Robinsons and the lodgers perceived them as a happy and affectionate couple. No one saw them quarrelling, and if there were private squabbles they were quiet enough not to disturb the other occupants of the house. There was certainly nothing to indicate that any tensions between the McCormacks might explode into murder. Based on subsequent events, it seems that Christopher McCormack resented the presence of so many lodgers in the house, and possibly also Annie's 'good neighbour' work, and the consequent diversion of his wife's energy from his own requirements. It is also probable that the rental income brought in by Annie's efforts exceeded his own pay, which could have hurt his pride. On the evening of 24 June, however, all was calm when Matthew Robinson saw his parents-in-law sitting together contentedly listening to the radio.

On the following morning, George Breen, one of the lodgers at No. 21, rose early, and, finding his breakfast was not ready, knocked on the door of the McCormacks' room at 6.20 a.m. Mrs McCormack was usually about at that hour but to Breen's surprise, it was her husband who answered his knock. McCormack asked Breen to wait a few minutes, which he did, then McCormack emerged, and said that he would get the breakfast as his wife was unwell. Breen noticed nothing unusual in his landlord's manner, and after eating breakfast he left for work, McCormack remaining in the house.

Later that morning McCormack went out, and that afternoon he was spotted by PC Heyworth sitting on the pavement in Elizabeth Street by Victoria coach station with his hand over his head. Heyworth asked him if anything was wrong and McCormack said, 'I have been all over the place.' He was obviously drunk and incapable and so Heyworth took him to the nearest police station in Gerald Road. The properties in Gerald Road are particularly impressive, standing five storeys high, and McCormack cannot have been too drunk to notice this. He asked for bail and, while waiting to be charged with drunkenness, announced, 'I can buy this place tomorrow.' (When the station closed in 1993 it was converted into an elegant private house known as 'The Old Police Station'.)

Unknown to Heyworth, the police must already have been looking for McCormack. Just before 8 a.m. that morning Mary Robinson, finding that her mother was not up and about as usual, entered her parents' bedroom and found her mother lying diagonally across the bed, her head covered in blood. It must have been apparent that she was dead and had been so for some time.

The first doctor to see the body was Dr Florance O'Sullivan of Boxtree Road, Harrow Weald, who was there at about 8 a.m., and stated that Annie had then been dead for about three or four hours. She had been attacked with a heavy blunt instrument, and there was a cut on the left forehead and a depression on the left temple. There had been profuse bleeding from the mouth and nose. An attempt had also been made to strangle her, as one of her own stockings was wound tightly around her neck.

Divisional Detective Inspector W. Barkell arrived at the scene and saw a bloodstained hammer lying by the side of the bed, which Matthew Robinson said was usually to be found around the house. On learning that the wanted man was at Gerald Road police station, Barkell went there to interview the suspect. Initially McCormack denied any knowledge of his wife's death. 'I didn't do it,' he said, adding, 'she was one of the best women in the world.'

Barkell decided to take McCormack to Wealdstone police station for further questioning. On the way there, his prisoner suddenly burst into tears. 'Do you want the truth?' said McCormack. 'I hit her on the head with a hammer. She was everlasting nagging me till I could not stand it any longer. I never had a wink of sleep.' At Wealdstone police station that evening he made a full statement in writing.

'I did kill my wife,' he admitted. 'It was the continual nagging she gave me every time we were alone. It got on my nerves.' He said he had got up early on the morning of 25 June and, seeing a hammer, he had picked it up on a sudden impulse and took it into the bedroom. When he entered the bedroom his wife said, 'Never a moment's peace,' and began to talk about all the work she had to do. He asked her what she wanted to keep lodgers for when he could keep her.

Wealdstone police station.

Methodist church,
Locket Road,
Wealdstone.

McCormack told Barkell he gave his wife £5 a week. 'She never smoked or drank, all she wanted was pounds, shillings and pence,' he said. 'I hit her several times. She turned over and was bleary-eyed; she looked terrible. I want to make everybody sure I did this on the spur of the moment; she was one of the finest women on the face of the earth.'

On the following day McCormack appeared at Hendon police court, where he was charged with the murder of his wife and remanded in custody. McCormack was granted legal aid and asked that Mr John Alfred Morley of local solicitors Pierron and Morley at 1 High Street, Wealdstone, should represent him.

Meanwhile, Mr Daniel Hopkin, presiding magistrate at Marlborough Street Court, was concerned at the absence of Christopher McCormack, who had failed to appear to answer a charge of being drunk and disorderly. He was informed that McCormack was at another court on a more serious charge. The register was marked 'no appearance'.

The inquest on Annie McCormack opened at the Methodist church hall, Locket Road, Wealdstone, on Tuesday, where Matthew Robinson gave evidence of identification. The pathologist who had examined the body was one of the best known and respected of his day, Dr (later Professor) Keith Simpson, whose notable cases include some of the most celebrated crimes of the era. Simpson said that the cause of Annie McCormack's death was shock due to multiple blunt injuries to the head and partial strangulation. The inquest was adjourned to 14 October.

Christopher McCormack appeared at Wealdstone magistrates' court on Friday 9 July and was remanded to Hendon court pending the full medical report to be provided by Dr Simpson. At Hendon Mr Crump appeared for the prosecution but had only a routine task to perform as McCormack had nothing further to add beyond his initial confession. Mary Robinson told the court that her parents were an affectionate couple and that as far as she was aware they did not quarrel. Her husband supported her testimony, saying that on the evening before the murder the McCormacks had both seemed well and happy. George Breen said that the household was a peaceful one. McCormack was committed for trial at the Old Bailey.

It must have been one of the shortest trials on record. McCormack appeared in the dock on 13 September, and asked by Sir Wilfred Knops, the clerk of the court, if he was guilty or not guilty of the charge, he said simply 'Guilty'. Sir John Cameron, counsel for the defence, told the presiding judge, Mr Justice Sellers, 'I am quite satisfied that the accused understands the plea he has made and the position has been properly explained to him.'

The judge spoke to the defendant. 'You have heard what your counsel says, do you agree with that?'

'Yes, my lord,' replied McCormack.

Wealdstone magistrates' court.

Only one more thing remained to be done. The judge put the black cap on his head and pronounced sentence of death. The entire trial had taken less than two minutes.

McCormack's only hope of a reprieve now lay with the Home Secretary, and, as it turned out, with the timing of events. James Chuter Ede was the son of a shopkeeper and a former teacher and trade unionist. In 1945 he became Home Secretary in the Labour administration of Clement Atlee. He had helped draft the 1948 Criminal Justice Bill, which abolished the rights of courts to impose corporal punishment. The Bill also proposed to suspend the imposition of capital punishment for a period of five years. Ede had once opposed capital punishment, but in 1948, in the light of a recent increase in violent crime, he did not feel that the time was right for such a reform. The Bill was passed by the House of Commons, and on 16 April Ede caused a great deal of astonishment and a certain degree of outrage by making a public announcement that while the legislation was under consideration he intended to commute future death penalties to life imprisonment, since it appeared very probable that the death penalty for murder might be suspended for five years. This policy had been hotly debated in the weeks immediately prior to McCormack's murder of his wife. As Lord Simons pointed out in a letter to *The Times*, ' . . . neither the Crown nor the Home Secretary, as the Crown's advisor, can promise a qualification of the penalty prescribed by statute for a murder *before the murder takes place.*'

Early in June the anti-hanging clause was deleted by the House of Lords. On 11 June Ede stated that in view of subsequent Parliamentary discussions on the issue he intended that in future he would treat each case on its own merits as he had done previously. Ede, while prepared to allow hanging to continue, was sensitive both to public opinion and the feelings of the House of Commons. He believed that there was scope to limit or modify the operation of capital punishment, and introduced a Royal Commission later that year to examine the issue. It was no very great surprise when McCormack was reprieved.

At the time of McCormack's murder of his wife, therefore, the question of capital punishment was being widely debated, and no convicted murderer had been hanged for some months. On 10 June the *Daily Mirror* forecast that hanging would come back for some murders, such as second murders, the murder of a policeman or warder, murder while committing a crime, and poisoning, and on the following day the *Daily Express* stated, ' . . . no murderer will be hanged in Britain, at least until the new Criminal Justice Bill becomes law.'

Whether McCormack had ever contemplated murder before the 25 June is unknown, but the publicity given to the Criminal Justice Bill and its implications might just have focussed a previously unformed intent.

16

HAVERING

The Third Man

O n Tuesday, 20 January 1885, 37-year-old Inspector Thomas Simmons of Romford was travelling to Rainham in a horse-drawn trap accompanied by 22-year-old Constable Alfred Marden. Simmons was in uniform, but Marden was in plain clothes. The weather was clear and visibility good, but by 4 p.m., as they passed through the south end of Hornchurch, only half an hour of daylight remained. Three men were walking along the road in the direction of Romford, and Simmons recognised one as 53-year-old David Dredge, a hay carter who had served several terms in prison including five years for horse stealing. One of his companions was 6ft tall and clean shaven, wearing a long dark overcoat and a white wrapper, while the other was about 5ft 7in with short, clipped whiskers, wearing a dark jacket. Certain that the men were up to no good, Simmons told Marden to get out of the cart and keep an eye on them while he went on to complete his business at Rainham. Marden followed the men as far as Ford Lane, and on the way met up with a uniformed constable called Emery, who commented that the men were 'funny-looking characters'. Marden eventually lost sight of the three and when Simmons returned, his companion mounted the cart and they drove on, while Emery was sent to Hornchurch to get back-up. On the Romford Road, near the sewage farm, Simmons and Marden caught up with the suspicious trio. It was after 5 o'clock and almost dark. The men stopped, turned around and stared at their pursuers, then David Dredge darted through a gap in the hedge leading into a meadow, while the others ran up the road, confirming the police suspicion that they had been on some criminal excursion. At that moment, three labourers called Matthews, Kemp and Sawkins, who had just ended their day's work on the sewage farm, arrived on the scene.

Simmons ordered Marden to go after Dredge on foot, while he drove the cart onwards, catching up with the other two about sixty yards further on, as they reached the gate leading to the sewage farm. 'Where are you men going?' he asked. 'Home,' said the tall man. Simmons got out of the cart, and approached the speaker with the intention of searching his coat pockets, where he must have suspected he would find burglary tools.

Meanwhile, in the field, Marden had caught up with and confronted his quarry. 'What are you doing over here David Dredge?' demanded the constable. Dredge uttered an oath and Marden suddenly found himself looking down the barrel of a pistol. 'I will blow your brains out with this,' said Dredge. At that moment, Marden heard the report of a firearm behind him. Looking back to the roadway he saw the tall man pointing a revolver at Inspector Simmons. Smoke was coming from the barrel.

'Come, they have shot me,' exclaimed Simmons. Marden ran back to help the Inspector, who had been wounded in the stomach. Simmons leaned against the cart and Marden asked if he was able to stand there. Simmons said he could, adding that it was the tall man who had shot him.

The two fugitives were now running across the sewage farm in the direction of Dagenham and the unarmed constable followed them, calling upon the three labourers in the name of the Queen to assist him. Simmons, in pain but still able to walk, told Kemp to mind the horse and also set off after the men together with Matthews and Sawkins. It was hard going on the boggy soil. About a hundred yards across the field the tall man threw off the wrapper and

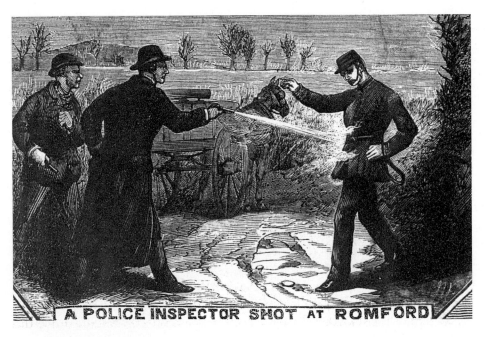

A POLICE INSPECTOR SHOT AT ROMFORD

The shooting of Inspector Simmons.

his long coat, which Marden picked up and briefly searched before running on.
The men ran between some haystacks and as Marden rounded the stacks he found
that both men had stopped and turned, pointing revolvers at him. They fired, and
Marden tried to get out of the way but his feet stuck in the mud and he fell, and
as he did so he felt a bullet pass over the right side of his face. The men ran on
again and Marden got up and chased them, despite again being threatened with
revolvers. The two eventually plunged into the reeds and marshes that bordered the
River Rom and vanished into the darkness. Marden went back to find Simmons,
who had had to stop and lean on some railings. 'I think I am done for this time,'
said the Inspector, clutching Marden's arm for support. 'Don't leave me any more.'

Back in the roadway, Kemp was standing with the horse and cart when a
man came up and spoke to him. It was David Dredge. Kemp, unaware that
Dredge was a suspect, told him about the shooting, and Dredge said that he had
been walking along the road with two men who had asked him for directions.
He added that since he had done nothing he would stay there until the
policemen returned in case they wanted to speak to him. He offered to take
charge of the horse and cart, but Kemp said that as he had waited so long he
would continue. They stood talking for about fifteen minutes, and then Dredge,
who may have been hoping to use the cart to make a rapid escape, accepting
that Kemp would not give it up, said that he would resume his journey, and
walked on in the direction of Romford.

Scenes from the Romford murder.

Marden arranged for his injured colleague to be taken home, while Matthews and Kemp handed in the coat at Romford police station. Dr Wright, a Romford surgeon, was brought to Simmons' bedside, and found a gunshot wound in the abdomen from which he was unable to remove the bullet.

Daylight searches revealed other items dropped by the fleeing men; a saw and socks with felt soles for the purpose of covering their boots to deaden footfall. The coat contained some revolver cartridges, a black cap with an eyehole cut in it, and a pair of glasses in a case which bore the name and address of Mrs Elizabeth Salmon, an optician's wife of 24 Seymour Street, London. Mrs Salmon confirmed that the sale had been entered in the firm's daybook on 30 December last, to a man she knew by the name of Manson. The police already had a good idea of who this man might be. He also went by the name of Adams, and was wanted for other offences.

Thomas Simmons died of peritonitis on 24 January. The Inspector, who had served in the Essex Constabulary for over nineteen years, had been an exemplary officer, often praised for his courage and hard work. A charitable subscription was at once opened for his wife and two children.

On 3 February, David Dredge was arrested in Limehouse. His wife gave the police an address for Manson, but when they went there he had gone. At the Romford petty sessions Dredge was charged with the wilful murder of Inspector Simmons. Mr Bachelor, prosecuting, observed that it did not matter which of the three men fired the fatal shot as 'they were each and all as guilty as if they had stood in a row and fired at him.'

The police, surmising that the missing killer might be short of funds, made enquiries at pawnbrokers' shops. On 16 February they learned from Edward Baxter, manager of a shop in Seymour Street, that a man called Manson and describing himself as a commercial traveller, had pledged a revolver in July and taken it out of pledge in October. Baxter was asked to inform the police if the man should enter the shop again. On 10 March the suspect, his newly bearded face muffled, returned to the shop with the same revolver and asked for an advance of 10s. Baxter detained him in the shop while sending an assistant to the Platt Street police station. In ten minutes Constable Day arrived, and, on seeing the revolver, said he would have to take the customer to the police station on suspicion of having shot Inspector Simmons. The man said he would go quietly but as they left the shop he tripped Day and ran off. Day and another officer gave chase and eventually caught the suspect and took him to Somerstown police station, their prisoner resisting violently all the way. At the station, he was not searched immediately and took the opportunity to throw some cartridges into the fire, which exploded. Ten more cartridges were found on him, and they fitted the revolver.

The prisoner was now calling himself John Lee. He had recently read about executioner James Berry's failure, due to a malfunctioning drop, to hang John

Lee (a butler who had murdered his mistress the previous November). Delighted by the idea of 'the man they could not hang', Manson had changed his name at once. When his house was searched the police found burglary tools and a sock with felt on the sole.

Both Dredge and Lee applied to have their trials transferred to the Central Criminal Court, the Old Bailey. Dredge was particularly aggrieved that the county newspapers had described him as a 'determined burglar' and a poacher. He claimed to be a hay and straw dealer who had made enemies in the county due to his failure in business.

Lee was forty-five, a blacking maker born in County Cork, who had served prison terms in Ireland before coming to London. He had been living in West Ham, but on 23 January he had abruptly left without giving notice and removed to Ferdinand Street, Chalk Farm. Constable Marden identified Lee from a line-up of about twenty men as the man who had shot Inspector Simmons. When charged with murder at Romford on 12 March, Lee was accompanied to court by no less than six constables, partly because of his belligerent manner but also for his own protection from the violently hostile crowd demonstrating outside.

Charles Woodcraft of Caistor Park Road, West Ham, gave evidence, saying that Lee lived two doors from him. He knew him by sight and identified the coat and wrapper dropped in the meadow as ones worn by the prisoner. Lee was an angry man. He complained loudly and insistently of the gross injustice done to him by the police and the calumnies about him that had appeared in the press. He was taken to Chelmsford Gaol by train, handcuffed between two officers and with several others in attendance. A crowd of about 500 gathered to hoot and yell at him.

The trial opened on 27 April with both Lee and Dredge charged with murder. Dredge's defence was that he had met the other two men on the road and they had asked him for directions. He claimed he did not know what kind of men they were or their business, and said he had never had a revolver in his possession. Lee's defence was that it was a case of mistaken identity and he had been nowhere near the scene of the murder.

The prosecution urged that if Dredge and the other two men had gone out on an unlawful expedition together, and he knew they had revolvers, he could be held responsible for the crime even if he did not fire the shot.

Constable Frederick Wilderspin of the Dagenham police stated that he was at Rainham railway station in plain clothes when the London train arrived, and three men got out of the same carriage. One of them was Dredge and one of the others was Lee.

Mrs Salmon had failed to pick out Lee at an identity parade, but claimed that she had been confused by his beard, and now thought that he was the purchaser of the spectacles found at the murder scene. Constable Emery identified Lee and Dredge as two of the three men he had seen on the road. The three labourers who had witnessed the shooting all stated that it was the taller man who had fired the shot, but none of them were able to identify Lee. Mr Grain, defending Lee, pointed out that at the time of the shooting it had been dark, and a carman called Shaw testified that anyone standing in the field would not have been able to see down the road sixty yards away to where the shooting took place. The hedge that bordered the road was 10ft in height.

Mr Stern, defending Dredge, suggested that Marden had been mistaken about his client having a revolver, and maintained that Dredge's conversation with Kemp and lack of hurry to get away was proof of his innocence. Evidence was given supporting Dredge's claim that he had travelled to the area because he had been offered a job tying straw at Romford.

Mr Justice Hawkins, summing-up, said that the evidence that Dredge was in any way a party to the shooting was very slight, and there was no proof before him of Dredge having been in contact with the other two men before 20 January. The fact that Mrs Dredge had been able to advise police of Lee's former address, clear proof that the two men knew each other, cannot have been mentioned in court. Lee demanded to make a statement and accused the police of persecution and perjury. The jury had no difficulty in finding him guilty of murder, but Dredge was acquitted. Lee, belligerent to the last, declared himself to be a 'helpless, unjustly-used, persecuted man', and denied having committed the murder even as he was being sentenced to death. Alfred Marden's courage was commended by the judge. The young constable rose to the rank of Superintendent in 1911, but after an internal enquiry, his promising career ended in demotion and early retirement soon afterwards.

The execution was fixed for 18 May at Chelmsford. The executioner was James Berry and he was using the same rope he had employed at the failed hanging of John Lee in November. The prisoner met his end bravely, and just before Berry pulled the lever, cried out, 'I die an innocent man; remember that!'

In July, Dredge was found guilty at Chelmsford assizes of assaulting Constable Marden and sentenced to twelve months in prison with hard labour. His narrow brush with death may have reformed him. He went back to his old trade of hay dealing, and raised a family. He died in 1913 aged 79.

The police suspected that the missing third man in the enterprise was a known villain, a man with short clipped whiskers named John Martin. In October 1885 he took part in a burglary at Netherby Hall, Cumberland, during which three policemen were shot and injured. Another policeman was shot dead as the burglars made their escape. Martin and two of his gang were caught and convicted of murder. Berry hanged them in February 1886. As he was led to the scaffold, Martin said he had not committed the murder, though innocent men had been hanged for his crimes. Asked who they were, Martin would give only one name – Lee. 'He was innocent,' he said. 'That crime was committed by me.'

HILLINGDON

The Fifth Bullet

Early on the morning of Saturday, 15 November 1884, 63-year-old James Gibbons of Orchard Cottage, Hayes, kissed his wife Elizabeth goodbye and set off to Fitzhead, Somerset, on a family visit. He returned on the 9.25 p.m. train, arriving at Hayes railway station where he appeared to be both in good health and sprits as he chatted to stationmaster Abraham Adams, who had known him for some seven or eight years. Gibbons then walked home where, after a late supper, he started getting undressed for bed.

Between 11 o'clock and midnight that night, Diana Sowman, the Gibbons' neighbour, was at home with her husband Thomas when she heard Elizabeth calling her. She went outside and found Elizabeth in her nightdress, standing in the lane at her gate. The front of the nightdress was stained with blood.

'Do come in, Mrs Sowman,' said Elizabeth. 'My husband has shot himself.'

Mrs Sowman followed her into the house and went upstairs to the bedroom, where she saw James Gibbons lying face down on the floor. He was wearing only a calico shirt, a flannel undershirt and some drawers. The two women tried to lift him, to see if he was dead, but he was too heavy. There was a great deal of blood on his clothing and he did not appear to be breathing. Thomas Sowman came to the front door and his wife called down, telling him to go for a doctor, while she stayed with Mrs Gibbons. Mrs Sowman then noticed a revolver lying by the left side of the body and picked it up and put it on a chest of drawers.

Twenty minutes later local surgeon Dr Parrott and his assistant Mr Hathaway arrived. During that time, Mrs Gibbons was too grief-stricken to speak, and Mrs Sowman decided not to question her.

The initial examination confirmed that Gibbons was dead. There were three gunshot wounds, one in the middle of the left cheek, one on the left side of the body, just below the nipple, and the other four inches above. A fourth bullet was later found on the bedroom floor. Parrott informed the police and a constable arrived and took possession of the revolver. Kindly Mrs Sowman stayed with Elizabeth all night, and later washed the body and laid it out.

There was no obvious reason why Gibbons should want to take his own life. He was comfortably off, having for many years been a contractor to the Great Western Railway for the creosoting of sleepers. He owned three horses, and employed twelve men. His will, in which he left everything to his wife, showed that he was worth £435. A prudent man with money, the previous March he had paid his annual rent in advance. James and Elizabeth, who had been married for thirty-seven years, were childless. There were tensions in the marriage, and it was well known in the district that husband and wife quarrelled.

Two and a half years previously, Lucy Venn, the daughter of James' cousin Mary, had come to stay with the couple and had helped Elizabeth with the housework. Mary Venn was the wife of a stonemason with five children and, until 1883, had an elderly father-in-law to care for, and may have found it difficult to manage financially. To the childless James, the presence of the girl may have brought some happiness to a humdrum home life. In September 1884 Lucy was 15, and not long afterwards, she was sent home to her family. James had not wanted her to go, but his wife had insisted. Even at a distance James maintained an interest in Lucy's future, arranging for her to go to school at Taunton, and planning in due course to get her apprenticed in a business. He had written to Lucy's mother to arrange the visit on 15 November, and Mary and Lucy had met him at the station on his arrival. He was his usual cheerful self, and had suggested that Lucy should come and stay at Orchard Cottage during her school holidays.

The inquest opened on Wednesday 19 November at the Royal Oak public house, not far from the Gibbons' home, where Elizabeth said that on James' return they had discussed his visit and she had asked if he had seen his cousin Mary at Taunton station. When he said that he had, she complained that he had kept this secret from her and he ought to have taken her there. According to Elizabeth, James had become annoyed, saying she had no business saying anything about his relatives. He then took the gun from under his pillow and began to wave it at her in such an agitated manner that she became alarmed and ran downstairs. Moments later she heard four gunshots, and, hurrying back to the bedroom, found her husband lying wounded on the floor. She tried to lift him, but failed, and ran next door to her neighbour, Mrs Sowman, for help.

Elizabeth told the coroner that her husband often got over-excited, and had not been sleeping well recently as he had been very depressed and suffered frequent headaches. He did not eat well except at supper time. She thought he had not been 'right' for some months and often acted as if he were insane. Sometimes he would get up in the middle of the night and dress himself and go into the yard and walk about. She could not explain his behaviour, except that he had suffered a bad fall from a truck three or four years ago after which he had been unconscious for a time, and had also had an episode of sunstroke.

Unfortunately, the coroner did not ask why the couple had found it necessary to keep a loaded revolver beside the bed. Annie Wall, the Gibbons' general servant, who lived nearby in Fleet Lane, had often seen the revolver wrapped in flannel on a table at Mrs Gibbons' side of the bed. The inquest was adjourned for medical evidence.

Dr Parrott and Mr Hathaway carried out the post-mortem on James Gibbons on 20 November, and paid particular attention to the three wounds. The one in the cheek had fractured the upper part of the jaw, the bullet being found near the left ear. The wound in the upper chest had been made by a bullet which had

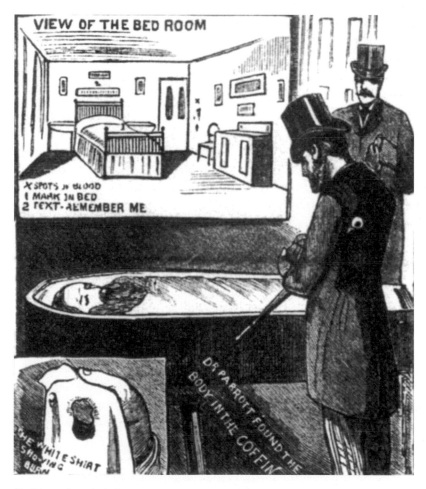

Dr Parrott views the body.

lodged in the muscle in front of the blade bone of the left shoulder. Neither wound would have been fatal. The lower chest wound had damaged both the heart and liver and would have been so rapidly fatal that this bullet must have been the last one fired. James Gibbons was right handed, and the surgeons had to consider whether it was possible for him to have fired all three shots, and also if he could have fired the last one after receiving the first two wounds. Their initial reaction was that it was an unlikely, but not impossible, suicide. It was when they turned the body over that everything changed. There was a fourth wound, and this one was in the back. The bullet had gone straight into the left shoulder and lodged in the flesh in front of the chest. There were powder burns on the back of the shirt and flannel undershirt, which showed that the gun had been held very close. This was not the case with the other wounds.

When the inquest reconvened Annie Wall revealed that while both she and James had been teetotal, Mrs Gibbons liked a drink. On the morning of 15 November, Annie had fetched a quart of sixpenny ale from the Royal Oak. At 1 o'clock she and Elizabeth had been driven into Uxbridge by one of James' employees, where Mrs Gibbons drank four pennyworth of either gin or brandy with water. After tea Annie had fetched another pint and a half of ale, and not long before James returned home, another pint. Despite this she did not believe Mrs Gibbons was the worse for drink. When James returned he complained about the front door being left open, but no other words were said and Annie left shortly afterwards.

On the first day of the inquest Mrs Gibbons had been regarded simply as a witness, but when the second day closed she was arrested on a charge of wilful murder and taken to Uxbridge police station.

The murder charge was heard at Uxbridge Town Hall on 8 December, with Elizabeth Gibbons sobbing convulsively throughout the proceedings. It emerged that she had given more than one account of what had happened on the fatal night. Stationmaster Abraham Adams told the court that on the morning after Gibbons' death, he and two employees of the creosoting works had gone to Orchard Cottage and found Elizabeth desolate from grief. She said that on the night of his death James had complained about a horse not being properly groomed, and that one of the fowls had died. He had taken the pistol from under the pillow, twisted it around in the air and said, 'I can't stand it any longer.' She then said that two shots had been fired while she was in the room, and she had closed with James and tried to get the pistol from him and they had fallen. She had then gone downstairs to raise the alarm, and it was while she was undoing the front door that she heard the other shots.

Mr Bachelor for the public prosecutor asked on what terms the couple appeared to be, and Adams replied, 'Rather middling, I should think.'

'Did they not agree well?' asked Bachelor.

In court at Uxbridge.

'No Sir.'

'Did Mr Gibbons complain to you?'

'Very often.'

Elizabeth was committed for trial, which opened at the Central Criminal Court, the Old Bailey on 18 December. The newspapers described her as 'stout and comely looking'. Mr Poland for the prosecution maintained that the decision before the jury was a simple one – since Elizabeth and James had been the only people in the house it was clear that either James had committed suicide or Elizabeth had murdered him. The crucial evidence was the position of the wounds, and a plaster cast was made of James's body to enable the medical men to show the jury where the bullets had entered.

There was little evidence of motive either for murder or suicide. James's will had been held by his solicitor which, the defence suggested, meant that Elizabeth did not know its contents. Some effort was made to corroborate Elizabeth's assertions that James had been of unsound mind. Mary Venn told the court that an aunt of James's had committed suicide after being disappointed in love, although on further questioning she admitted that this had happened forty or fifty years ago. Mary also believed that another relation was in a lunatic asylum, but knew nothing of the circumstances. Lucy Venn said that her aunt and uncle had been kind to her, but intimated that she had left because of something she had done wrong although she claimed she could not remember what this was. Two or three days before she went, her aunt had hit her in the mouth.

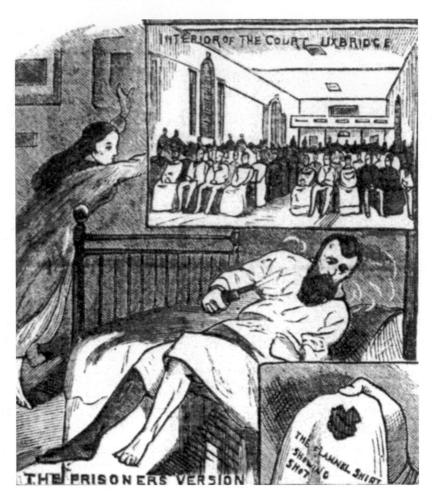

Mrs Gibbons' version of events.

Elizabeth Gibbons never deviated from her story that her husband had committed suicide, but the medical experts were unanimous in stating that it was impossible for the wound in the back to have been self-inflicted, and the inescapable conclusion was that she had shot him. The defence tried to suggest that the gun had gone off when James had fallen, but it was thought extremely unlikely that this could have produced such a neat horizontal wound.

It took the jury just half an hour to deliver a verdict of guilty and Mr Justice Hawkins sentenced Elizabeth Gibbons to death. The prisoner listened to the judge's words with her eyes closed, and then, in an almost inaudible voice, said that she had no reason to urge why the sentence should not be carried out. The execution was fixed for 5 January.

The Times, while agreeing with the verdict, commented that 'it is rare to see a capital sentence so completely unsupported by what may be called direct or primary evidence.' Other newspapers declared that the public conscience was uneasy about the case. There was no apparent motive, the main evidence was the position of the wounds, and even if she was guilty the crime had been committed in the heat of passion.

A surgeon called Miller wrote to the newspapers about a case of suicide in which a student had first shot himself in the chest, the ball passing through the left ventricle, and then reloaded his pistol and shot himself in the head. The student had not however managed to shoot himself in the back. Other correspondents suggested that the wound in the back had been caused when the revolver was dropped or from a ricochet. Most saw Elizabeth as a woman to be pitied rather than punished.

William Garner, Elizabeth's solicitor, prepared two petitions, one for signature in London and one in Uxbridge, which omitted any criticism of the local doctors. Many people in Uxbridge, Hayes, West Drayton, Hillingdon, Cowley and other towns in the vicinity signed the local petition. Both were presented to the Home Secretary, Sir William Harcourt, asking him to consider a reprieve on the grounds that Elizabeth had no motive to murder her husband, whose death was more likely to be a case of suicide. Elizabeth, awaiting execution in Newgate Gaol, only showed emotion when visited by a nephew and niece from Hayes, otherwise she remained impassive and did not discuss the case at all. She achieved a brief celebrity when her likeness appeared in Madame Tussaud's, and the case opened up a fresh round of correspondence in the newspapers recommending the establishment of a Court of Criminal Appeal.

To the relief of the public, the Home Office confirmed on 31 December that the sentence on Elizabeth Gibbons had been commuted to penal servitude for life.

It was later reported that 500 people had 'chiefly from morbid curiosity' attended the sale of James Gibbons's goods, which did not realise 'fancy prices'. The dead man's favourite retriever dog, which had been chained up at the time of the funeral, was said to have visited the grave daily ever since.

Elizabeth served part of her sentence at Woking District female prison, and was later transferred to Aylesbury convict prison. In May 1900 the Home Secretary gave orders for her release. She went to live with a nephew in Brighton, and died in 1911 aged 83.

Mr Poland probably came closest to the facts when he theorised that there had been an altercation, after which Elizabeth had snatched up the revolver and 'angrily and recklessly' fired it at her husband. It seems probable that the first shot was the one in the back, fired as James sat on the edge of the bed, causing a flesh wound in the shoulder. If Elizabeth had thought she might kill or disable him with that she might well have been shocked to see him jump up and turn

H.B. Poland.

to face her. Perhaps he tried to walk around the bed to snatch the gun away. As he came at her, she fired until she could fire no more.

Poland also alluded to a possible motive – jealousy of the attention and financial support James was lavishing on Lucy Venn. Elizabeth might have known that she was the sole beneficiary of James's will, and at nine years his junior she would have expected to outlive him. Had she felt that James was squandering her inheritance on Lucy, or even feared that the girl was becoming a favourite and that he would change his will in her favour? James's visit to his cousin was the trigger which finally unleashed his wife's rage.

18

HOUNSLOW

The Poppy Day Murders

On Wednesday, 12 November 1941, the front page of *The Times* was
dominated by war news. There was hard fighting on the Russian front,
the Admiralty had issued a statement that six Axis ships had been sunk by HM
submarines, while in Tokyo, Prime Minister Tojo declared that Japan was 'at the
crossroads'. Tuesday had been Armistice Day, marked by a stirring speech from
President Roosevelt, while in Britain volunteers had sold millions of poppies,
the proceeds going to the Earl Haig Fund for the assistance of ex-servicemen.
At the bottom of the page was a short feature. The headline was 'Eight People
Shot in London'.

Shortly before 9 a.m. on 11 November, Leslie Ernest Ludford, a 28-year-old
solicitor, waved goodbye to his parents and left his home at 11 Foster Road,
Chiswick to go to his office. Ludford suffered from a severe curvature of the
spine and walked slowly with the aid of a stick. A quiet and well-liked man,
he was known for his kindness and eagerness to help others. His disability had
not prevented him from doing a great deal of voluntary work, and he acted as
a 'poor man's lawyer 'in Paddington and Willesden. Sometimes his work kept
him out late at night but he claimed to have no fear of the 'blitz'. He also took
a keen interest in local politics and served on the committee of the Brentford
and Chiswick Junior Conservative Club, which was a hub of social activities in
the area.

At approximately 8.50 a.m., Ludford reached the corner of Hadley Gardens
and Duke's Avenue. Mrs Violet Pender, also of Foster Road, had left her home
at about the same time as Ludford, and was walking a few yards behind him.
Also in Hadley Gardens that morning were Mrs Matilda Alice Mott and Arthur
Henry Burgess and his wife Violet, who had paused near No. 11 to buy a poppy.
There were two poppy sellers in the street; local resident Mrs Dancy at the

Leslie Ludford.

junction with Duke's Avenue and her friend Miss Redfearn further down the road. It was Mrs Dancy who first saw the dark blue saloon car turn the corner from Duke's Avenue. After travelling a few yards, it stopped, and a man got out. Mrs Dancy was waiting to see if he would buy a poppy from Miss Redfearn, when a shot rang out. Leslie Ludford had almost reached Duke's Avenue, when he was hit. 'Don't! Don't!' he cried out, and tried to escape, staggering through the side gate which separated Nos 1 and 3 Hadley Gardens. Coolly and relentlessly, the gunman pursued him. Mr Stanley Randall of 1 Hadley Gardens heard the shots and, peering out of his front bedroom window, saw a man with a gun to his shoulder aiming at something in the corner of the front garden. Randall rushed downstairs.

As the wounded man lay helplessly where he had fallen, the gunman fired another shot point blank into his body, then turned and walked back to the car. On the way he paused and casually fired at Mrs Pender, hitting her in the thigh. He then fired off another shot at Ludford, got into the car, and drove away. Mrs Mott, seeing the car coming towards her, crouched down behind a hedge, but as it passed she peered out and made a note of the number, GGC 83. Arthur Burgess saw the car head off in the direction of Sutton Court Road and was also able to take the number. Mrs Mott then ran to the surgery of Dr Morgan Evans at 7 Duke's Avenue, where Mrs Pender, who was able to walk, was being taken.

Stanley Randall bent over the wounded man, who was barely conscious and struggling to speak.

'He has shot me,' Ludford managed to say.

'Who has?' asked Randall.

'Brent.'

Randall asked Ludford if he knew the man's address and Ludford made a great effort to say the words, but his head sagged and his voice failed. Randall telephoned for the police and an ambulance, and Ludford was taken to West Middlesex Hospital, accompanied by Police Sergeant Percy Hammond. On the way Ludford managed a few more words, 'Brent. It was Brent,' before losing consciousness. On admission to hospital he was found to have gunshot wounds in the abdomen, left arm and left groin, and was suffering from severe shock and haemorrhage. He died a few minutes later.

The corner of Hadley Gardens and Duke's Avenue.

At 9 a.m. there was a loud knock at the front door of 1 St Mary's Grove, Chiswick. Two of the residents, Mrs Annie New and Mrs Emma Crisp, thinking that the caller was the milkman, came to the door with empty bottles in their arms, and were surprised to see no one there, although a dark blue car stood at the kerbside. There was a sudden flash and an explosion, and Mrs New felt a stinging pain in her arm. Looking down, she saw blood. 'I'm shot!' she exclaimed, and the words were hardly out of her mouth when there was a second loud report and Mrs Crisp collapsed. Mrs New caught her as she fell and laid her down, then called her husband.

The milkman, Mr William Lloyd Jones, was about two doors away when he heard the shots and screams. Looking up he saw a gun pointing from the window of a car, which then drove off, 'in a casual fashion', up Harvard Hill. Jones made a note of the car number and while his girl assistant went to tend the injured women he raced to a nearby grocer's shop, whose proprietor telephoned the police. Mrs Crisp, who had suffered gunshot wounds to the chest and abdomen, was carried into a nearby doctor's surgery.

Minutes later, in Hamlet Gardens, Kathleen Guyver, a gas collector, was shot in the right arm and abdomen. She was taken to DuCane Road Hospital.

At 9.15 Mrs Henrietta Sell was walking down Bollo Lane, Ealing, and as she passed a stationary car shots were fired and she was twice wounded in the arm. 'The Germans have got me!' she screamed. She was taken to Acton Hospital. Five minutes later in Hartington Road, Winifred Allenby of the WAAF saw a man leaning out of a car firing a gun at her. She jumped back quickly and escaped injury. He drove on.

St Mary's Grove, Chiswick.

The shootings had attracted the attention of some workmen in a corporation lorry, who gave chase and had almost caught up with the blue car when they were held up at some level crossing gates, and it got away.

It was 9.50 when the car reached Rathgar Avenue, Ealing, and shots were fired at Agnes Grace Hunt, who was uninjured. Twenty minutes later the car stopped in Bruton Way, Perivale, and there was a knock on the door of No. 33. Fifty-seven-year-old Mrs Edith Barringer was just about to go out. She opened the door, and was shot. Mrs Barringer staggered forward and fell wounded in her front garden. A doctor went to her assistance, and as he waited for an ambulance he saw a sporting gun cartridge on the ground, and picked it up. Mrs Barringer was admitted to King Edward's Hospital. She had a deep wound in the thigh and died of shock and haemorrhage later the same day.

The police now had a good description of the car driven by the gunman, which was circulated to all divisions. Sergeant Frostick was at the police box in Station Road, Harrow, when he saw the wanted car, approached and signalled the driver to stop. As the car was passing, Frostick jumped on the running board and ordered the driver to pull in. For a moment Frostick thought the man was complying, but then the driver suddenly shouted, 'What do you want?' at the same time accelerating the car so the policeman lost his balance and fell into the road. A few minutes later Sergeant Sutton and Constable Cook saw the car in Headstone Lane, Hatch-End. Not having a car handy they commandeered a lorry and gave chase, and tried to block it at Brooks Hill, but the lorry was too slow as it was carrying a load of bricks and the car was able to accelerate past and get away. At 12.10 p.m., Constables Percival and Laver were on duty in a patrol car when they saw the saloon approaching them in Stanmore Broadway. They immediately turned their car around and gave chase. The saloon swerved dangerously and passed three traffic islands on the wrong side. A police barrier had been placed across the near side of the third island, but the car was able to pass this and continued along Stanmore Road. Percival had been issued with a rifle, and while Laver drove the car, Percival opened the windscreen of the police car, thrust the barrel of the rifle through the aperture, and took aim at the other car. At the Watford Bypass, they were able to overtake the saloon and called on the driver to stop. The order was ignored and Laver forced the car to stop by ramming it into the side of the road. The occupant was a young man. Laver dragged him from the driving seat and searched him for weapons while Percival covered him with the rifle. 'All right,' said the prisoner, 'I give in.' He was cautioned and taken to Edgware police station. When he was searched an army pay book was found in the name of Phillip Ward.

In the back of the car there was a brown fibre case in which was found a single and a double barrelled shotgun, and several boxes of shotgun cartridges as well as a number of loose cartridges. In the front seat was a spent cartridge. When the police later made a search of Ward's lodgings more cartridges were found. Four empty shotgun cartridges were later picked up in Hadley Gardens, which were similar to the one found in the car, and two cotton wads of the type found in sporting gun cartridges were found in St Mary's Grove.

The prisoner, Phillip Joseph Ward, was a gunner in a searchlight battery of the Royal Artillery and a serving soldier, having been called up for military service on 16 September 1940. Ward was born on 16 April 1910. He had been a normal cheerful boy until the age of 12, when he had suffered a head injury, and from that time his behaviour was unpredictable, irritable and violent. He had first shown signs of a serious mental disorder at the age of 16. He had been admitted to mental institutions on a number of occasions, and in 1931, after a suicide attempt, he was taken to the City of London Mental Hospital, where he was certified insane. Ward was convinced that everyone was talking about him and laughing at him behind his back, and that there was an organised conspiracy to spoil his life. The diagnosis was paranoid schizophrenia. He left the hospital without permission in June 1933 and returned to live with his parents in Acton. By law, the hospital could do nothing except grant him an automatic discharge. In 1939 Ward left home, drawing an allowance. When examined by an army doctor in 1940, he was considered to be of normal stability and graded A1.

In 1937 Ward had become a member of the Brentford and Chiswick Junior Conservative Club, calling himself Philip Ross Brent. The chairman of the committee was then Leslie Ludford. Ward had exhibited unacceptable behaviour at club events, especially in relation to a young woman member, Miss Barbara Newark, to whom he had also written some letters. Repeated complaints had been made to the committee about Ward, and a number of members had threatened to resign because of him. The committee met and passed a resolution cancelling Ward's membership. As it was known by then that he went under two names, the memberships of both Brent and Ward were cancelled to avoid any misunderstanding. He was notified of the decision in a letter dated 30 November 1937, which closed with the words, 'Should you endeavour to enter the club such action will be taken by the officers to ensure your removal as may be deemed advisable.' The letter was composed at Ludford's address and signed by Ludford and the two vice chairs of the committee. The letter was handed to Ward at the club, where he was attending a whist drive. In Ward's disordered imagination, the cancellation was just one incident in the global campaign against him. Incensed by the letter, he overturned his table, made a dash for Ludford and tried to grasp him by the throat, exclaiming, 'Just because you are a cripple you think you can do what you like.' The other members of the club overpowered Ward and removed him from the room. It was not the only occasion when Ward had been violent to Ludford. There had been an earlier incident when he had slapped Ludford's face.

Time had not dimmed Ward's anger and resentment, which he focussed primarily on Ludford. Ward had left a trunk at Liverpool Street station, and amongst other things it contained some notebooks with extensive rambling notes relating to the Brentford and Chiswick Junior Conservative Club, with frequent mentions of Leslie Ludford. Almost four years after his expulsion from the club, he had determined on revenge.

Another member of the committee with whom Ward felt he had a quarrel was Miss Phyllis Ena New who, in 1937, had lived at 1 St Mary's Grove. Ward must have been expecting to find her there, but she had married and moved to Greenford. Mrs Annie New was her mother. Although the murder of Mrs Barringer appeared to have been a targeted killing, there was no evidence that she or anyone in her house had ever known Ward.

In December 1940, Ward had ordered a double barrelled shotgun from John Rigby and Co. of Sackville Street, London, which cost £26 and was delivered the following month. On 7 November 1941 he was granted seven days leave, and on the following day he arrived at a guesthouse at 78 Barrowgate Road, Chiswick, where he had stayed on a previous occasion. On 9 November he paid £9 9s for the four-day hire of a Hillman saloon car, number GGC 83. When he collected the car, he was carrying a large, brown-fibre suitcase.

Barrowgate Road, Chiswick.

At 2.30 p.m. on 11 November, Divisional Inspector Frederick Young cautioned the prisoner at Edgware police station. Ward claimed that he was innocent and that he did not know Ludford.

When Ward appeared in the dock at Acton police court, on 12 November, every seat in the public gallery was filled. Although a serving soldier, it was commented upon in the press that he was not in uniform, but wore a neat grey suit without collar or tie. Mr Laurence Dennis, solicitor, said that he would reserve cross-examination, but Ward was having none of this. He objected to Inspector Young's testimony, announced in a loud voice that he wanted to ask some questions, and told the magistrate that he had not appointed the solicitor to act for him. Dennis explained that he had been appointed by Ward's father. 'My father is not me,' said Ward, insisting that he had something to say. Mr Kent, the presiding magistrate, told him sharply that he would be remanded for three weeks. Inspector Young suggested that during that time Ward should undergo a medical examination, and the magistrates agreed. On the same day, 56-year-old Mrs Crisp died in the West Middlesex Hospital.

When Ward was brought before the magistrates at Acton on 3 December he was charged with three murders, and pleaded not guilty. Mr Vincent Evans was prosecuting. The shotgun was brought to court in three parts and Mr Frank

Wallace of Rigby and Co. assembled it and tested the triggers, testifying that all was in working order, a procedure which Ward followed with keen interest. Ward's defence queried the admissibility of Sergeant Hammond's statement regarding Ludford's dying words identifying his killer, but the bench decided that the statement was admissible.

By the third hearing on 10 December, Ward, neatly dressed in a striped blue suit, was taking an increasingly lively interest in the proceedings, constantly scribbling notes for Mr Dennis. As evidence was given of his earlier assault on Ludford, Ward leaned forward, laughed, and exclaimed 'Really!'

Ward was committed for trial, however Dr H. Grierson, the senior medical officer of Brixton Prison, reported that Ward was suffering from schizophrenia and while he would be able to follow the course of the trial, he would not be able to instruct counsel. 'I am of the opinion that when received he was insane, that he was insane at the time of the alleged crime, and he is still insane.'

In January, at the Central Criminal Court, Ward was found unfit to plead, and the recorder, Sir Gerald Dodson, directed that he should be detained until His Majesty's pleasure be known.

19
ISLINGTON

The Secret in the Cellar

Shortly before he was executed in November 1910 for the murder of his wife, Dr Crippen wrote a letter to his mistress, Ethel le Neve, expressing the hope that someday evidence would be found to prove him innocent. As the years passed there were few serious challenges to the view that Crippen was guilty, but in 2007 that was all to change.

Dr Hawley Harvey Crippen, known as Peter to his friends, was a quiet and unprepossessing man born in Michigan in 1862. In 1893, he was a widower when he met 17-year-old Cora Turner, a vivacious girl with ambitions to be an opera singer. After their marriage, Crippen paid for Cora to have singing lessons, but by 1900 it was apparent that her talents were better suited to the music hall. Crippen was working as a consultant for Munyon's, a patent medicine company, when he arrived in England to manage their London office. His American medical qualifications did not permit him to practise medicine in the UK. Cora, resplendent in elaborate gowns and jewellery, tried to establish herself as an artiste under the name Belle Ellmore, but met with little success, and made no appearances after about 1907. She did however retain a great many friends in the world of the music hall, and was the honorary treasurer of a charitable society, the Music Hall Ladies Guild.

Ethel le Neve was a typist who began working for Munyon's in 1902. Born in 1883, she was a quiet reserved girl, a refreshing contrast to the flamboyant Cora. She and Crippen gradually developed an understanding which, in time, became a love affair.

In January 1910, Crippen and Cora were living at 39 Hilldrop Crescent, and Crippen was working from offices at Albion House, New Oxford Street. Crippen was later to claim that while he and Cora had made an outward show of happiness, all had not been well. There had been frequent arguments,

Mrs Cora Crippen.

The Crippens' home at 39 Hilldrop Crescent.

during which Cora threatened to leave him, and the couple had ceased to sleep together.

Apart from Crippen, the last people who saw Cora alive were Paul Martinetti, a former music hall artist, and his wife, Clara, who came to dinner on the night of 31 January. After a pleasant evening, the Martinettis left at 1.30 a.m. They noticed nothing unusual in the manner of either Dr or Mrs Crippen.

When Cora did not attend the Guild meeting on 2 February the secretary, Melinda May, went to 39 Hilldrop Crescent, and was met at the door by Ethel le Neve, who handed her two letters; one to herself and one to the committee, together with the treasurer's documents. The letters were apparently from Cora, in which she stated that the illness of a relative had compelled her to resign as treasurer and go to America. Neither letter was in Cora's handwriting. On the same day, Crippen pawned some of Cora's jewellery. A week later he pawned some more. Cora's friends waited to receive a card or letter but were puzzled when they heard nothing further. On 20 February, Crippen attended a ball accompanied by Ethel le Neve, and Clara Martinetti noticed that Ethel was wearing a brooch which she thought very like one that had belonged to Cora. Clara asked Crippen about Cora, and he said that he had heard from his wife and that she had reached California but had been taken ill. On 20 March

Crippen wrote a letter to the Martinettis, telling them that he had heard that Cora was dangerously ill with pneumonia. Three days later he told Clara that he was expecting any day to hear that Cora had died, and on the following day he sent Clara a telegram to say that Cora was dead. He later informed her that Cora had died in Los Angeles, attended by her relations. On 26 March a brief obituary notice appeared in a theatrical magazine, *The Era*, at the request of Crippen.

The members of the Ladies' Guild were not satisfied with Crippen's account of Cora's death. Crippen's son by his first marriage, Otto, lived in Los Angeles, and when the Guild contacted him he said that Cora had not died there, it being his understanding that Cora had died in San Francisco. The Guild made further enquiries and found that no woman of the name of Crippen had died in San Francisco.

John Nash, a theatrical manager, and his wife were friends of Cora's who had been abroad at the time of her disappearance and on their return learned to their surprise that Cora had abruptly gone to America and died there. The Nashes were friends of Superintendent Froest of Scotland Yard. They called on him at the Yard on 30 June, outlining the suspicious circumstances of Cora's reported death, and were introduced to Inspector Walter Dew.

Dew thought that given the 'Bohemian character' of the people involved there could be a simple explanation, however he agreed that the mystery needed to be cleared up. He interviewed Cora's friends, and on 8 July, accompanied by Detective Sergeant Mitchell, went to 39 Hilldrop Crescent. Ethel le Neve, who greeted them wearing one of Cora's brooches, had been living there as Crippen's wife since 12 March, although she told the police that she was a housekeeper. Crippen was at Albion House, and Dew insisted that Ethel, who was becoming increasingly agitated, should take him there. Reluctantly she agreed and all three went to Crippen's office, where he made a lengthy statement. Crippen told the police that Cora was not dead, but had left him. He believed that she had gone to Chicago to join Bruce Miller, a musical artist with whom he felt sure she had been having an affair. He admitted that the story of her going to America and dying of pneumonia was a lie, told to conceal a scandal.

Dew was impressed by Crippen's cool and collected manner and initially he thought that his account was not unreasonable, however on reflection he believed that Crippen, anticipating that Cora's friends might report her disappearance to the police, had only appeared convincing because he had told a carefully prepared story. Ethel also made a statement admitting that she had been on intimate terms with Crippen for two or three years and that he had told her that Mrs Crippen had gone to America.

Dew decided to make a thorough search of 39 Hilldrop Crescent and he, Mitchell, Crippen and Ethel returned there. Every room in the house, including the cellar, was carefully examined, and everything appeared to be in good order. Crippen was most co-operative throughout. Dew left, but as a parting comment he told Crippen that in order to finally clear the matter up what he really needed was to find Mrs Crippen.

The more Dew thought about the mystery, the more he was convinced that Crippen was hiding something. On 11 July he and Mitchell returned to Albion House, but neither Crippen nor Ethel were there. They then went to 39 Hilldrop Crescent and were admitted by the maid, but Crippen and Ethel were not at home. They had left the morning after Dew's visit. The police searched the house again, and found a loaded revolver and some cartridges in a wardrobe. They had not been there on the earlier search and Dew could not help wondering if they had been in Crippen's pocket three days previously.

Dew was now convinced that Crippen, possibly in collaboration with his mistress, had murdered Cora and that the couple had fled, probably overseas. Descriptions of the missing couple were circulated, and port officials were especially asked to look out for them. Crippen was described as 5ft 3 or 4 inches tall with sandy hair going bald on top, a 'scanty straggling moustache', and 'rather slovenly appearance'. Ethel, more flatteringly, was 5ft 5in tall, with a 'pleasing appearance, quiet subdued manner.'

The police now had the full run of 39 Hilldrop Crescent, and on 12 July a further search was carried out without anything of interest being discovered. Dew was later to claim that the cellar held a peculiar fascination for him. On 13 July, after another fruitless round of digging up the garden, he and Sergeant Mitchell probed the cellar floor with a poker. Some of the bricks were loose and after pulling them up a layer of clay was found, which, when removed, revealed a mass of decomposing flesh wrapped in a pyjama jacket. The smell was appalling. When the remains were excavated they were found to be boneless portions of a human body, with no clue as to the gender, let alone the identity of the victim. There was nothing obvious to indicate the cause of death, but there were however significant clues to suggest that these were the remains of Cora Crippen. A number of items were found buried with the flesh – a hair curler with some hair attached, dyed in the same colour as Cora's hair, and some ladies' underclothes. The pyjama jacket was found to be a match with pyjama trousers found in Crippen's bedroom.

The summer was a quiet season for the press, and the Crippen case was the perfect opportunity to fill the newspapers with something sensational. The story was soon the topic of conversation everywhere, and men with a close resemblance to Crippen's description were, to their extreme annoyance, being reported to the police and arrested. Three days after the couple's disappearance, Dew learned that Crippen had called at Albion House on the morning of his departure, and sent an employee, William Long, to purchase a set of boy's clothes.

METROPOLITAN POLICE

MURDER

AND MUTILATION.

Portraits, Description and Specimen of Handwriting of HAWLEY HARVEY CRIPPEN, alias Peter Crippen, alias Franckel; and ETHEL CLARA LE NEVE, alias Mrs. Crippen, and Neave.

Wanted for the Murder of CORA CRIPPEN, otherwise Belle Elmore; Kunigunde Mackamotzki; Marsangar and Turner, on, or about, 2nd February last.

Description of Crippen. Age 50, height 5 ft, 3 or 4, complexion fresh, hair light brown, inclined sandy, scanty, bald on top, rather long scanty moustache, somewhat straggly, eyes grey, bridge of nose rather flat, false teeth, medium build, throws his feet outwards when walking. May be clean shaven or wearing a beard and gold rimmed spectacles, and may possibly assume a wig.

Sometimes wears a jacket suit, and at other times frock coat and silk hat. May be dressed in a brown jacket suit, brown hat and stand up collar (size 15).

Somewhat slovenly appearance, wears his hat rather at back of head

Very plausible and quiet spoken, remarkably cool and collected demeanour.

Speaks French and probably German. Carries Firearms.

An American citizen, and by profession a Doctor.

Has lived in New York, Philadelphia, St. Louis, Detroit, Michigan, Coldwater, and other parts of America.

May obtain a position as assistant to a doctor or eye specialist, or may practise as an eye specialist, Dentist, or open a business for the treatment of deafness, advertising freely.

Has represented Munyon's Remedies, in various cities in America.

Description of Le Neve alias Neave.—A shorthand writer and typist, age 27, height 5 ft. 5, complexion pale, hair light brown (may dye same), large grey or blue eyes, good teeth, nice looking, rather long straight nose (good shape), medium build, pleasant, lady-like appearance, Quiet, subdued manner, talks quietly, looks intently when in conversation. A native of London.

Dresses well, but quietly, and may wear a blue serge costume (coat reaching to hips) trimmed heavy braid, about 1 inch wide, round edge, over shoulders and pockets. Three large braid buttons down front, about size of a florin, three small ones on each pocket, two on each cuff, several rows of stitching round bottom of skirt; or a light grey shadow-stripe costume, same style as above, but trimmed grey moire silk instead of braid, and two rows of silk round bottom of skirt; or a white princess robe with gold sequins; or a mole coloured striped costume with black moire silk collar; or a dark vieuxrose cloth costume, trimmed black velvet collar; or a light heliotrope dress.

May have in her possession and endeavour to dispose of same:—a round gold brooch, with points radiating zig-zag from centre, each point about an inch long, diamond in centre, each point set brilliants, the brooch in all being slightly larger than a half-crown; and two single stone diamond rings, and a diamond and sapphire (or ruby) ring, stones rather large.

Absconded 9th inst, and may have left, or will endeavour to leave the country.

Please cause every enquiry at Shipping Offices, Hotels, and other likely places, and cause ships to be watched.

Information to be given to the Metropolitan Police Office, New Scotland Yard, London S.W., or at any Police Station.

E. R. HENRY.
The Commissioner of Police of the Metropolis.

Metropolitan Police Office,
New Scotland Yard.   16th July, 1910.

Police wanted notice for Dr Crippen and Ethel le Neve.

Although the press theorised that Crippen and Ethel were in London, where it was easy to disappear, they were in fact in Belgium, with le Neve in boy's clothing, masquerading as John Robinson and son. On 20 July they boarded the steamship *Montrose*, bound for Canada. Captain Kendall soon became convinced that Master Robinson was a woman in disguise, and suspected that the Robinsons were Crippen and le Neve. He arranged for a message to be sent by wireless telegraph, the first time that invention had been used to catch a criminal. As soon as Dew saw the message he felt sure he had his quarry and asked for authority to pursue them by a fast steamer that would arrive in Canada before the *Montrose*. On 23 July he departed on the *Laurentic*. The news of the chase was leaked to the newspapers and the public eagerly followed the story, with Crippen and Ethel remaining unaware that they were the objects of international attention. When the *Laurentic* arrived in Canada on 29 July, a mass of press reporters were waiting to greet Dew. On 31 July, Dew was rowed out to the newly-arrived *Montrose*, where he confronted Crippen in the captain's cabin and formally arrested him for the murder of his wife. Ethel was also placed under arrest. When Crippen was searched, some of Cora's jewellery was found on him. A note was also found suggesting that Crippen intended to commit suicide by jumping overboard. Dew was not convinced by his prisoner's explanation that

Dr Crippen and Ethel le Neve in the dock at Bow Street.

the note was all part of an escape plot. Dew escorted Crippen and Ethel back to England on the *Megantic*.

Although extensive further searches were made of 39 Hilldrop Crescent, no more human remains were found, however the dustman recalled that in the early part of February he had been asked to remove unusually large amounts of rubbish, including burnt material. Neighbours reported having heard screams some time at the beginning of February, and two ladies even said they had heard gunshots.

At the police hearing on 6 September, the Home Office analyst reported that he had detected traces of a highly unusual alkaloid in the remains – hyoscine, a drug which Crippen was known to have purchased on 19 January.

The prisoners were tried separately, and Crippen's trial opened on 18 October. Crippen's counsel, Marshall Hall, believed that Crippen should admit to poisoning his wife but only in order to sedate her. The defence would then be that he accidentally gave her an overdose and dissected the body when he panicked. Crippen refused to do this. He knew that if he admitted to a crime then Ethel would be deemed an accomplice, and to protect her he insisted on pleading not guilty.

The identification of the mass of flesh as the remains of Cora Crippen was crucial to the entire case. Cora had had an operation scar on her abdomen, and the prosecution provided a convincing witness, a young pathologist Bernard (later Sir Bernard) Spilsbury, who stated unequivocally that a mark on one piece of flesh was an old scar, and not, as the defence suggested, a crease. Crippen was found guilty of murder and sentenced to death. On 25 October, Ethel le Neve was tried as an accessory after the fact and acquitted.

In the ensuing years, Crippen's guilt has been generally accepted, but some queries and anomalies remained. Poisoners do not as a rule dismember their victims; their object is to make the death appear to be from natural causes. Why would someone go to so much trouble to conceal the identity of the remains then carelessly throw in a hair curler and clothes? Why carefully dispose of most of the body and then bury pieces of flesh in the cellar?

On 22 November 1910, the day before his execution, Crippen wrote a long letter to Ethel, a large portion of which was devoted to asserting that the remains found in the cellar were not those of his wife. In 2007 forensic toxicologist, John Trestrail, was able to demonstrate that DNA taken from the original slides made from the cellar remains showed that the body was not that of Cora Crippen. In the following year it was confirmed that the remains were male. Had that fact come to light during Crippen's trial then he would automatically have been acquitted.

Inevitably, a suspicion must arise that the remains were planted in the cellar by someone who, convinced that Crippen had murdered his wife, was frustrated by lack of concrete evidence. The new revelations do not, as many have claimed, mean that Crippen did not murder Cora. An examination of Crippen's behaviour after 31 January 1910 demonstrates that he knew that Cora was not going to return home, contact her relatives or write to any of her friends. Crippen knew that his wife was dead, and the only way he could have known that was if he had killed her, probably on or around 1 February. Between that date and Ethel moving into 39 Hilldrop Crescent, Crippen had almost six weeks to dispose of Cora's body.

It has been suggested that a woman recorded under the name of Belle Rose in the New York census returns of 1910 and 1920 could be Cora, based partly on the claim that her profession in 1920 was 'singer'. A close examination of the return shows that the profession was actually 'designer' and this fits with the same woman's profession in 1910 of 'milliner'. The age is also incorrect.

There is no confirmed sighting of Cora Crippen after 31 January 1910. Had she been alive after that date, the international hue and cry, not to mention the rewards offered for information, would have brought her out into the place she had always wanted to be – in the limelight.

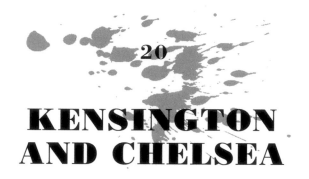

20

KENSINGTON
AND CHELSEA

House of Horror

On 15 November 1949, Timothy John Evans went to stay with his uncle and aunt in Merthyr Vale, unaccompanied by his young wife, Beryl, and 14-month-old daughter Geraldine. When asked about the whereabouts of his family, Evans' evasive answers and frequent changes of story caused increasing concern. Evans, his wife and child had been living in the top flat of 10 Rillington Place, a cul-de-sac of three-storey houses; mean, narrow and shabby. On 27 November, Evans' sister, Eileen, spoke to the occupants of the bottom flat, John Christie and his wife Ethel, and was told that Beryl and Geraldine had left on Tuesday 8 November. On the following day Evans' other sister, Maureen, visited while Christie was out. Ethel told her that Beryl had left saying goodbye and had promised to write, but then Christie arrived home and told Maureen that Beryl had left without saying goodbye. When Maureen pointed out that one of them must be lying, and threatened to go to the police, Christie became so angry she thought he was going to hit her.

On 30 November, under pressure from his family, Timothy Evans made a statement to the police. He said that Beryl had recently found out she was pregnant and wanted an abortion. He had been given some abortion pills by a stranger in a café and Beryl had taken them and died. He had put her body down the drain outside his house. After arranging for Geraldine to be looked after, he sold up his furniture and came to Wales.

The police checked the drain, but it was obvious that Evans' story was impossible, as it took three men to lift the cover. They found nothing suspicious inside. When Evans was confronted with these developments, he said that he had lied to protect Christie, and made a second statement.

According to Evans, Christie had found out that Beryl wanted an abortion, and approached him offering his services, but warned that the 'stuff' he used would kill one person in ten. Evans told Christie he wasn't interested, but Beryl was determined to go through with it. On Monday 7 November Beryl told her husband that she had made arrangements with Christie for the next day. Evans went to work early the following morning. When Evans returned that evening Christie met him with bad news; Beryl was dead. He said her stomach was 'septic poisoned' and showed him Beryl's body lying on the bed. There was blood on her nose and mouth and from what Evans called 'the bottom part'. As a temporary measure, Christie forced the door of the first floor flat, which was empty, and put the body in there. He told Evans that he intended to put it down the drain. On 9 November Evans went to work. Christie offered to look after Geraldine, saying that he knew a couple in East Acton who would take her. That night Christie told Evans that the couple from Acton would come and take the baby on Thursday. When Evans returned from work on Thursday evening Geraldine had gone and Christie said that the people from Acton had called. He advised Evans to leave London.

The first impression of the police when they heard this second story was that Timothy Evans was not quite right in the head. Evans was born in Wales in 1924, and his family moved to London in 1935. Illness had kept him out of school for many months at a time, a deprivation that had never been corrected. As a result he scored poorly on reading and IQ tests. He sometimes told wild lies and fantasies to boost his confidence. He met 18-year-old Beryl Thorley on a blind date in 1947, and they were married later that year. In the spring of 1948 they moved to 10 Rillington Place, and in October, baby Geraldine was born. Evans was working long hours as a van driver, and bringing in a modest wage. The new baby put extra pressure on their resources and the couple quarreled. In the summer of 1949, Beryl found that she was pregnant again. This was unplanned, and financially, it was a disaster. She tried douching and syringing to procure an abortion, but without success.

The police, suspecting that Evans had killed his wife, made a search of 10 Rillington Place. They probably didn't check the rear garden, a piece of wasteland some 20ft square, or they might have spotted the human thighbone propping up the fence, neither did they look in the wash house, which could only be accessed from the yard at the back. In Evans' flat they found a stolen briefcase, and a newspaper cutting about the Stanley Setty torso murder. Evans was arrested and brought back to London. Christie told the police that Evans and his wife were always arguing and Evans had attacked her by grabbing her throat, and Mrs Christie suggested that Beryl might have gone away for an abortion.

The police learned that a friend of Beryl's, Joan Vincent had come to see her on 8 November, and found the front door open. Some workmen had been

Old walling thought to have once been a part of the garden wall at Rillingon Place.

carrying out renovations to the property that day, and could have been taking materials into the house. Joan went up to the top flat, but was unable to open the door to Beryl's kitchen, and got the impression that someone was inside holding it shut. She assumed that Beryl didn't want to see her and went away.

On 2 December the police carried out a more thorough search. On opening the wash house door they saw a stack of wood propped against the sink. Behind the wood was a package wrapped in a green tablecloth and tied with a sash cord. When the package was opened, Beryl's legs slipped out. The wrapped body of Geraldine was found under some wood behind the door.

It was estimated that both victims had been dead for about three weeks. Death was due to strangulation with a ligature, Beryl with a cord, Geraldine with a tie. Beryl also had bruising to her throat and neck, a swelling to her right eye and upper lip, and bruising inside her vagina. There had been no abortion. Unfortunately, no swab was taken. The police showed Evans the clothing of his wife and child, and said that they believed he was responsible for their deaths. He said only one word – 'Yes.'

That night Evans signed a confession to the murders of Beryl and Geraldine. This account stated that a row on 8 November had ended with Evans slapping Beryl and strangling her with a piece of rope he had brought into the flat from his van. He laid her on the bed with the rope still round her neck, and later that evening put the body in the first floor flat. After feeding the baby he waited until things were quiet, carried the body down to the wash house and put it behind the sink, then covered the body with pieces of wood. He then locked the wash house door. The following day he fed Geraldine, put her in her cot and went to work, feeding her again when he got home. The next day, 10 November, he again went to work after feeding Geraldine, but on returning home, strangled her with his tie. That night he put the body in the wash house.

There were some anomalies in this confession. It refers to Evans locking the wash house door, but the lock was damaged and didn't work. No rope was found around Beryl's neck. More crucially, it was not until after the confession was taken that the police interviewed the workmen, and discovered that the plasterer had completed the ceiling of the wash house on 9 November – the day after Evans was supposed to have put Beryl's body there – and they had seen nothing unusual. On 11 November, the wash house had been swept out and was left empty. The room measured just fifty-two by fifty-four inches, and it is hardly possible that two corpses could have been there without anyone noticing. The wood used to cover the bodies consisted of floorboards taken up from the front passageway in 10 Rillington Place, and this had not been done until 11 November. Evans' statement suggests he put the wood in front of the bodies on a day when the planks were still part of the floor. The carpenter said he had given the wood to John Christie on 14 November.

The workmen were interviewed at the police station and told that they must have been mistaken. Both were persuaded to modify their stories to match Evans' confession.

The trial of Timothy Evans opened at the Old Bailey on 11 January 1950. He was tried only for the murder of Geraldine. As the law then stood, both murder charges could not be heard together, and in the case of Beryl, Evans could have pleaded provocation. Evans had retracted his confessions, and his defence was that Christie was the murderer. The chief witness for the prosecution was Christie.

John Reginald Halliday Christie was born on April 8 1899 near Halifax, Yorkshire. At school he was considered above average in intelligence, but with a strict father and over-protective mother he became shy and withdrawn. When he was eight, his grandfather died and he was allowed to view the corpse. He later described his reaction as 'fascination and pleasure'. His first sexual adventure was a disaster, all the more so because the girl concerned told others about his deficiencies. While attracted to women, he also hated them.

Christie served during the First World War when he was gassed. On 10 May 1920 he married Ethel Simpson. Soon afterwards he committed his first recorded crimes. He had been working as a postman and, in April 1921, he was sentenced to three months in prison for stealing postal orders. In 1923 he received twelve months probation for obtaining money by false pretences, and violence. The marriage foundered. He neglected Ethel sexually and visited prostitutes. In 1924 Ethel went to live with relatives in Sheffield and Christie moved to London, where, that September, he was sentenced to nine months in prison for larceny.

In 1929 he was living with a prostitute, and presumably living off her, too, as he was not working. During an argument he struck her over the head with a cricket bat. For this crime he received a sentence of six months hard labour. In 1933 he was sentenced to three months for stealing a car from a priest who had befriended him. While in prison he wrote to Ethel, asking her to come and live with him again, and she agreed.

In 1938 the couple moved to 10 Rillington Place. On the outbreak of war, Christie enrolled as a volunteer special constable. He enjoyed the respect this position gave him, and was hard working and efficient. He also began an affair with a young woman working at the police station, whose husband was a serving soldier. This period of Christie's life was his highest point of self-esteem, but in the summer of 1943 the soldier returned, found Christie and his wife together, and gave him a severe beating.

At the trial of Evans, Christie's war record was introduced to demonstrate his good character. He frequently referred to being ill and in pain, and probably made quite a pathetic figure in the witness box, appearing too weak to carry out the actions attributed to him by Evans. It wasn't until later cross-examination that his history of petty crimes came to light, but the prosecution persuaded the court that these minor offences were irrelevant. Unknown to anyone at the time, Christie was also a murderer.

Christie's first known murder victim was Ruth Fuerst, an Austrian student nurse born in 1922, and reputedly a part-time prostitute. In August 1943, while Ethel was away visiting relations, Ruth went to 10 Rillington Place. After having intercourse, Christie strangled her with a rope. Knowing that Ethel would be home that evening, he put the body under the floorboards in the front room. The next day, with Ethel out at work, he dug a hole in the back garden, and moved the body to the washhouse. At ten that night, under cover of darkness, he buried the body. The clothing was burned in a dustbin.

Christie left the police force in 1944 and worked in an electrical factory, where he met Muriel Eady, a respectable spinster, who suffered from chronic catarrh. The next time Ethel was away Christie lured Muriel to his flat, saying that he had an inhalation device which could cure her catarrh. The inhaler was connected to a gas tap. Once Muriel was unconscious Christie had intercourse with her and strangled her. The body was placed in the wash house, and later buried in the garden. Muriel's thigh bone later worked loose from the soil and was used to prop up a garden fence.

On 13 January 1950, Timothy Evans was found guilty of the murder of his daughter. He was sentenced to death and hanged at Pentonville Prison on 9 March.

Christie had been working for the Post Office again, but the trial had uncovered his past record, and he was dismissed. His relationship with Ethel became increasingly strained. Early on the morning of 14 December 1952, Christie strangled her with a stocking, and hid the body under the floorboards. He wrote to relatives explaining that Ethel had rheumatism and couldn't write. He subsisted by selling furniture and cashing in Ethel's savings.

In January 1953, Kathleen Maloney, a 26-year-old prostitute, was seen leaving a public house, very drunk, with Christie. Back at 10 Rillington Place, Christie gassed her and strangled her with a rope. On the following day he pushed her blanket-wrapped body into an alcove in a corner of the kitchen, behind the washhouse.

A few days later, Rita Nelson, a 25-year-old prostitute, was reported missing by her landlady. Rita was twenty-five weeks pregnant, and Christie may well have offered his services as an abortionist. He tried to gas her but when she struggled, he strangled her. He body also went into the alcove.

Pentonville Prison, where both Evans and Christie were hanged.

Hectorina McLennan met Christie in March 1953, when she and her boyfriend came to look at a flat. Hectorina later visited Christie alone, and her body joined the others in the alcove.

Time was almost up for Christie. He had no money and no job. After subletting the flat and taking three months advance rent, he packed his case and left. On 24 March a tenant discovered the papered-over alcove, peeled back the covering and shone his torch inside.

Christie wandered aimlessly about London for a few days, and on 31 March he was recognised by a police constable, and arrested. He confessed to killing all the women, excusing his actions by saying that some had forced themselves on him, while Mrs Christie, Muriel Eady and Beryl Evans had been suffering and depressed and he had put them out of their misery. He did not confess to the murder of Geraldine. A tobacco tin was found containing four samples of pubic hair. Christie said that they were, as far as he could recollect, from Mrs Christie and the three women in the alcove, but it was impossible to prove who they were from.

In May, Beryl's body was exhumed. Christie had claimed that he had given her gas and then strangled her, but there was no evidence that she had inhaled enough gas to render her unconscious. Her pubic hair was intact. Christie's

Site of what was once Rillington Place.

trial for the murder of Ethel opened on 22 June 1953. He was found guilty and hanged at Pentonville on 15 July.

In 1966, after a lengthy campaign spearheaded by writer and broadcaster Ludovic Kennedy, the Brabin enquiry granted Timothy Evans a posthumous free pardon for the murder of Geraldine, although it was still officially believed that he may have been guilty of killing Beryl.

Whose signature was on the crimes? If Evans had killed Beryl during a quarrel it would have been in the heat of the moment. If he had strangled her it would have been with his bare hands. The use of a ligature suggests a premeditated crime, and that is Christie's signature method. All his victims were killed in that way.

The fact that Beryl was not gassed is cited as evidence that it was Evans and not Christie who killed her, but a possible scenario is that, as in the case of Rita Nelson, Beryl panicked and struggled before inhaling significant amounts of gas, and Christie then strangled her. The facial bruises could have been either from Christie or a previous fight with Evans.

Did Evans kill his daughter? He was a notably inept liar, but after 10 November he gave every impression, in both word and deed, that he believed Geraldine to be alive, right up to the moment the police told him they had found her body. It would not have fitted Christie's self-image to confess to the murder of Geraldine. In all the other cases he had claimed either that the victim had been a sexual aggressor, or he had carried out mercy killings. It would damage his self esteem to admit to the killing of a child.

At the request of the residents, Rillington Place was renamed Ruston Close in 1954. This is not to be confused with present-day Ruston Mews. The street was demolished for new development in the early 1970s.

21

KINGSTON

'In an Evil Moment'

The opening of the mainline London and South-Western Railway in 1838 provided a much-needed fast rail link from Southampton to Victoria. One station on the route was Surbiton, and as a result, the little settlement, now part of the Royal Borough of Kingston-upon-Thames, became a popular commuter town. At 11.15 on the morning of 17 January 1901, Mrs Rhoda King, the 54-year-old wife of a printer, was travelling to London to see her daughter-in-law, who was very ill, and boarded the train at Southampton, entering an unoccupied third class compartment. There were no corridors on the train, and passengers in each compartment were unable to see or communicate with the people in the next one. For the few minutes between stations therefore, travellers were highly vulnerable to crime. Mrs King, apparently preferring quiet and privacy despite the risk, was alone until the train reached Eastleigh, when a respectable looking young man entered the carriage. He seemed restless and said nothing, only coughed a great deal. At Winchester they were joined by another passenger. He was 48-year-old William Pearson, a gentlemen farmer who was travelling to London on business. The three passengers did not converse, and Mr Pearson, after reading his newspaper, laid it aside and dozed. As the train drew out of Surbiton station, Mrs King checked her ticket and stood up to look out of the window. There were two loud bangs, and at first Mrs King thought they were fog signals, then she felt blood pouring down her face.

She turned to the young man who was standing behind her. 'My God! What have you done?' she exclaimed. 'Why did you do it?'

'I did it for money,' he said. 'I want some money. Have you got any?'

Mrs King had a shilling in her purse which she handed over, and then she looked down at the other passenger. There was blood on Pearson's face, and a gurgling sound in his throat. She felt sure that he was dead. The young man

Scenes from the South-Western Railway murder.

took papers and valuables from Pearson's pockets then he sat down and started counting the money.

Mrs King, trapped in a moving railway carriage with a murderer, and the only living witness to the crime, was, in her own words 'extremely alarmed'. Going down on her knees she asked the young man if he had a mother, and implored him to spare her life for the sake of her two sons. As she reached out to him he exclaimed, 'Keep your hands down; don't touch me!' and she realised that her hands were covered in blood.

'I'm sorry I hurt you,' he said, and reassured her that he would not hurt her any more if she kept quiet about what had happened. Perhaps the mention of his mother by a woman who was ten years her senior had softened his desperate mood. When Mrs King tried unsuccessfully to staunch the blood on her face with two handkerchiefs, the young man gave her his. He then offered her a sovereign from Pearson's purse, asking, 'Is this any use to you?' but she refused to take it.

Mrs King tried to keep the murderer talking. She asked him where he had come from and he said that he was from Birmingham and was going to Liverpool on his way to South Africa. He mentioned his brothers and added that he had had some very bad luck. Suddenly he remembered the revolver and started looking around him. 'What have I done with that damned thing?' It was on the seat, and he picked it up. 'I must not keep it about me. I have a good mind to put it in his hand, and then they will think that he did it himself.'

'If I was you, I would throw the revolver out of the window,' said Mrs King. He was about to do so but hesitated, saying that there were some men working on the line.

'Wait till you get a little further on,' advised Mrs King. As the train passed by some sheds she suggested that he should throw the pistol out there, and he did. He then took a small parcel of bullets out of his pocket and threw that out also. Mrs King next suggested that Pearson's face should be covered with a handkerchief, and he complied.

The train was by now approaching the next stop, which was Vauxhall. 'As soon as I get to Vauxhall I shall make a run for it,' said the young man, 'mind you don't say anything about it.' Mrs King reassured the nervous murderer that she would say nothing of what had happened. As the train slowed he opened the door, hesitated for a moment on the footboard because there were porters on the platform, then jumped out and hurried towards the exit. 'Stop him!' screamed Mrs King. She staggered out of the train gasping, 'Stop that man; he has murdered someone in that carriage!' and the hue and cry was raised.

The murderer bolted down the station steps, pursued by several porters, and headed in the direction of old Vauxhall Bridge. Here he encountered police constable Thomas Fuller on point duty at Vauxhall Cross, who joined in the chase.

With this escape route blocked, the fugitive changed direction and ran into a nearby gasworks. Almost knocking down a doorkeeper, he fled across a small creek into a yard and eventually entered a tunnel which led into number 4 retort house and hid behind a coke truck. By now there was quite a crowd of pursuers outside the gasworks and the engineer in charge gave orders that the gates leading into Wandsworth Road, the only other exit, should be closed. The police were informed of where the man was hiding, but the tunnel was dark, so lanterns were sent for; while officers kept watch to prevent an escape. When the lanterns arrived, officers approached the entrance to the tunnel, demanding that the man give himself up. Alfred Atkins, a fire-raker, found the fugitive in number 10 archway, standing between a truck and the wall, and called out 'here he is!' Hearing the cry, Constable Fuller came up and took the man into custody. The prisoner was silent until he arrived at Larkhall Lane police station, then he said:

> I shot him to get my own back. The woman pushed her face near the trigger. Afterwards it went off again, the shot grazing her cheek. I wish I had killed her, and then I should have got away.

Sergeant Thorley searched the prisoner and found a purse containing £5 in gold, a watch and chain, and a cigar case, all later identified as the property of the murdered man, and some of Pearson's personal papers.

The flight and capture of Parker.

Dr George Albert Simpson of South Lambeth Road had been called to Vauxhall station, where he saw the body of Mr Pearson laid out in the waiting room. There was a single wound through the left eye and lid. The bullet had passed through the eye into the brain. The eyebrow was singed and there were burn marks, which showed that the pistol had been fired from only inches away. The pockets of the dead man contained three shillings and some copper coins.

The tragic news was conveyed to Pearson's family; his 34-year-old widow, Isabella, and two young daughters. In Southampton, the home of the King family, there was considerable excitement. Mr King was at work in the ordinance survey office, when a report reached him that his wife had been shot and had died of her injuries. On hearing this, King fainted.

Mrs King, who was very much alive, had been taken to St Thomas' Hospital, where an examination using the relatively new medical miracle, the Roentgen ray, found that she had had a lucky escape. A bullet, split into three pieces, was lodged in her lower jaw, but the bone was not broken. Powder blackening showed that she, like Pearson, had been shot at close range. It is possible that an involuntary movement on hearing the shot that killed Pearson had saved her life. The revolver used in the murder was later found by a plate-layer fifty yards to the west of Wandsworth Road Bridge. When handed in, four chambers were found to be still loaded.

The prisoner originally told the police his name was George Henry Hill, but it was later found that his real name was George Henry Parker. He was 22, and the eldest of eight children born in Studley, Warwickshire, to James Parker, a needle pointer, and his wife Catherine, who worked in a cycle factory. In recent months his parents had been living apart. Parker had been sent to a reformatory at the age of 14, but on his release he had stayed with his parents only a few weeks before disappearing, and thereafter they had seen very little of him.

Parker, described as 'a young man of fine physique … of very dark complexion, 6ft in height', had recently enlisted in the Royal Marine Artillery but shortly afterwards, letters had gone missing from his barracks. A watch was kept and it was found that he had stolen his comrades' letters for the postal orders enclosed and forged their signatures. He served twenty-one days in prison, after which, unsurprisingly, the Royal Marine Artillery no longer required his services. He had then gone to London and worked as a dresser in the Lyceum Theatre, where he was soon suspected of carrying out a robbery. He disappeared before he could be arrested, arriving in Portsmouth with a great deal of jewellery in his possession.

There he met 23-year-old Elizabeth Sarah Rowland, a laundrywoman, and the wife of a private in the Scottish rifles, who was away in India. Lizzie, as she was known, did not mention that she was married and Parker told her his name was Hill. The two started keeping company, and going to places of entertainment, for which he paid. On 16 January they went to Southampton together, where they spent a great deal of money on drink. On the following day, having both sobered up, they wanted to return to Portsmouth and Parker told Lizzie he had only enough money to get their rail tickets. They travelled together as far as Eastleigh, where she changed to the Portsmouth train, but he told her he was going on to London to get some things he had left there.

Under questioning, Parker told a series of wild and often contradictory stories. On being charged with the murder of Pearson and attempted murder of Mrs King, he claimed that he had killed Pearson because of an old grudge, for injuries done when he was in the army and also after he left. He then asked to be allowed to write to his father. 'I must have been mad,' he wrote. 'I do not know what I did it for … Had you not broken up the home … I might have been a better man.' He attributed his crimes to craving for money and being led astray by pretty girls, although he professed his love for Lizzie, who he said was 'not good-looking.'

On 18 January, Parker wrote to Lizzie from prison. With assurances that he had always loved her dearly and that he was truly sorry for having 'in an evil moment' allowed himself to be carried away into committing the crime, he said that he had bought the revolver in Southampton with the intention that when he returned to Portsmouth, he could end both their lives if he had not been successful in getting money from his father. He said he knew Lizzie had not been happy at home (she was later to deny this) and he too had been unhappy, 'mostly on account of the false charges brought against me at barracks,' for which he declared he was 'as innocent as the dead'. Accepting the fact that he would probably be hung for the crime, he added, 'I believe I was mad. I know I was drunk.'

On 25 January, Parker wrote a letter of apology to Mrs Pearson, saying that he was 'really and truly sorry' for the crime, and had never intended to shoot her husband, having bought the gun with the intention of shooting Lizzie and himself. The crime had been committed 'on the spur of the moment'. He finally admitted that he had never seen Pearson before in his life.

On 7 February, Parker saw Lizzie at the police court and told her yet another version of the crime, that the shooting had been an accident.

There was little that could be said in Parker's defence at the trial, which opened on 25 February. Dr Simpson, who was not an expert on mental disorders, was nevertheless questioned on the subject and stated that 'a man predisposed to the attacks of an unhinged mind, or weak-minded, might, from alcoholism or disappointment, be led away in a moment to do an act which he

The execution of Parker.

is not responsible for.' He could only speak generally, however, and admitted he knew nothing of Parker's case.

The incident prompted a letter to *The Times* concerning the dangers of travelling in trains without corridors.

Parker was hanged in Wandsworth Gaol on 19 March 1901.

22

LAMBETH

In a Lonely Place

Near the junction of Lavender Gardens and Battersea Rise to the north of Clapham Common is the start of an asphalt path that leads diagonally across the common to the central bandstand. During the wintry nights of December 1910 the Common was usually deserted, its pathways unlit.

On the morning of Sunday, 1 January 1911, police constable Joseph Mumford was patrolling the Common when he discovered the body of a man lying in a clump of bushes about halfway between the bandstand and Lavender Gardens. There was a pool of blood near some railings on the other side of the path, and a trail of blood and drag marks showing that the man had been killed on the path and the body pulled along by the coat collar into the bushes. Mumford called for assistance and at 9 a.m. surgeon Joseph Needham arrived to examine the body, and estimated that the man had been dead for approximately six hours. Papers found in the dead man's pocket identified him as 48-year-old Leon Beron. Beron was Russian by birth, but when he was a year old the family had moved to France, where his two younger brothers, Solomon and David, were born. The family came to England in 1894. Leon, who was a widower, had lived with David at 133 Jubilee Street, Stepney, which ran parallel to Sidney Street, while Solomon lived in a nearby lodging house, and their father, Max, was in a residential care home for aged Jews.

Leon had lived a hand-to-mouth existence. He owned nine small rented houses, on which he made a profit of about £25 a year. Out of this he spent 2s a week on his own rent and between 1s 3d and 1s 6d a day on food. On most days he ate at a kosher restaurant called the Warsaw, at 32 Osborn Street, just off the Whitechapel Road, about fifteen minutes walk from his home. He usually arrived at the restaurant at about 2 p.m. and spent the rest of the day there, eating, drinking tea, smoking his pipe and talking to other customers, leaving at about midnight.

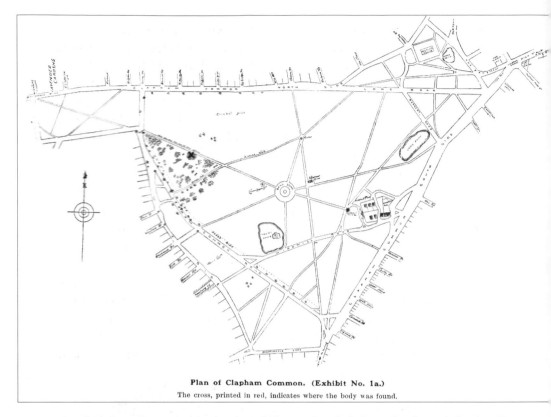

Plan of Clapham Common. (Exhibit No. 1a.)
The cross, printed in red, indicates where the body was found.

Plan of Clapham Common exhibited at the trial. The site where the body was found is marked with an X.

Beron had no bank account. He changed the silver he received for the rents into gold at the restaurant, and kept his money in a wash-leather purse secured inside his coat with a safety pin. It was estimated that on the night of his death he was carrying between £12 and £30 in gold coin. At one time he had had money to invest and he had bought an eighteen carat gold watch and chain, from which hung a £5 gold piece. The value of the watch and chain was about £30. When his body was found, Leon's money and the watch and chain were all missing.

There was no obvious reason why Leon should have been on Clapham Common, especially at night. Max Beron lived in Nightingale Lane, south of the Common, but Leon was not on good terms with his father and never visited him. If he had done, then he would surely have taken a cab to Nightingale Lane and not to the north of the Common. His murderer might, however, have convinced him of some profitable scheme which involved a visit to Clapham. Police searches revealed no clues as to the murderer. A bloodstained handkerchief was found not far from the murder scene, but although it had a laundrymark, its owner was never traced.

The body was taken to Battersea mortuary, where it was examined by pathologist Frederick Freyburger. He found eight wounds caused by blows to the head, which he thought had been made by a blunt metallic instrument like an iron bar. In his opinion, the first wounds to be inflicted were two in quick succession on the right side of the forehead, which would have caused rapid unconsciousness. The location suggested that the assailant was left handed. The victim would have sunk to the ground, and the other blows to the scalp and forehead had followed. Beron had then been stabbed three times in the chest, probably shortly after death. There were also seven shallow cuts on the victim's face, some quite short, two of which attracted particular attention. They were later referred to as S shaped, although one was a greatly elongated S and the other a rough mirror image. Needham described them as more like the f-holes on a violin. The cuts were undoubtedly inflicted with a knife and could not have been produced when the body was dragged.

Beron's stomach contained the remains of bread and meat, and smelt of alcohol, the stage of digestion suggesting that he had died three or four hours after he last ate. It was estimated that Beron's last meal would have been eaten at approximately midnight, and he was killed about three hours later.

In the previous two weeks a man had been seen in almost daily company with Beron. His name, or at least the one he was then using, was Steinie Morrison. Morrison was a distinctive figure, some 6ft 3in tall, 29 years old, handsome and smartly dressed. He was especially adept at charming young women, giving them presents and hinting at marriage within days of meeting them, as a preliminary to seduction. He claimed to make his living by dealing in jewellery, but he had also been seen more than once with a black pistol. Morrison had begun to frequent the Warsaw restaurant at the start of December, and about a week or two before the murder, it was noticed that Morrison and Beron had struck up a friendship, and spent a great deal of time in conversation. They made an odd couple, the quiet diminutive Beron,

Leon Beron.

who looked older than his years, and the tall, young, more flamboyant Morrison. On one occasion Morrison had been seen admiring Beron's watch and chain. Morrison may have been short of ready money, as he had pawned a watch for £4 10s shortly before Christmas.

Several witnesses had seen the two men in the restaurant together on the 31 December. Morrison had arrived at 6 p.m. and handed a parcel to the waiter, Joe Mintz, asking him to look after it for him. The paper-wrapped object was about 2ft long. Rebecca Snelwar, the restaurateur's ten-year-old daughter, asked what it contained, and Morrison said it was a flute. It was certainly the right size for a flute but Mintz thought it was too heavy. It felt more like a bar of iron. Morrison joined Beron at his table and the two men spent the evening together, drinking tea and lemonade, but they did not buy any food. At about twenty minutes to twelve, Morrison collected the parcel and he and Beron left together. The location where Beron ate his last meal and had his last alcoholic drink were never identified, but the remains of a sandwich were found in his pockets, so it seems that he did not enter a restaurant.

The men were still together in the Whitechapel area later that night. At a quarter to one, Jacob Weissberg and Israel Zaltzman were at the corner of Black Lion Yard near Whitechapel Road and saw Beron and Morrison, both of whom were known to them, walking in the direction of Osborn Street. Shortly after 1 a.m. Nellie Deitch and her husband were walking along Commercial Road on their way home from a party. Nellie had known Beron for twelve years, and recognised him as he walked towards her in the company of another man she later identified as Morrison. Jack Taw, a waiter at the Warsaw who knew both men by sight, said he had seen them at about a quarter to two in Whitechapel Road, not far from Osborn Street.

At 2 a.m., cab driver Edward Hayman picked up two men at the Mile End corner of Sydney Street. He had good reason to remember this journey as he had never picked up a fare in the East End before and was usually only in the area when he had taken someone there. He later identified Steinie Morrison as one of the two passengers, and described the other as being about 5ft 5in. The taller man had asked to go to Lavender Hill, mentioning the Shakespeare Theatre at No. 168. Hayman had dropped them at the Clapham side of Lavender Gardens. It was then about a quarter to three and from that spot to where Beron's body was found was about a ten minute walk.

The cab rank at Clapham Cross was about half a mile from the murder scene. Cabman Andrew Stephens was there at approximately a quarter past three, when a man who had been walking alone asked to go to Kennington and was dropped next to Kennington Church, a journey of just over ten minutes. Stephens later identified this fare as Morrison, saying he was well dressed and clean shaven, and looked like someone in the theatrical profession, but estimated his height at only 5ft 10in. Alfred Catlin was a cab driver on a rank near Kennington Church and picked up two men there at 3.30 a.m. and took them to Finsbury Park station. He later identified Morrison as one of the two men.

Morrison was very familiar with Clapham and the Common. On 21 September 1910 he had started work as a baker with Thomas Pithers, whose shop was at 213 Lavender Hill, about fifty yards from Lavender Gardens. He worked there until 10 November and during the last ten days he had done a bakery round in the area, which had involved him crossing the Common to streets on the other side.

On 1 January, Morrison deposited his gun and cartridges at St Mary's railway station, Whitechapel. On the same day he was seen to have £28 in his pocket in gold and notes. He ceased to patronise the Warsaw restaurant and moved to new lodgings. Morrison was a convict on licence and should have notified the police of his change of address, but failed to do so. As a result, he was arrested on 8 January at a restaurant in Fieldgate Street, Whitechapel. He immediately assumed he was being arrested for murder and offered to make a statement. Morrison denied being especially friendly with Beron or having walked about the streets with him, but after being identified as the man seen with Beron on 31 December, he was charged with murder. Some tiny spots of blood were found on his shirt, but a man who owned several shirts and took a pride in his appearance would not have been wearing the same shirt on 8 January as he had worn eight days earlier. It was suggestive, however, that the spots were on the left cuff and collar, since Morrison was left handed and Beron had been struck on the right side of the head. There was an innocent explanation for the blood – Morrison suffered from nosebleeds. The trial opened at the Central Criminal Court, the Old Bailey on 6 March 1911 and lasted for nine days. Defence counsel Mr Abinger tried to discredit Mintz by asking him about his attempt at suicide nine months previously. Mr Justice Darling saw the danger of this line of questioning and interrupted to warn Abinger. Under the Criminal Evidence Act of 1898, Morrison was permitted to give evidence in his own defence, but could not be questioned about past crimes unless witnesses for the prosecution had also been so questioned. Attempted suicide was then a felony. Despite the warning Abinger persisted, and also attacked Mrs Deitch by accusing her of running a brothel.

Abinger brought witnesses to provide an alibi for his client. Morrison's landlady, Mrs Zimmerman, said he had come home shortly before twelve on New Year's Eve and had gone straight to bed. The street door had been locked and bolted at midnight. Although Morrison had his own key, she thought she would have heard if he had gone out. She saw Morrison again at ten the next morning. She had taken his linen to the laundry and had seen no bloodstains on either his clothes or sheets.

Steinie Morrison.

Twenty-three-year-old Esther Brodsky and her sister Jane, who was sixteen, testified that they had gone to a performance at the Shoreditch Empire at nine o'clock on New Year's Eve and had sat in the orchestra stalls, the seats costing 1s each. There they had recognised Steinie Morrison, a man they knew by sight. The performance finished between eleven and half past. They saw him again two days later and on the following Friday he gave Jane a silver watch for her birthday and asked to continue seeing her with a view to marriage.

Morrison was in the witness box for about a day and a half. He stated that after leaving Pithers' bakery with savings of £4, he began to deal in cheap jewellery, earning about £2 a week. He was in no need of money as his mother had sent him sums of £15 and £20 from Russia, and – a story he told for the first time in court – on 1 December he had won £28 gambling. He denied being with Beron at the restaurant on the evening of 31 December, saying he had called there at 8 p.m. only to leave the flute. He then went to the music hall, where he saw Jane and Esther Brodsky in the audience. He was back at the restaurant before twelve, and after some refreshments, collected the flute and went home. On the way he had seen Beron talking to a tall man.

Abinger's error now came home to roost as Mr Muir for the prosecution questioned Morrison about his past prison terms for burglary and receiving stolen goods. Muir's trump card was Hector Munro, manager of the Shoreditch Empire, who exposed Morrison's alibi for the evening of 31 December as a lie. There had been no unsold seats at the time Morrison and the Brodsky girls claimed to have arrived and tickets cost 1s 6d and not 1s. Morrison had described seeing a singer dressed as a Scotsman on 31 December, but that act had not commenced until 2 January. Abinger countered by producing his own surprise witness, a Constable Greaves, who contradicted his colleagues by saying that Morrison was told he was suspected of murder before he offered to make his statement. Abinger also attacked the identification evidence, since the cab drivers had identified Morrison only after pictures of him were published in the newspapers. He suggested another motive for the murder. Beron might have given information to the police following the murder of three policemen in Houndsditch on 16 December 1910 by a gang of anarchist burglars, and he had been killed by the gang members as an act of revenge.

In his summing-up, Mr Justice Darling hypothesised that Beron may have been murdered by two men, differently armed. As to the lines on the face, which it had been suggested, had stood for 'spy' in more than one language, only someone with a more vivid imagination or better eyesight would make a letter S out of them. The jury, possibly swayed by the false alibi, found Morrison guilty, and he was sentenced to death. Considerable doubts had been raised in the public mind about the weight of the evidence used to convict Morrison, and Home Secretary Winston Churchill was inundated with letters and petitions. On 12 April the sentence was commuted to life imprisonment.

An enquiry into police procedures concluded that the evidence given by Constable Greaves was untrue. An Englishwoman living in Paris later claimed she had overheard a conversation which suggested that another man had been guilty of the murder, but no useful information emerged from this.

Steinie Morrison was a violent and refractory prisoner, constantly protesting his innocence. Convinced that prisoners who were quiet and well-behaved were simply forgotten, he wrote, 'I am going to make myself the thorn in their eye continually until justice is done me.' He frequently refused to eat and sometimes had to be placed under restraint. At Dartmoor Prison in January 1921, he was force-fed because of his refusal to take food. A few days later, he died. The cause of death was 'aortic disease aggravated by voluntary abstention from food.'

No connection has ever been proven between the Berons and the events in Houndsditch, neither have the cuts on Leon's face been conclusively explained. If Beron was simply murdered for his gold, the cuts could have been made by his killer to put investigators off the scent, either by suggesting another motive, or in an attempt to disguise the identity of the victim. Only someone Beron knew would have done this. The question that should be asked is, who did Beron trust enough to lure him onto lonely Clapham Common at 3 a.m. – a member of a criminal gang – some stranger – or his new friend, the respectable looking Steinie Morrison?

On 3 April 1925, Home Office official Sir Ernley Blackwell wrote a letter to Winston Churchill regarding allegations that the Beron murder had been political:

It was a sordid murder for robbery by two men, Stinie [sic] Morrison being one, and a man named Hugo Pool being the other. All mystery in the case was completely cleared up two years later in August 1913, when I got from Ethel Pool, the wife of Hugo, a full statement as to the part her husband had played, with Stinie [sic] Morrison, in the murder of Beron.

Blackwell, who believed that Pool was the man who accompanied Morrison at Kennington Church as described by cab driver Alfred Catlin, had no doubt that had that information been available at the trial, both men would have hanged.

23

LEWISHAM

The Print of a Thumb

The murder of Thomas and Ann Farrow in 1905 was one of shocking brutality, but when the Stratton brothers were put on trial, there was more at stake than just the lives of the defendants. Everyone involved in the case knew almost from the start that it could herald a new era in forensic science.

Seventy-one-year-old Thomas Farrow and his wife Anna, 65, had managed George Chapman's oil and colour shop at 34 Deptford High Street since 1902. The Farrows lived above the premises and kept business hours of 8 a.m. to 9.30 p.m., but Farrow would often open up the shop earlier to sell paint to decorators on their way to work. The average net weekly takings were about £12 to £13.

There was one assistant, William Jones, and on Monday, 27 March 1905, Jones arrived at the shop as usual, but was unable to gain entry. He went to another of Chapman's shops and returned with one of the assistants. They managed to get in though the back, and found Thomas Farrow lying dead in the parlour, his head covered in blood. Upstairs, Mrs Farrow was in bed, badly injured and unconscious. The cash box lay on the bedroom floor, its tray pulled out. It was empty. Jones immediately went to get the police. Sergeant Atkinson arrived, and in the downstairs parlour found two masks with eye holes cut in them, made from stockings.

Police surgeon Dudley Burnie examined Thomas Farrow and found six severe wounds to the head, probably inflicted with an iron bar or jemmy. The old man had been attacked some two or three hours previously and had died only about an hour before he was found. Mrs Farrow had suffered two similar head wounds, and was taken to hospital.

The next policeman on the scene was Sergeant Crutchett, who recognised at once that the most important piece of evidence was the cash tin, which had been handled by at least one of the murderers, and might yield fingerprints. In September 1902, in a ground-breaking trial, Harry Jackson had been found guilty of burglary at the Old Bailey on evidence which included the relatively new science of dactylography – the study of fingerprints. It was the first such conviction in the United Kingdom, although the case did not rest entirely on fingerprint evidence. It was an encouraging victory for the fingerprint department of Scotland Yard, founded in 1901, but as the police, notably Assistant Commissioner Melville Macnaghten, were well aware, the real test of the acceptability of the system in the eyes of the public would be a high profile murder case.

Crutchett took charge of the cash tin, making sure to handle it through some sheets of paper, and at 11.30 Chief Inspector Frederick Fox of Scotland Yard and Melville Macnaghten arrived. The shop had not been broken into, and since both the Farrows were in nightclothes, it was believed that the old man had got out of bed having been woken by what he thought were early customers. He had been knocked unconscious, and his attackers had then gone upstairs, bludgeoned Mrs Farrow as she lay in bed, and rifled the cash box. Farrow had later regained consciousness, but he had then collapsed and died of his injuries.

Careful examination of the cash box revealed a mark on the underside of the tray, which looked like a partial thumbprint. The box was carefully wrapped and taken to be examined by Detective Inspector Charles Collins, who had been employed in the fingerprint department of Scotland Yard since 1901. The print did not match either of the Farrows, or the policemen who had been present. Unfortunately there was no match with any of the prints he already had on file. There was an anxious wait for Mrs Farrow to regain consciousness, in the hope that she could provide a description of the attackers but she died on 31 March.

A number of witnesses had come forward reporting sightings of possible suspects early on the morning of 27 March. Professional boxer Henry John Littlefield had seen two men running in the street at about 2.45 a.m. and thought it strange. A few minutes later he encountered the running men again and recognised one of them as Alfred Stratton, whom he had known for the last five or six years, and his brother Albert, whom he had known only a few months. They were behaving in a suspicious manner; Alfred looking to and fro, his brother fumbling with something under his coat. When Littlefield read about the murder in the newspapers on the following day, he went to the police.

Ellen Stanton, who was on her way to work at 7.15 a.m., had seen two men running from the High Street and recognised one of them as Alfred Stratton. He was dressed in a dark brown suit. Shortly afterwards, Alfred Purfield, a painter, passed by Chapman's shop and saw Mr Farrow standing in the doorway with blood on his hands, face and clothing. The old man gave him a vacant look and closed the door. Not seeing a policeman nearby, Purfield hurried on to catch his train to work.

Chapman's oil and colour shop, 34 Deptford High Street.

Alfred and Albert Stratton, 22 and 20 years old respectively, were known to the police as shady characters who somehow subsisted without having to work, although both had thus far avoided being arrested. Tough, brutal young men, they had cohabited with a series of women, sponging off them and beating them. Until the previous February, Albert had been lodging with Kate Wade, a married woman. The landlady, Sarah Tedman, had seen the brothers with a chisel and jemmy. After Albert left the lodgings, she found some stocking tops with holes cut in them and string and elastic attached to form masks.

Twenty-two-year-old Hannah Cromarty had been living with Alfred for a year. She described herself as an 'unfortunate' – a euphemism for a prostitute – and was pregnant by Alfred. On the day before the murder they had quarreled and he had given her a black eye. At about midnight on the night of the murder she heard tapping on the window, and Alfred got out of bed and spoke to the

MRS FARROW
THE MURDERED WOMAN.

MR FARROW
THE MURDERED MAN

Mr and Mrs Farrow, the murdered couple.

person outside, saying, 'Shall we go out to-night, or leave it for another night?' Hannah went back to sleep and was unable to confirm if Alfred had gone out or not. On the following day she noticed that his brown coat was missing. He had cleaned his trousers with paraffin and was putting blacking on his brown boots. When she later mentioned to him that people were saying that he was suspected of murdering the Farrows, he told her to say he was with her all that night. Hannah knew that Alfred had buried some money near the waterworks and on her information the police were able to recover the sum of £4.

The Strattons must have been confident that there was insufficient evidence to incriminate them, for they made no attempt to leave the area. On 2 April, Detective Sergeant Frank Beavis saw Alfred Stratton in the tap room of the King of Prussia public house, and took him to Blackheath police station. Alfred, claiming that he was in bed with Hannah Cromarty on the night of the murder, said that his brother had gone to sea.

On the following day Detective Inspector Arthur Hailstone saw Albert in Deptford High Street, took him by the arm, and said, 'Come along'. On the way to the police station he told his prisoner that he should consider himself in custody together with Alfred for the murder of Mr and Mrs Farrow and the theft of £13.' 'Is that all?' said Albert.

There was little convincing evidence against the brothers apart from the eyewitnesses and not all were in agreement. A milkman and his boy who said they had seen two men running from the shop on the morning of the murders failed to identify the Strattons.

At the magistrates' court hearing on 3 April it was ruled that the Strattons could be held one more week for fingerprint evidence to be taken. When Collins took the prints the prisoners seemed amused by the proceedings and commented that it tickled. About two hours later, Collins made a dramatic announcement to Macnaghten. The mark on the cash box tray matched the thumbprint of Alfred Stratton. Both brothers were charged with murder.

With two men's lives hanging on a single print, the police knew that the choice of prosecutor was crucial, and at once contacted Richard Muir, a meticulous and hard working barrister, who had been the prosecuting counsel in the Jackson burglary case. On that occasion he had spent four days being briefed by Collins in the technique and theory of fingerprinting. Muir again went to Scotland Yard to discuss the fingerprints with Macnaghten and Collins before he agreed to take the case. Appearing at the committal proceedings, he set out his stall early, placing the cash tin on his table where it was guarded by two policemen. Everyone who came near it was warned, 'careful, don't touch. There are fingerprints on it.' No one was left in any doubt as to the importance of this piece of evidence.

The trial opened at the Central Criminal Court, the Old Bailey on 5 May, and while the fingerprint evidence was central to the prosecution's case, Henry Littlefield and Ellen Stanton were important eyewitnesses. Kate Wade testified that Albert had been lodging with her at the time of the murders but had not stayed with her that night. She also said that he had asked her for some old pieces of stocking, which she had been unable to give him. Police surgeon Dudley Burnie confirmed that the injuries suffered by the Farrows were consistent with their having been attacked with a weapon like the jemmy known to have been in the brothers' possession.

Hannah Cromarty stated that on the day before the murder there was no money, food or fuel in the house. On the day after, Alfred had bought coal, wood, tea and sugar, as well as a daily paper.

Muir was fully prepared to explain the science of fingerprinting to both judge and jury, but he saw that the defence had called two expert witnesses to rebut his evidence. John George Garson was a doctor of medicine and a supporter of the Bertillon system, which classified prisoners by means of physical measurements, such as height and head size. Garson had experience of the fingerprint system and testified that he did not agree with Collins' conclusions. Under cross-examination, he was obliged to admit that the Bertillon system had been abandoned by Scotland Yard in 1901 and that his services had then

R.D. Muir.

been dispensed with. Worse was to come when Muir brought out a letter which Garson had written to him on 26 April, offering his services as a witness for the defence. Garson had written to the Director of Public Prosecutions on the same day, expressing his willingness to give evidence for the prosecution. Asked to reconcile the two letters, Garson said, 'I am an independent witness.'

'An absolutely untrustworthy one, I should think, after writing two such letters,' observed the presiding judge, Mr Justice Channell.

The defence had also secured the advice of Dr Henry Faulds, the man who had suggested the use of fingerprints to identify criminals as long ago as 1880. In the intervening years his work had been overlooked, and credit had gone to others, leaving him an embittered man. Based on Faulds' suggestion, the defence challenged Collins's evidence, pointing out the difference between the print on the cash box and the one taken on paper by the police. Collins, at the request of a juryman, took an impression of that gentleman's thumb, and was able to demonstrate that the minor discrepancies resulting from the means of taking the print did not invalidate the identification.

Faulds squabbled with defending counsel in court then sat in silence and fumed. He was not asked to give evidence. Alfred Stratton was then called to the witness box and claimed that he had slipped out on the night of the murder after being woken by his brother, who wanted to borrow money. He admitted having been out after 2.30 a.m., but claimed that both had gone back to his lodgings at 3.30 without waking Hannah, and Albert had slept on the floor. He denied the murder, and said that the £4 had come from a boxing contest he had won a few months previously.

The prosecution then called William Gittings, who was on duty as assistant gaoler at the Tower Bridge police court when the brothers were there on remand on 18 April. Albert had beckoned him to the cell door and asked, 'How do you think I shall get on?' to which Gittings replied, 'I do not know.' 'Is he listening?' asked Albert, referring to his brother in the adjoining cell. Gittings checked and told Albert that Alfred was sitting down reading a newspaper. 'I reckon he will get strung up, and I shall get about ten years,' said Albert, '. . . he has led me into this.'

In summing-up, Mr Justice Channell observed that the statement made at the police court was the most important piece of evidence against Albert,

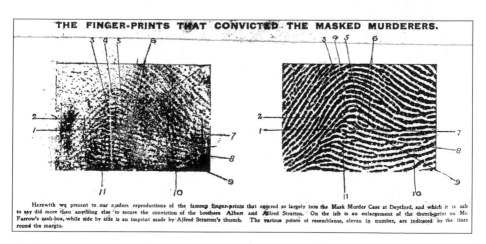

THE FINGER-PRINTS THAT CONVICTED THE MASKED MURDERERS.

Herewith we present to our readers reproductions of the famous finger-prints that entered so largely into the Mask Murder Case at Deptford, and which it is safe to say did more than anything else 'to secure the conviction of the brothers Albert and Alfred Stratton. On the left is an enlargement of the thumb-print on Mr. Farrow's cash-box, while side by side is an imprint made by Alfred Stratton's thumb. The various points of resemblance, eleven in number, are indicated by the lines round the margin.

The fingerprints that convicted the Stratton brothers.

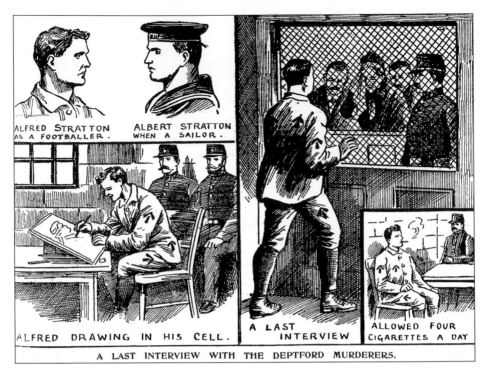

ALFRED STRATTON AS A FOOTBALLER.   ALBERT STRATTON WHEN A SAILOR.

ALFRED DRAWING IN HIS CELL.   A LAST INTERVIEW   ALLOWED FOUR CIGARETTES A DAY

A LAST INTERVIEW WITH THE DEPTFORD MURDERERS.

Alfred and Albert Stratton.

although he directed that it should not be regarded as evidence against his brother. As to the fingerprint, 'to a certain extent it was corroborative evidence in regard to Alfred, though he did not think the jury would like to act on it alone.' The jury deliberated for just under two hours before finding both brothers guilty of murder. On 23 May, Albert and Alfred Stratton were hanged at Wandsworth Prison.

The public acceptance of, and interest in, the new fingerprint system was demonstrated in July 1905, when the *Penny Illustrated Paper* ran a competition in which its readers were invited to test their skill in recognising the similarity between fingerprints portrayed in its pages.

MERTON

Monkshood

On 16 October 1878, a 26-year-old American doctor, George Henry Lamson, married Swansea-born Kate George John, who was 25. Lamson had left New York with his parents in 1858 and lived in Paris until 1870. He studied medicine first in Paris and then in America, graduating at the University of Pennsylvania. Much of his career had been spent at military hospitals on the continent of Europe, including a spell at Bucharest from August 1877 to March 1878.

Kate's mother, the widow of a linen merchant, had died in 1869, and Kate, her sister and two brothers, had been placed in the care of a guardian. On Kate's marriage she became entitled to claim her portion of her parents' legacy, which automatically became the property of her husband. Her sister had married and inherited her share in the previous year. Kate had two brothers, Hubert, born in 1861, and Percy in 1862. On 24 June 1879, 18-year-old Hubert died suddenly at the Lamsons's home, and his share of his parents' bequest passed to his two married sisters and brother. Percy was still too young to take possession of his legacy, which now amounted to £3,000. He was due to inherit either on marriage or achieving his majority, but if, like Hubert, he died unmarried before reaching the age of 21, his share would be distributed equally between his sisters.

In 1881 Percy was boarding at Blenheim House School, St George's Road, Wimbledon, which had been his home for the last three years. He suffered from a curvature of the spine, and had lost the use of his legs, but was otherwise in good health and was not under any form of medical treatment. Percy was well cared for, and both masters and pupils made sure he was involved in the life of the school, and had plenty to occupy his mind. Two wheelchairs were kept for him, one on the second floor where he slept, and one in the basement where he spent his day. He was carried downstairs in the morning and up again at night.

George Henry Lamson.

It was only natural that Percy became depressed from time to time, being unable to take part in sports which he loved to watch, but he generally bore his difficulties with cheerful acceptance.

The Lamsons had been living in Ventnor, Isle of Wight, but in 1880 George purchased a medical practice in Bournemouth. A man of his profession should not have been in financial difficulties, but early in 1881 his affairs were in such a state that he was obtaining small sums of money by pawning his watch and medical instruments, borrowing from acquaintances, and trying to get cash advances on cheques from an account already overdrawn, and in one instance on a bank with which he had no account. In March 1881, the Bournemouth Medical Society removed him from its rolls after finding that he was not entitled to a number of qualifications he had been claiming, and in April he sold his practice and left Bournemouth.

Even a half share in Percy's legacy must have been looking very attractive, but the boy showed every sign of living long enough to inherit. Lamson, under the guise of concern for his brother-in-law's health, began dosing him with a variety of medications, which invariably made him feel worse. Lamson had once sent a box of pills to William Bedbrook, the headmaster of Blenheim House School, saying that they would benefit Percy's condition. Bedbrook had given Percy one of the pills, but the next morning the boy complained of feeling unwell and had said he would take no more of them. Lamson had given Percy a pill during a family visit in August 1881, and the boy had felt very ill afterwards. Lamson also supplied powders, said to be quinine, together with medicinal wafers made of flour paste intended to enclose the powders so that they could be swallowed without tasting them, but there is no evidence that Percy took any of these. No one appears to have suspected that Lamson was deliberately trying to harm Percy, but the boy may have learned to distrust medicines from that source.

On 1 December, George Lamson wrote to Percy saying that he would shortly be going abroad and would like to call to see him before he left. On Saturday 3 December, Percy had his breakfast and dinner as usual, and in the afternoon he joined in a game of charades with the other pupils. After tea, which was at six o'clock, he was looking through some examination papers. Lamson called at five to seven and was shown into the ground-floor dining room while Percy was carried up from the basement. It was some weeks since Lamson had last called and he was so much thinner and paler than on his last visit that Bedbrook did not at first recognise him and remarked on the change in his appearance. Bedbrook offered Lamson a glass of sherry, and Lamson accepted, saying that he always took sugar with it to counteract the effect of the alcohol. Bedbrook thought this odd, and commented that he understood it would have the opposite effect, but he sent for the sugar, and a basin of powdered white sugar was brought and placed on the table. Lamson put a little sugar into his glass and stirred it with his penknife.

Lamson was carrying a black bag which he opened and brought out a Dundee cake and some sweets, which he said he had brought from New York. He then cut up the cake with his penknife, handed pieces to Percy and to Bedbrook and took one himself. Both Percy and Bedbrook helped themselves to some sweets. Lamson then produced two boxes containing gelatine capsules, which he said he had brought back from a recent trip to America, thinking Bedbrook would find them useful in giving medicines to the boys. When he placed the boxes on the table one was much nearer to Bedbrook. 'See how easily they can be swallowed,' said Lamson. The master took a capsule from the nearer box, and examined it, checking that it was empty before swallowing it. Bedbrook later recollected that the capsules were of different sizes. He then saw that Lamson was spooning sugar from the basin into another capsule, although he had not noticed which box this capsule came from. Lamson handed the filled capsule to

Percy, saying, 'here, Percy, you are a swell pill taker, take this.' Percy obediently took the capsule and swallowed it. A few minutes later Lamson announced that it was time for him to leave to catch his train. Bedbrook saw him to the door and as he departed, Lamson said that he did not think Percy would live much longer, a comment the master thought quite unjustifiable from the boy's appearance and state of health.

Ten minutes later Percy began to complain of heartburn, saying that he felt just the same as he had when Lamson had given him a quinine pill on a previous occasion. Percy grew rapidly worse and was carried up to bed, where he suffered painful convulsions and vomited violently. The matron was called, and a visiting doctor, Otho Windsor Berry, who had just arrived, was brought to see the boy. Another doctor, Edward Stephen Little, was summoned by Bedbrook. Percy was suffering from intense irritation of the stomach, and both doctors, suspecting he may have been poisoned, made sure to preserve some of his vomit for testing. There was little they could do for him beyond injecting morphine to relieve the pain. Eventually the tormented boy fell into a coma and at 11.20 p.m., just four hours after Lamson's visit, Percy died. The police were notified and enquiries were made as to the whereabouts of Lamson.

The death of Hubert John was now beginning to look highly suspicious, and there was speculation that his body might be exhumed, although in the event this was not done.

The post-mortem examination was carried out on 6 December by Dr Thomas Bond, lecturer in forensic medicine at Westminster Hospital, assisted by Berry and Little. He concluded that Percy had died from a vegetable alkaloid poison. The medical samples were examined by Home Office analyst Dr Thomas Stevenson. From the contents of the stomach he obtained an extract which, when he placed it on his tongue, produced a burning, tingling sensation, which he said was 'as if a hot iron had been passed over it or some strong caustic applied'. This reaction was characteristic of a specific alkaloid – aconitine, obtained from monkshood. His examination of the organs and vomit produced a similar result. He found no trace of poison in the cake or sweets or in the gelatine capsules. Some pills and powders had been found amongst Percy's effects, which were supposed to contain quinine, which Lamson had been recommending Percy should take. Stevenson found that the pills and three of the powders produced the effects of aconitine.

On 8 December, Lamson returned from Paris and went to Scotland Yard. He said he was unwell and upset, but he had come home after reading about the death of Percy in the newspapers, and had called to give his address, after which he planned to go to Chichester. He did not seem surprised when he was arrested, charged with the murder of Percy John and taken to Wandsworth police court. 'Do you think they would accept bail?' he asked, hopefully.

THE WIMBLEDON MYSTERY: LAST SKETCHES OF DR. LAMSON AND WITNESSES AT BOW-STREET.

George Henry Lamson at Bow Street.

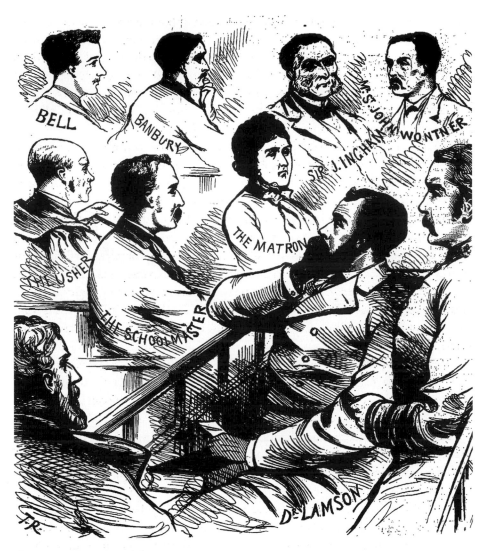

George Henry Lamson and the witnesses at Bow Street.

The case attracted enormous public interest: the story of a helpless youth who had borne his disability with such courage being cruelly murdered by his own relative for money creating a particular sense of outrage.

The trial opened at the Central Criminal Court, the Old Bailey before Mr Justice Hawkins on 8 March 1882, where the evidence demonstrated a chain of circumstances that pointed only to murder by the prisoner. An assistant at Plough Court pharmacy, Lombard Street, stated that on or about 24 November, Lamson had bought two grains of aconitine, a powerful alkaloid poison. A few days previously Lamson had tried to buy aconitine at another chemist, who had declined to sell it to him. He had succeeded in buying aconitine on the Isle of Wight on 28 August, the day before Percy had been taken ill after Lamson gave him a pill. The defence counsel, Mr Montagu Williams, who called no witnesses, did his best, trying to cast doubts on the medical evidence and asking for the jury's sympathy for Lamson's devoted wife and their daughter, Agnes, but the evidence was too strong. The jury took only half an hour to deliver a verdict of guilty, and Lamson was sentenced to death.

The execution was fixed for 4 April, but Lamson remained hopeful of a reprieve, and following the intervention of the US President, the Home Secretary delayed execution until the 18th and again to the 28th to allow time for affidavits and letters to be transmitted from the United States regarding the prisoner's state of mind. Family and friends in England also supplied further information which they felt should have been produced at the trial. Kate Lamson stated that she had been concerned about her husband's soundness of mind for over a year. His erratic disposition had made him incapable of attending to his business. Several letters described Lamson's paranoid delusions, hallucinations and lack of ordinary self-control. The superintendent of Bloomingdale Asylum for the Insane, New York, revealed that Lamson's aunt, grandmother and great-uncle had all died in the asylum.

While it had been mentioned at the trial that Lamson had purchased morphine and atropine for his own use, the extent of his addiction to those drugs was now revealed. By 1881 Lamson was suffering pain, dizziness and insomnia, his arms exhibiting scars and abscesses from his frequent injections. He had developed a peculiar lurching walk, and his behaviour and speech were so erratic as to convince those who knew him that he was a possible danger to himself and others. None of this evidence suggested homicidal mania, and, as *The Times* pointed out:

> . . . the immediate circumstances of the murder pointed to the exercise of a crafty deliberation . . . if Lamson could appreciate the benefit he would derive from Percy John's death – and why else should he have selected him as his victim? – he could realise the wickedness of his act.

There was to be no reprieve for Lamson, who did, before he died, admit to the murder of Percy John, although he denied murdering Hubert. Lamson was executed by William Marwood at Wandsworth Gaol on 28 April 1882.

Blenheim House School, possibly because of the unwarranted notoriety, was renamed St George's School and was amalgamated with Kings College School in 1897. Kate Lamson, who changed her surname and that of her daughter to George, later became the manageress of a convalescent home.

Only one question needs to be addressed. How did Lamson administer the poison under the nose of William Bedbrook? The simple and obvious answer is that it was in the capsule, but this has long been disputed. Sir Henry Hawkins, writing about the case in 1904, believed that the poison was in the cake, the capsules being just a clever smokescreen. He suggested that the poison was injected into one of the raisins in the cake, so that the skin would delay its effect, although he admitted that there was no evidence to support this theory. H.L. Adam, editor of the *Notable British Trials* volume, first published in 1912, stated, quoting the authority of an unnamed person present at the trial, that Lamson was able to apportion the poisoned slice to Percy because he brought the Dundee cake to the school already cut in slices.

The essential evidence on this point is that of Bedbrook, recorded by the court stenographer and newspaper reporters at the trial, his statements at the inquest and police court and his original deposition. Bedbrook said he noticed nothing unusual about the cake except that it was wrapped in newspaper, and that he saw Lamson slicing it into portions with his penknife. Bedbrook never said that the cake arrived pre-cut, and if he had, the Solicitor General Sir Farrer Herschell, prosecuting, would surely have mentioned it – but he did not. Adam also stated that the stomach contents included a raisin skin found to be impregnated with aconitine. This is untrue, as may be seen from Dr Stevenson's evidence. Stevenson said that he had received a bottle containing some of the stomach contents, which were mainly fluid and included a raisin. He had found aconitine not in the raisin but in the fluid. Lamson was well aware that aconitine has a burning taste. He had made use of it at the military hospital in Bucharest, and after his trial two doctors signed affidavits about his reckless use of the drug when practising there. The ideal methods of supplying it as a poison was as a coated pill, in a powder meant to swallowed enclosed in a wafer, or in a capsule. The raisin idea would only work if Percy gulped it down whole and unchewed, hardly something on which a would-be poisoner could rely. Biting down on the raisin would cause immediate pain.

Lamson's method shows careful planning and forethought. He first ensured that Bedbrook took a capsule from a box of empty ones. He had primed one of the capsules in the other box with poison and had only to select the right one to fill with sugar while Bedbrook's attention was directed towards the capsule he was examining. If Bedbrook's observation – that the capsules he saw were of different sizes – was correct, then selecting the primed capsule should not have been difficult. The cake did have a part to play. It was intended as an early birthday gift for Percy, who would have been nineteen on 18 December, and formed part of Lamson's excuse for his visit. Lamson might also have thought that the presence of a heavy fruit cake in Percy's stomach would delay the operation of the poison enough for him to make a rapid exit.

25

NEWHAM

Here Comes a Chopper

On the afternoon of Tuesday, 8 November 1864, shipwright's apprentice Richard Harvey was out wildfowling with some companions near Silvertown, where the North Woolwich road runs parallel to the River Thames past the Victoria Graving Dock. Between the road and the Thames was a quarter of a mile of marshland on which the reeds stood over 7ft high, forming an almost impenetrable mass, apart from some narrow pathways accessible by crossing a plank over a deep, muddy ditch. Harvey plunged into the reed-bed to drive up birds for the guns, but soon came running out saying he had found a dead body. The corpse lay on its back, and was clad only in black trousers and Wellington boots, with a small fragment of white shirt on one arm. The head was missing. One of the men went to find a policeman, and brought Constable Bridgeland to the spot. He noticed a dent in the earth where the head had been, and some small pieces of bone and part of the brain. In the trouser pockets he found some paper with writing in German and a farthing. He had the body removed to the Graving Dock Tavern, where it was examined by Plaistow surgeon Edward John Morris.

Morris thought that the deceased, a well nourished man, had been dead for several days. The muscles of the neck, and one shoulder and both hands had been much gnawed by rats. The head had been removed using both a knife and an axe.

The absence of the head and most of the clothing made identification of the remains difficult, and many local residents – the newspapers estimated 4,000, some of whom may just have been there for the diversion – came to view the body. The situation appeared hopeless until Heinrich Zuelch, a German shoemaker of 2 Hoy Street, recognised the boots which were of German manufacture and which he had not long ago repaired. The dead man, known locally as 'German John', had recently lodged at No. 4, the home of Ferdinand Edward Karl Köhl and his English wife Hannah.

Köhl, also a German, was 26 or 27 years old, a 'short thick-set man with dark brown hair and a somewhat florid complexion'. He had arrived in England early in 1864 and, following a brief employment with a butcher, he worked for a sugar-baker (a sugar refiner). In September he had been living in Plaistow, lodging at 3 Nelson Place, the home of James and Elizabeth Warren. He then went to Germany for about two weeks, returning in the company of a good-looking, gentlemanly and well-dressed German aged about 21, who was looking for lodgings and spoke very poor English. Köhl introduced 'John', as he was known, to the Warrens, telling them they had been brought up together almost like brothers. This was a lie, as the two men had first met on board the steamer from Germany.

John, who was on his way to New York, was a trusting young man. He had four boxes of clothing with him, and on his arrival gave six sovereigns as well as a watch and chain and a ring to Mrs Warren for safekeeping.

On 2 October Köhl married 18-year-old Hannah Williams. Despite his new responsibilities, he made no effort to look for employment. He was always short of funds and borrowed money from friends and his wife's family, which he was unable to repay.

On 10 or 11 October, Köhl began renting a house in Hoy Street, which he sublet to lodgers. He then arranged for John to come and lodge with him. John settled his bill with Mrs Warren, who returned his property, and it is probable that John then entrusted his valuables to his new landlord.

Police Superintendant Daniel Howie went to question Köhl, who confirmed that his lodger had gone missing. He said that he and John had gone to the docks together on 3 November to look for a ship but not finding the required passage, they went to the Commercial Road, some five miles away, where Köhl was looking for work. He said he had gone into a sugar-bakery, leaving John outside, but on emerging from the bakery found that John had gone, and he had not seen him since. He had been to see the body found in the reeds but was not sure if it was John. Köhl told the Superintendent that when John had left Mrs Warren's he had no money and had pawned his clothes. Howie was suspicious and sent both Köhl and his wife in a cab to Plaistow police station for questioning. Köhl was cautioned and said, 'I know well where I was on that – ' then abruptly stopped. When Köhl's house was searched a number of pawnbrokers' tickets were found, showing that he had pawned some of his German lodger's property during October. The police also learned that when Zuelch had asked Köhl if he could borrow a pair of shoes, he had been handed a pair which later turned out to belong to the dead man.

It had originally been thought that the murder had taken place where the body lay, but when searches were made of the little pathways through the reed beds, a pool of blood 4ft long by 1ft wide was discovered at the bottom of the muddy ditch. The footprints of the dead man as he stood in the ditch were clearly visible, as were the marks of the murderer's feet as he lifted out the lifeless body of his victim. Blood smears showed where the body had been dragged to its eventual position, and about two thirds along the way was a circular patch of blood, as if the severed head had been put down for a moment on its oozing surface. On 9 November, the police found the head buried twelve inches deep in a mangold wurzel field about thirty yards from the body. The cause of death was two violent blows, which had fractured the skull.

Dr Morris examined the head and thought that two weapons had been used, one resembling a hammer and one a chopper.

Köhl and his wife appeared at the Stratford police court on 9 November where a youth, Henry Lee, told the court that at 10 a.m. on Thursday 3 November he had seen Köhl and the deceased walking together towards the reed bed where the body was eventually found. No one had seen the young German alive after that time. Köhl had been at Zuelch's house at midday and back at his own home an hour later, which seemed to leave him insufficient time to walk to Commercial Road to visit the sugar-baker's and return. There was no evidence to incriminate Hannah, who was discharged. She was carried away in a swoon by her brother, Joseph. Köhl was handcuffed and taken to Ilford Gaol in a cab, a task of some difficulty because of the large and excited crowds that had gathered around the court. On the same day, Detective Sergeant Clarke searched Köhl's house, and removed a chopper. During Köhl's time in Ilford Gaol he was attended by Dr Louis Cappel, minister of the German Lutheran church in Alie Street, Goodman's Fields. When in court, a German constable was sent to act as an interpreter.

On 10 November, engineer John Atkinson was visiting the reed-bed and halfway between the places where the body and head had been found, he saw a white-handled clasp knife, which he picked up and took home. He showed it to his wife and she pointed out it had some hairs stuck to the back. Realising it might be connected with the murder, he handed it over to a policeman.

Later that evening the inquest opened at the Bell and Anchor Tavern, Plaistow. The murdered man had now been identified as Theodore Christian Fuhrhop, a clerk from the firm of Messrs Neumann and Co. of Hamburg. He was buried on 16 November at West Ham cemetery. On the journey from the Bell and Anchor, the hearse was stopped after a message was received from the analyst Dr Letheby, and the coffin was opened, and some hair removed for comparison with that on the knife.

On 17 November, Mary Wade, who lodged in the front parlour of Köhl's house, told the adjourned inquest that she had seen her landlord and Fuhrhop go out together at half past nine on the 3 November, and Köhl came back

Pastor Louis Cappel. (By kind permission of the Trustees of the German Lutheran Chapel, Alie Street)

alone at 1 a.m. Seeing that there was mud on the legs of his trousers, the back of his coat and elbows, she exclaimed, 'Good gracious, Charley, where have you been in the mud?' Mrs Wade particularly noticed that it was a light-coloured clayey mud, like that on the reed-bed, and unlike that on the streets of London, which were, in any case, dry at the time. Köhl said he had picked up the mud travelling in a butcher's cart, and went out to the back yard and brushed his clothes. He went out about half an hour later, saying he was going to look for

The Bell and Anchor, Plaistow. (By kind permission of Newham Heritage and Archives)

John, but returned just after 3 p.m., saying that if John was not home in two hours he would break his boxes open. Two hours passed and Köhl, asking a cousin of Hannah's who was visiting, to be a witness, broke open the boxes with a poker and expressed astonishment that John's clothes were missing. Returning downstairs he told Mary that John would not be coming back as his clothes had gone. He went out again and came back at 5 p.m., looking pale and agitated. Another lodger Eliza Whitmore, confirmed this, and identified the white-handled knife as one she had seen in Köhl's possession after John went missing.

Mary owned a chopper, a formidable looking implement, one side of which formed an axe and the other a hammer, mounted on a handle 2ft long, which Köhl had borrowed from her before 3 November. When he returned it on the following day, the part of the handle above the iron had been painted red. He said he had done so to keep the iron part on as it was loose.

Another witness, Thomas William Hudson, appeared to say he had seen Köhl and John together, going towards the reed-bed on 3 November.

Köhl's clothing as well as the knife and chopper had been handed to Dr Henry Letheby, professor of chemistry at the London Hospital. Removing the handle of the chopper, he examined the hole where it had been fitted and found what he believed to be dried blood mixed with clothing fibres, human skin and rust. He also found blood spots on Köhl's clothing. It was impossible to say if the blood spots were human, but he believed them to be so. When Dr

Morris saw the chopper he said that it could have produced the wounds on the head. He was also of the opinion that the head had been severed from the body some time after death, how long he could not be sure, but it had certainly been done when the body was already cold.

It was thought that Köhl had returned to the body early on Monday 7 November in order to remove and bury the head. On the previous day Köhl had asked Eliza Whitmore's husband, who usually went out at 5.30 a.m., to wake him before he went out. Whitmore did so and Köhl got up and went out. He was back home between 7 and 8 a.m. He may have gone back to the scene a second time, since Mary Jane Cooper, who knew Köhl, saw him on the Thames bank, near the reed-bed, at 3 o'clock in the afternoon of Monday 7 November.

Representatives of the police were sent to Germany to make enquiries about Köhl's history, which was reported to be 'generally bad'. It was found that he had been born in Prussia, although his family later removed to Hanover. In 1860 he had enlisted for ten years in the King's regiment of hussars, but after two-and-a-half years he was convicted and sentenced to three months in a military prison for stealing from his comrades, and dismissed. Early in 1864 he was charged with stealing some harness, but absconded to avoid punishment and came to England.

Some of the clothing and jewellery pawned by Köhl and his wife in October were identified as the property of the deceased. James Warren identified as Furhop's a key of distinctive design which was found in Köhl's pocket. Hannah's brother, Joseph, said that the prisoner had shown him pawn tickets for his lodger's watch and chain, which he said he had pawned for him. On 5 November Köhl had entered a fancy goods and grocery store in Nelson Terrace, and when he pulled out his money to pay, the proprietor, William Jackson, saw that he had several sovereigns.

On 23 November the inquest jury brought in a verdict of wilful murder against Köhl, who was committed to take his trial at the Old Bailey.

Köhl had been busy thinking up ways of saving himself. After the inquest he asked his brother-in-law, Joseph, to come and see him in gaol, and said, 'Bring my cousin Bill.' When Joseph asked him what for, Köhl said, 'Why he was with me all day on that Thursday.' 'No he was not,' said Joseph, to which Köhl replied, 'He must say so.' Bill declined to assist him.

The trial of Edward Köhl opened at the Central Criminal Court, the Old Bailey on 11 January 1865. The prisoner had taken advantage of the privilege granted by English law of being tried by a jury including six of his own countrymen. Witnesses were called who stated that Köhl had not been at the sugar-bakery on the morning of 3 November. It was also pointed out that the attempt to prevent identification of the body was only relevant if the murderer was someone who the dead man had known.

The jury took only half an hour of deliberation to bring in a verdict of guilty, and Köhl was sentenced to death. He awaited his fate at Springfield Gaol, where he was visited by Dr Cappel. At first his manner was subdued but as the day of his execution approached, his mood swung violently between anger and hysteria. He repeatedly asserted his innocence and demanded Cappel's assurance that he believed him innocent, something Cappel was unable to give. January 26, the date appointed for Köhl's execution, was bitterly cold with a thick sleet falling, nevertheless, large crowds assembled outside Springfield Gaol. As he waited, the prisoner fainted in his cell, and had to be restored with cold water. Köhl was asked to sign a final letter to his father, but instead seized a penholder and pushed it into his mouth, saying he would kill himself. When the penholder was wrested away from him, he tried to knock himself against the wall. After that he was kept handcuffed. Several times he asked to be told when his last moment had come, and Cappel believed he intended to confess in the final seconds before he died. As Köhl stood on the scaffold, Cappel said, 'This is the last moment,' but even as he spoke the drop fell, and the prisoner was silenced forever.

Köhl was the last man to be publicly executed at Springfield.

26

REDBRIDGE

'Do Something Desperate'

Shortly after midnight on Wednesday, 4 October 1922, John Webber, of De Vere Gardens, Ilford, heard a woman screaming, 'Oh don't, don't!' When he left his house to see what was happening, he found a small group of people standing around the figure of a man who had collapsed and lay propped against a wall in nearby Belgrave Road.

A few moments earlier, Miss Dora Finch Pittard had been walking towards her home in Endsleigh Gardens, together with Mr Percy Cleveley and his wife, when they were accosted by a well dressed young woman in a state of hysteria. 'My God, will you help me? My husband is dying on the pavement!' They asked her what had happened, but the woman, who was almost incoherent, could only say that he had fallen down. While Miss Pittard went to fetch a doctor to the stricken man, the Cleveleys asked if he had been attacked and she said someone had rushed past, after which her husband had blood coming out of his mouth. Dr Noel Maudsley, of Courtland Avenue, who was in bed when alerted to the emergency, quickly threw on some clothes and rushed to the scene. His examination, made by the light of a match, confirmed that the man had been dead for about ten minutes. 'Why did you not come sooner and save him!' exclaimed the hysterical widow. Seeing no injuries, Maudsley assumed, based on her statements, that the deceased had had a seizure of some kind. The police were called and the body was removed. Sergeant Mew escorted the grieving woman home, only yards away in Kensington Gardens. She gave her name as Edith Thompson, and her husband was Percy. She said she thought he had had 'one of his attacks'.

Richard Thompson, the dead man's brother, lived in nearby Seymour Gardens and later that morning he called on Edith and asked what had happened. She said that Percy had had an attack and simply fallen forward. When Percy's body was examined by the police surgeon, however, three stab wounds, all over two inches deep, were found in the neck and throat. One was on the right side of the back of the neck, penetrating to the spine, another on the right side of the neck below the angle of the jaw, the knife passing into the floor of the mouth. The third and undoubtedly the fatal wound was a little below and in front of the second, severing the carotid artery. There were also a few superficial cuts to the abdomen and right arm. It was apparent that Edith must know a great deal more than she was telling.

Edith was born Edith Jessie Graydon in 1894, the daughter of a Scottish-born despatch clerk, William Eustace Graydon, and his wife Ethel. In 1916 she had married shipbroker's clerk Percy Thompson, who was four years her senior. The couple had no children. For the last ten years Edith had worked for a wholesale milliner's business in Aldersgate Street, most recently in the capacity of bookkeeper and manageress. Her employer judged her to be a very capable businesswoman. There was however another side to Edith, beyond the reliable worker and middle-class wife. Edith had a passionate nature, which fed off romantic and sensational novels in which she imagined herself at the centre of great emotional dramas. It was a need which had had no outlet, but as soon as Edith found a channel for her imagination, she entered a world in which fantasy and reality became dangerously intertwined.

On the Wednesday morning, Detective Inspector Hall saw Edith at her house and told her that Percy had been stabbed to death. Edith, who was in a highly agitated state, told him that she and Percy had just passed the corner of Belgrave Road and Kensington Gardens when Percy had suddenly cried out and fallen against her. As she put out her arms to save him she saw blood coming from his mouth. She had tried to hold him up but he had staggered several yards and fallen against a wall, then slid to the ground. His clothing was wet with blood. Shortly before the incident they had been walking side-by-side and talking about going to a dance. Edith said she had not seen anyone about.

There was no trace of the murder weapon. The police searched all the gardens in the area, and also the drains, and on 9 October their efforts were rewarded when a bloodstained knife was found in a drain in Seymour Gardens. It was a double-edged blade, tapering to a point, and five and half inches long.

When the police questioned Mrs Fanny Maria Lester, a widow who lodged with the Thompsons, they learned of a suspect, and a motive. Mrs Lester had heard the Thompsons arguing, and seen bruises on Edith's arm. She told the police of a young man, Frederick Bywaters, who had been friendly with the Thompsons and stayed at the house the previous summer, but had left after an altercation with Percy.

Frederick Edward Francis Bywaters was born in 1902. He worked as a storekeeper on the SS *Morea,* a steamship which travelled to and from the Far East.

Percy and Edith Thompson.

He had known Edith for seven years, as he had been at school with her two brothers, and in 1921 he had been courting Edith's younger sister, Avis. In June he had accompanied Percy, Edith and Avis on a holiday to Shanklin, after which, on 18 June, he had gone to stay with the Thompsons. For the first week he was a guest but after that he had paid rent of 25s a week. Early in August, however, Frederick had witnessed a row between Edith and Percy, during which Percy had thrown his wife across the room. Frederick had felt compelled to intervene. As a result of this incident Frederick left the Thompsons' house the following morning, and returned to live with his mother.

Mrs Lester heard the Thompsons having 'high words' every evening for a week after Frederick's departure. 'They had high words often right up to the time of the tragedy,' she added. Between 5 August and 9 September, Frederick and Edith met in secret, and the relationship developed into a passionate affair. Edith was desperate for a separation so she could be with Frederick. Although she could have left Percy, the 20-year-old steward had no money or a home of his own to which Edith could go.

When Frederick was away with his ship Edith wrote letters to him; long, newsy, romantic, wordy, gushing letters of love and desperation. Some of the incidents she reported may not have been true, but were devised to add a dramatic garnish to the situation. On one occasion she wrote to Frederick, saying that Percy had told her father about the rows they had had about the illicit relationship, something William Graydon later said was 'imagination entirely'. He said he had had no idea that Edith and her husband were not on good terms.

Frederick, who was living with his widowed mother, Lillian, in Westow Street, Upper Norwood, was questioned at Ilford police station and could not provide a convincing alibi for the time of the murder. He said that he had last seen Edith on the Monday when they had lunched together, and claimed to know nothing of the murder.

Initially, neither Frederick nor Edith knew of each other's presence at the police station. After Edith had made her statement she was taken past the room in which she could see that Frederick was being questioned. This may well have been a deliberate ploy by the police to provoke a reaction, and if so, it was an immediate success. 'Oh God! Oh God!' Edith exclaimed. 'What can I do? Why did he do it? I did not want him to do it!' She then made another statement saying that she had been pushed away from Percy by a man who had scuffled with him. As the man ran away she recognised him as Frederick Bywaters.

Faced with Edith's statement, the young steward soon confessed that he had been the attacker, but from the very start he was adamant that Edith had known nothing about his plans. 'The reason I fought with Thompson was because he never acted like a man to his wife,' he told the police. He always seemed several degrees less than a snake. I love her and could not go on seeing her lead that life.'

Frederick Bywaters.

Frederick, claiming that he had only intended to injure and not kill Percy, said that near Endsleigh Gardens he had pushed Edith to one side and pushed Percy up the street, saying, 'you have got to separate from your wife.' When Percy refused, they had fought. Frederick was describing a face-to-face encounter, hoping to sustain a claim that he acted in self-defence, but Dr Percy James Prout, the divisional surgeon who examined the body, stated that he believed the first blow struck was the stab wound in Percy's back.

A crucial development in the case was the discovery of a cache of love letters written by Edith to Frederick, some of which he kept on board ship, with others at his home or in his pockets. Edith had also kept some of Frederick's letters in a box at her place of work. At the magistrates' hearing, Edith's counsel, Mr Stern, recognised the dangerous nature of these documents and made every effort not to have them admitted in evidence. It was obvious from the letters that Edith and Frederick had been having an affair, and that Edith desperately wanted to be separated from Percy. She was sure that her husband suspected that she and Frederick were lovers. She wrote of how helpless and frustrated she felt in a loveless marriage, and fantasised about Percy's death. 'Darling you must do something this time,' she wrote, about a year before the murder. 'I am not really impatient but opportunities come and go by.' She then revealed that Percy had told her that someone had given him a draught for insomnia which had made him feel ill. Edith had told a friend about the incident, 'only I told her as if it frightened and worried me, as I think perhaps it might be useful at some future time that I had told somebody. What do you think, darling?' Edith also enclosed newspaper cuttings about poisoning cases.

In February 1922 she wrote about 'this thing that I am going to do for us both,' asking Frederick if he would feel differently towards her because of it. In April she wrote claiming that she had put something in Percy's tea and he had complained of it tasting bitter. Mentioning a story Percy had told about how he had once been nearly suffocated by gas, she wrote, 'I wish we had not got electric light. It would be easy.' According to her letters, however, Edith had another plan – she was going to put ground glass in Percy's food. On 1 April 1922 she wrote, 'I am going to try the glass again occasionally when it is safe, I have got an electric light globe this time.' In a letter postmarked 24 April she reported further, 'I used the "light bulb" three times but the third time he found a piece so I have given it up until you come home.' According to a letter postmarked 3 May, 'I was buoyed up with the hope of the light bulb and I used a lot, big pieces too, not powdered, but it had no effect, I quite expected to be able to send that cable, but no, nothing has happened from it.' It is hard to believe that Edith could have put large pieces of glass in Percy's food without him noticing, and the entire incident could well have been a colourful story, devised to demonstrate both her devotion and desperation.

Edith also told Frederick she had been reading books about poisons, looking into the properties of belladonna, opium and digitalis. On 1 June she wrote that Percy had tried to persuade her he was having a heart attack and when she made it clear that she didn't believe him: '... he got up and stormed. I said exactly what you told me to and he replied that he knew that was what I wanted and he was not going to give it to me.' This probably refers to a request for a separation. Her final letter to Frederick is undated, but was probably written between 19 and 21 September and read, 'He has the right by law to all that you have the right to, by nature and love. Yes, darlint, [Edith's abbreviation of darlingest] be jealous so much that you will do something desperate.'

On 2 November at the City of London cemetery, Manor Park, the body of Percy Thompson was exhumed and organs were removed and sent to Dr Bernard Spilsbury for analysis. The post-mortem revealed 'no indications of poisoning or of any previous attempts at it'. The only drug present was morphine in small medicinal quantities, and there was no sign that Percy had ever eaten ground glass.

The trial opened at the Central Criminal Court, the Old Bailey on 6 December 1922 before Mr Justice Shearman. Both prisoners pleaded not guilty. A substantial portion of the trial was taken up by readings from Edith's letters.

Shearman's summing-up strongly addressed the doubts of the jurors. He said that historically there had been many cases where a person was charged with murder, even though they had not themselves dealt the blow. Referring to Edith's claim that Percy had the right by law to all that Frederick had by nature and love, he told the jury, 'I think you will feel disgust at that observation.' Reminding the jurors that Frederick and Edith had met just hours before the murder, and that she had told him where she and Percy would be later that night, he added that they would not convict her unless they were satisfied that they had jointly agreed to murder Percy, and she knew Bywaters was going to do it, and she directed him to do it. He emphasised the fact that after the murder Edith had lied to protect her lover.

The jury, white-faced with strain, found both prisoners guilty, and made no recommendations to mercy.

There was a public campaign for a reprieve for Edith. The Home Secretary, William Bridgeman, had not believed she would be found guilty, but on reviewing the case could find no mitigating circumstances. Frederick and Edith wrote each other letters in prison. Frederick accepted his fate but was hopeful that Edith would be spared and tried to encourage her to keep her spirits up. The letters were not delivered, but were retained by the prison authorities. Neither prisoner was told of this. Flowers were sent to Edith anonymously. They were not passed to her and it was ordered that they should be destroyed.

Frederick and Edith were hanged on the same day, 9 January 1923, he at Pentonville Prison and she at Holloway. Frederick met his end stoically. Many allegations have been made about Edith being in a state of collapse or hysterical before she was hanged. The governor of Holloway later made a statement saying that he had decided to give her sedatives before the execution. Although he felt she could have walked to the scaffold without assistance, he had thought it more humane to spare her that, and had had her carried there. Apart from that, he said, nothing unusual had occurred.

The fact that Dr Maudsley had failed to notice that Percy had been stabbed may have weighed upon his mind. In 1928 he attracted adverse comment from a magistrate after signing sick notes for a patient he had not seen for some time. A few days later he committed suicide.

In 1956, when the question of abolition of capital punishment was being debated in parliament, Edith's case was frequently mentioned. In 1971, Holloway Prison was rebuilt and the bodies of women executed there were removed to Brookwood cemetery. Edith's remains and those of three other women are interred at plot number 117, and a memorial was placed there and a service of dedication held on 13 November 1993.

History and the passage of time have judged the execution of Edith Thompson to be unjustified. She was undoubtedly an accessory, in that she lied after the murder to protect Frederick, but that lie is the clearest evidence that she did not know in advance that Frederick planned to attack Percy. No one could have planned in cold blood to pass off a stabbing as a natural death. Had there been collusion, the couple would have thought up a far more convincing story.

27

RICHMOND

'A Perfect Virago'

On the morning of 5 March 1879, a wooden box was found in the River Thames near Barnes Bridge by a passing coal porter. When he opened it he saw to his horror that it was packed with a mass of flesh he felt sure was human, and he at once informed the police. The pieces comprised most of a body of a woman. Only one foot and the head were missing. A lack of decomposition and the parchment-like appearance of the flesh suggested that it had been boiled. It was impossible to identify the deceased, and despite the fact that dismemberment had been carried out in a very rough manner, newspapers speculated that the remains might have been planted by medical students playing a prank. The truth was far grimmer, and as the story unfolded before an appalled public, the perpetrator of the crime was revealed as a bold, manipulative and remorseless woman.

Kate Webster had been born Katherine Lawler in Killane, County Wexford in 1849. It is hard to establish many facts about her early life, partly because her family and friends were reluctant to talk about her, and also because she was such a proficient and profuse liar that it is impossible to know how much of her own statements can be believed. Her story of a marriage to a sea-captain called Webster was probably false. The name was one of many aliases she used during her criminal career. She served a number of prison sentences for larceny, one in Ireland before the age of 20; and soon after her arrival in Liverpool in 1867, she was sentenced to five years in prison, obtaining her release in January 1872. She moved to London, supposedly to look for work as a general servant, but more probably to make the most of the opportunities for theft offered by the teeming capital. In Hammersmith she became friendly with an honest hard-working family, the Porters, before moving on, saying she was going into service in Notting Hill. It was there, she later said, that she met the man who

*Kate Webster, from a
contemporary print.*

was the cause of all her misfortunes. Kate was adept at blaming others, usually
men, for the consequences of her own criminal behaviour. This man – and she
was to give him several different names – supposedly seduced her, and was the
father of the son born to her on 19 April 1874. Kate was being watched by the
police, who were suspicious of her activities, both in thieving and swindling, and
was obliged to change both her address and her name regularly. Between 1875
and 1877, she served two prison sentences for larceny. Major Arthur Griffith,
Governor of Newgate Prison, described her as 'a defiant brutal creature, who
showed no remorse, but was subject to fits of ungovernable passion, when she
broke into language the most appalling.' While she was in prison, her son was
cared for by a friend, Sarah Crease, who lived in Mitchell's Row, Richmond.

In January 1879 Kate was lodging with Sarah Crease, who was working as a
charwoman for a Miss Loder. Kate occasionally cleaned for Miss Loder when
Sarah was unable to attend. One of Miss Loder's friends was Mrs Julia Martha

Thomas, a 54-year-old widow who lived alone at 2 Vine Cottages (sometimes called Mayfield Cottages), Park Road. Mrs Thomas was a retired school teacher, with pretensions to gentility. She was always well-dressed and owned a gold watch and chain and several rings. Her eccentric and finicky ways meant that maidservants rarely remained with her for long, and in January 1879 Miss Loder knew that Mrs Thomas was looking for a new servant. She recommended Kate Webster.

The bold, tough-minded maid and the fussy dictatorial lady did not rub along well. Kate later said that she found her employer 'very trying . . . When I had finished my work in my rooms, she used to go over it again after me, and point out places where she said I did not clean, showing evidence of a nasty spirit towards me.' By the middle of February, Kate had been given her notice, and it was agreed that she would leave at the end of the month. She was already planning to rob her employer, for on 25 February Kate told a friend that she would shortly be leaving London as she expected to inherit some property.

Mrs Thomas, sensing the unspoken evil on Kate's mind, felt uncomfortable at being alone in the house with her. The gardener shared this view, and described Kate as 'A perfect virago and tyrant.' Mrs Thomas got a lady and her daughter to lodge with her for a fortnight. Kate should have departed once the lodgers had gone, but she asked Mrs Thomas if she could stay on a few days longer and, reluctantly, her employer agreed.

On Saturday 2 March, the leaseholder of Vine Cottages, Miss Elizabeth Ives, who lived next door with her mother, Jane, saw Mrs Thomas tending to the plants in the garden. On the following morning, Mrs Thomas went to the Presbyterian service at the Lecture Hall, Hill Street, Richmond. Kate was free to do as she pleased on Sunday afternoons, but with the proviso that she would be back in time for Mrs Thomas to go to church that evening. That Sunday Kate stayed out too long. She had spent her afternoon in a public house and returned to find Mrs Thomas ready to go out and angry at the delay. Hard words were said and Mrs Thomas left for church in a state of agitation that was noticeable to others in the congregation. Despite this, Mrs Thomas returned home alone. Perhaps she did not like to admit that she was afraid of her own servant.

Back at No. 2 Vine Cottages, there was no quarrel, no fight. Next door, Jane Ives, sitting in her drawing room on the other side of a thin wall, and with the quiet road outside, heard nothing more than a thump, like a falling chair, which she thought came from the hall or landing. Then silence. Although Kate Webster never admitted it, she probably attacked Mrs Thomas from behind, possibly with an axe. Mrs Ives must have heard the body fall without a groan. The question Kate now had to resolve was how to dispose of the corpse. If she had merely wanted to commit murder and petty theft she might have taken what she wanted and fled, but Kate was more ambitious. She wanted everything

Vine Cottages, home of Mrs Thomas.

that Mrs Thomas had owned, not only the jewellery and plate but the furniture too, and to achieve this she effectively had to become Mrs Thomas. The body had to disappear without a trace. It was no trouble for her to carry the body down the stairs and lay it out on the kitchen table. There she went to work, determined that most of her dreadful task should be completed before the following morning. She first removed the head with a razor, then cut open the stomach with a carving knife, removed the entrails and burnt them. She then cut up the body with the knife and razor, using a meat saw for the bones, and boiled the pieces in the kitchen copper. Next door, Miss Ives heard the sound of the boiling copper, which started early in the morning and went on for some hours and was accompanied by a strong smell. Eventually, Kate fell into an exhausted sleep. She was awoken by the knock of a coal agent, William Deane, who thought she looked flustered. She spoke to him very abruptly, saying that Mrs Thomas was not in, then slammed the door.

The body parts were packed into a box and the head in a bag, but there were still a few pieces left, one of which was a foot. Kate went out and disposed of these separately. The foot was later found in a manure heap on the Crop Hall allotments.

It may have been on the following day that Kate approached Mrs Pleasant Hayhoe, the proprietress of the nearby Hole in the Wall public house, at 3 Park Mews, offering to sell her two jars of fat which she said were the best dripping. In telling the story, Mrs Hayhoe did not relate whether or not she had purchased the dripping.

On 4 March, Kate finally finished the cleaning and was ready for the second and most daring part of the plan. That afternoon she arrayed herself in one of Mrs Thomas's silk gowns, with the gold watch and chain and several rings, and set out to see her old friends the Porter family in Hammersmith. She carried with her a large black bag which contained the boiled head of her mistress. The Porters lived in Rose Gardens, a narrow street of two rows of cottages, separated by an unpaved, poorly drained roadway. Kate had not seen the Porters for six years, yet she greeted them with delight, telling Henry, a 44-year-old painter, 'I have simply been longing to see you again, father.' The family entertained her to tea and she told them that she had married a Mr Thomas but was now a widow, and that an aunt had recently died leaving her a nice house in Richmond. She intended to dispose of the property and go to live with her parents, who, she said, lived in Scotland. She asked Porter if he could recommend a broker to assist her in disposing of the furniture and she also asked if Henry's 15-year old-son, Robert, could go with her and help carry a box. The Porters, impressed by their friend's good fortune, readily agreed, and Henry, Robert and Kate set off together to Hammersmith railway station, young Robert struggling with the unexpectedly heavy bag. At Hammersmith Bridge they all went into the Oxford and Cambridge Arms for some refreshment, and Kate asked the Porters to stay there while she took the bag to a friend. She returned twenty minutes later. They then went to the station, where Kate and Robert took the train to Richmond.

Young Robert must have been concerned at the size and weight of the box Kate wanted him to help her move. She said she had arranged to give it to a friend, and it must be carried across to the other side of Richmond Bridge. Bearing the heavy box between them they set off down Mount Ararat Road, resting every so often. One handle of the box was missing and Robert had to hold his end of it by the cord which was bound around it. As he walked, the broken fitting of the handle chafed his knuckles. Halfway across the bridge there are recesses on either side with seating, and it was in one of these recesses that they put the box down. Kate said that she was to meet her friend there, and told Robert to wait for her at the end of the bridge. He did not go far, and as he waited in the dark, he heard a splash. When Kate reappeared, she told him her friend had taken the box.

Kate still had the furniture to dispose of, but showed considerable reluctance to stay in the house alone. The next day she brought the Porters' eldest son,

*John Church, from a
contemporary print.*

William, to Richmond, and on some nights she stayed at Hammersmith. Henry also called to view the furniture. On 9 March Kate was introduced to John Church, proprietor of the Rising Sun public house, Rose Gardens, Hammersmith, who said he would make her an offer for the furniture. Church, an ex-soldier, was a happily married man with a daughter, popular, hardworking and respectable. Kate's masquerade as Mrs Thomas was by now so practiced and convincing that he was completely taken in. Church called at Richmond a number of times to examine the furniture and on 17 and 18 March he was there to help with the packing and removal of what he believed to be his property.

When Miss Ives saw the furniture being loaded into a van she naturally asked where her tenant was. Kate said she didn't know, and, rattled by the enquiry, decided to make a rapid departure. In her hurry she left behind two vital clues that were to be her undoing. Whatever the emergency, Kate would not abandon her child. She took her son, and fled to Ireland.

John Church, puzzled by Kate's flight, made enquiries, then his wife discovered a letter in the pocket of a dress of Mrs Thomas's that Kate had flung onto the van. It was addressed to Mrs Thomas from a friend of hers, a Mrs Menhennick. When Church visited Mrs Menhennick, he discovered that the lady from whom he had bought the furniture was not Mrs Thomas, and he and the Porters contacted the police. It was not until 23 March that Robert told the police about the box he had helped carry, and a connection was made between the disappearance of Mrs Thomas and the human remains found in the Thames. When shown the box that had been pulled from the Thames, Robert, remembering the missing handle and his chafed knuckles, was able to identify it as the one he had carried. The police searched 2 Vine Cottages and discovered a quantity of charred bones in the grate and some fatty deposits in the copper.

On 25 March the police issued the following notice:

Wanted, for stealing plate, &c., and supposed murder of mistress, Kate, aged about 32, 5 feet 5 or 6 inches high; complexion sallow; slightly freckled; teeth rather good and prominent.

The *Daily Telegraph* described her as 'tall, strongly made'. It was only later, when the full horror of what Kate had done became known, that Tussaud's created their waxwork figure, with its grim and forbidding stare.

It was not hard to trace Kate, as in her hurry to depart she had left behind one of her own dresses, in the pocket of which was a letter from her family in Ireland. She was arrested there on 28 March, and brought back to London. The journey gave her the time to think how she might contrive a way out of her difficulty, and she volunteered a statement in which she claimed to have had a close relationship with John Church for seven years, saying that on the night of 3 March she had come home to find that he had murdered her employer. Church was arrested and on 30 March he and Kate were charged with the murder of Mrs Thomas. Fortunately, Church had an unshakable alibi for that evening and he was soon released. Kate then made another statement, blaming Henry Porter. He too had a solid alibi.

Kate Webster had been notorious as a thief but now she was celebrated as a murderess, a fame she seemed to enjoy. When she saw the crowds outside the Richmond magistrates' court on 2 April her stern features relaxed into a smile of appreciation. On 17 April, when Henry Porter gave evidence of how she had made a fuss of him on her arrival on 4 March, Kate was so amused that she laughed out loud.

The trial opened at the Central Criminal Court, the Old Bailey on 2 July 1879 and was presided over by Mr Justice Denman. The prosecution was led by the Attorney-General Sir Hardinge Giffard KC. Mr Warner Sleigh for the defence

Kate Webster's effigy at Madame Tussaud's, 1879.

Mr Justice Denman.

made the best of what looked like a hopeless case from the start, pointing out that it had not been established that Mrs Thomas had been unlawfully killed, and that it was possible she had died of natural causes. The jury had no difficulty in returning a guilty verdict and Kate was sentenced to death. In Wandsworth Prison Kate was unusually docile, and hopeful of a reprieve. She made another statement on 10 July, in which she exonerated both Church and Porter, and claimed that in all her criminal activities she was entirely under the control of the man she named as the father of her child, and whom she now implicated in the murder of Mrs Thomas. On 28 July, learning that she would not be reprieved, she finally confessed her sole guilt and went to her death calmly the following day. The black bag containing Mrs Thomas's head was never found.

28

SOUTHWARK

'No More Mrs Chapman'

The precise date of the arrival in Britain of barber-surgeon Severin Klosowski from his native Poland is unknown. In 1887 he was living in Warsaw, but in either 1888 or 1889 he was recognised by an acquaintance when working as a hairdresser in Whitechapel High Street. This suggestive proximity in both time and place to the infamous murders of Jack the Ripper has led to considerable speculation that Klosowski was the Whitechapel murderer. In Poland, Klosowski, who was born in December 1865, had been apprenticed to a surgeon, but seems never to have been awarded his degree. He certainly had no qualifications to support a medical career outside Poland. In London he became a jobbing hairdresser, and later opened a small shop. Apart from the hairdressing, he had one major talent. Women found him very attractive, and he could charm them into unquestioning devotion. His techniques were simple; he used flattery, and extravagant gifts, pretended to be wealthier than he was, and constantly boasted about his adventures, travels and medical qualifications.

He may well have been married while in Poland, but if so, he had abandoned his wife, and had no qualms about finding another. While there is substantial evidence that he disliked women, whom he used, abused and abandoned without remorse, he was never without female companionship for long. In August 1889 'Seweryn Klosowski' married 'Lusie Baderksa' (spelling as per the marriage registers), whom he met at a Polish club in Clerkenwell. In that same year a woman claiming to be his wife arrived in Whitechapel from Warsaw with two children. Klosowski refused to acknowledge them, and they remained in the neighbourhood for a time. Lucy gave birth to a son, Wladyslaw, in the summer of 1890. Later that year the Klosowskis went to live in America, but the couple soon parted because Lucy could not tolerate her husband's constant womanising. In February 1891 she returned to England without him, and shortly afterwards Wladlyslaw died. When Klosowski reappeared in London the couple were reunited, and a daughter, Cecilia, was born in May 1892. Lucy soon found that her husband's old habits would not change, and left him, taking the child. From November 1893 Klosowski lived with a woman called Annie Chapman, but in 1894 he brought Lucy back to live with him, and told Annie that Lucy was his wife. He may well have tired of Annie and brought Lucy back to persuade his mistress to leave. The three lived in the same house for a few weeks before Annie took the hint, and left. It was then that Klosowski decided on a change of identity. He began calling himself George Chapman and claimed to be an American. Never again would he acknowledge that he was or had ever been Severin Klosowski. Annie was pregnant and early in 1895 she approached him asking for assistance but he ignored her demands, and she went away empty-handed. Eventually Lucy left him for good, taking their daughter.

George Chapman.

Later that year he started an affair with Mary Isabella Spink, a married woman whose husband had left her because of her excessive fondness for drink. Mrs Spink was irresistibly attractive to Chapman, because she had a legacy of almost £600, a substantial fortune to a man who earned only 30s a week. In 1897 the couple took the lease of a shop in Hastings and opened a hairdressing business, calling themselves Mr and Mrs Chapman. One of their customers was a chemist called Davidson, from whom Chapman, on revealing that he had some medical knowledge, was able to buy an ounce of tartar emetic, also known as antimony and potassium tartrate. Colourless, odourless, and readily soluble in water, a dose produces symptoms very similar to those of gastro-enteritis.

Mrs Spink's funds enabled Chapman to move up in the world. The couple left Hastings and together leased the Prince of Wales Tavern in Bartholomew Square. He had by now obtained possession of all Mrs Spink's property, and was left with a woman of 41 who was far healthier than he felt she had any right to be. Not long after the move to Islington, Mary developed persistent symptoms of vomiting and abdominal pains. A doctor was called in and prescribed medicines which were carefully administered by the doting 'husband', but the patient weakened, and on Christmas Day 1897 she died. The once robust Mary was so emaciated by her weeks of illness that the doctor gave the cause of death as 'phthisis' another name for tuberculosis.

Chapman was not without female companionship for long. A few months later he claimed that he and his new barmaid, 33-year-old Bessie Taylor, had married. Bessie had nothing but praise for her new husband, and when her parents visited the couple, Chapman easily charmed them. Bessie was hardworking and popular with the customers, and a great asset to the business, but before long she began to exhibit the same symptoms as her predecessor. She became thin and frail, and Chapman's manner changed abruptly. He was violent and abusive towards her, and once threatened her with the revolver he used for shooting rats in the cellar. The couple moved to a new public house, the Monument Tavern in Union Street, Borough. Several doctors were called to attend Bessie, but their treatment had little effect and they were mystified as to the nature of her illness. On 13 February 1901 she died, and the cause of death was certified by Dr Stoker as 'exhaustion from vomiting and diarrhoea'.

In August 1901, 18-year-old Maud Eliza Marsh advertised for a situation as a barmaid and received a reply from Chapman. Her parents visited their daughter's prospective employer to make sure that he was respectable. He informed Mr and Mrs Marsh that he was a widower, and in case they should be anxious that Maud would be living alone with a man twice her age, said that the upper part of the property was occupied by a family, which was true. On the Monday after Maud arrived, the family departed. Chapman soon began making amorous advances toward the new barmaid. He gave her a gold watch

George Chapman and Bessie Taylor.

and chain, and before long Maud was writing to her mother with a dilemma. 'George' had told her that if she did not let him have what he wanted he would give her £35 and send her home. What he wanted was in no doubt. '... still I am engaged,' wrote the girl, 'so it will not matter much, and if he does not marry me I can have a breach of promise, can't I?' Mrs Marsh wrote back at once ordering Maud to come home, but instead Maud and the charming George visited the Marshes in Croydon, where the plausible fiancé gave assurances of his honourable intentions, and asked Mrs Marsh and her son to witness a will in which he stated he would bequeath £400 to his wife. On 13 October, Mrs Marsh went to see Maud and was told that she and Chapman had been married that morning. When Mrs Marsh asked to see the certificate, Maud said, 'George has got it, and has put it with his other papers.' There was no certificate because the marriage was a sham. Maud said that the wedding had taken place in a Roman Catholic 'room' in Bishopsgate Street, which, if true, suggests that she had been duped by a bogus ceremony, Chapman not wanting to risk another bigamous marriage.

Shortly before the lease of the Monument Tavern was due to expire, the property was damaged by fire, and Chapman made an insurance claim, which was refused on suspicion of arson. Eventually he was obliged to withdraw his claim and his policy was cancelled.

In December the couple moved to the Crown public house, also in Union Street.

In June 1902 Chapman appeared as a prosecutor in a case against a commercial traveller, Alfred Clark, who was accused of having obtained £700 from him for some worthless shares. Maud corroborated Chapman's story, and Clark was found guilty and sentenced to three years in prison.

In June 1902, Florence Rayner was briefly employed at the Crown as a barmaid. Chapman soon made advances to her, kissing her and asking if she would be his sweetheart and go to America with him. When she pointed out that he was a married man, he said, 'Oh, I could give her that,' with a snap of his fingers, 'and she would be no more Mrs Chapman.' He said he would first send Florence to America, then sell the business and come on after her. Within days Maud became very ill, with vomiting, diarrhoea and pains in the abdomen. By then Florence had had enough of Chapman's advances. After he came upstairs into her bedroom one afternoon, she quickly obtained a new job in Twickenham, and left. Chapman went there to visit her once, and when she asked after Maud he told her that she was in hospital suffering from constipation. 'If you had not been such a fool, you would have been at the Crown now,' he said.

Maud was in Guy's Hospital, where the doctors were unable to identify the cause of her illness, however she improved under their care and was allowed to return home. There, the symptoms started again. Dr Stoker was called in, the same man who had signed the death certificate for Bessie. For a second time he was puzzled about the nature of 'Mrs Chapman's' illness. As before, the husband was devotedly attentive, insisting that all the patient's food should be prepared by himself.

Maud's condition deteriorated, and on 20 October Mrs Marsh came to stay and nurse her dangerously ill daughter, while the baffled Dr Stoker was a regular visitor. Maud was pitifully weak, unable to keep down anything she

George Chapman and Maud Marsh.

was given, complaining of thirst, and vomiting green bile. The only explanation offered for her illness was some rabbit she had eaten, yet no one else who had eaten this dish had been taken ill. Chapman provided some brandy, which was kept by the bedside for preparing drinks of brandy and soda. In the early hours of Tuesday morning Mrs Marsh made up a drink for Maud but the girl was unable to finish it. Mrs Marsh then took some of the brandy herself in a little water and became ill with vomiting and diarrhoea, which went on for an hour. Mrs Marsh began to suspect foul play, and consulted her own doctor, Dr Grapel of Croydon, who came to the Crown that afternoon, saw Maud, and spoke to Dr Stoker. On the way home to Croydon, Grapel thought hard about the case and by the time he had arrived he had decided that Maud was probably being poisoned with arsenic. He at once telegraphed Dr Stoker, telling him to look for signs of arsenical poisoning, but Stoker, who was out, did not receive the message until after Maud was dead. It was probably Grapel's visit that triggered Chapman into finishing what he had started sooner than he had planned. When Stoker called at the Crown at 3 p.m. on 22 October, finding the house open for business as usual, he was told that Maud had died at 12.30. This time Stoker refused to design a death certificate. Chapman tried to bully Stoker into signing, saying that death was obviously caused by the inflammation due to vomiting and diarrhoea.

'What caused the vomiting and diarrhoea?' asked Stoker, to which Chapman made no reply.

Stoker conducted a post-mortem and sent the organs for analysis. Small amounts of arsenic were found, and on 25 October Chapman was arrested and charged with murder. It was not until the police searched his papers that they discovered his real name. They also discovered a book on poisons, a label proving his purchase of tartar emetic, and a great deal of cash. Some of the currency notes were ones which Chapman had testified he had given to Alfred Clark. As a result, Clark's case was re-investigated and he was released in December 1902.

The coroner's enquiry revealed that Maud's death was due to poisoning with antimony, the arsenic probably being present as an impurity. The preliminary hearings at Southwark police court were adjourned to allow time for the exhumation of the bodies of Mrs Spink and Bessie Taylor. Antimony, like arsenic, has the effect of leaving bodies in an unusually good state of preservation and both bodies were found to be in very good condition. The bodies of Maud and Bessie contained substantial amounts of antimony; Mrs Spink's, because she had been in the grave rather longer, less so. A medicine bottle which had been rinsed out was found to contain traces of the poison.

Chapman's trial opened on 11 February 1903 at the Central Criminal Court, the Old Bailey and was presided over by Mr Justice Grantham. While a popular judge, Grantham did have the unfortunate habit of frequently interrupting counsel whenever anything unusual came to his attention, and when he believed the prisoner to be guilty he did not attempt to conceal his opinion from the jury. The prosecution was led by the Solicitor-General Sir Edward Carson, and the almost impossible task of defending Chapman fell to the amiable Mr George Elliott KC, who had appeared for the defence in many high profile cases. The public flocked eagerly to hear the case, but they were disappointed. Tickets of admission were already sold out and the galleries of the gloomy court were crowded. Chapman had been calm and confident at the police court hearings, but it was a subdued and depressed man who took his place in the dock. He must have known that there was very little hope.

Mr Elliott did his best, but there were no defence witnesses he could bring. As Chapman wept in the dock, Elliott appealed to the jury, claiming that there might be prejudice against his client because he was an alien. Mr Justice Grantham had no such qualms and delivered a lengthy speech which was virtually a direction to find the prisoner guilty. He was particularly scathing about the failure of the medical men to realise that they were dealing with a case of poisoning. It took the jury just ten minutes to return a verdict of guilty.

The convicted man was taken to Wandsworth Prison, where he continued to maintain that he was an American, and wrote letters claiming that he had been

convicted on perjured evidence. The Polish woman who was believed to be his legal wife called repeatedly at the prison, but he refused to see her. He was executed on 7 April 1903. Shortly afterwards, Lucy remarried.

Chapman's motives for the murder of Mrs Spink are not hard to fathom. He was tired of her drunken ways, and had extracted all her money, so he removed her. In the past he had simply abandoned his unwanted women, but when his Polish wife and children and the pregnant Annie Chapman came after him for support he had had to take desperate steps to evade his responsibilities. Only death would avoid that complication. Perhaps he tired of Bessie, too, and Maud, fatally for her, had been hinting that she wanted to start a family. He already had designs on her replacement: Florence Rayner. Chapman may have got a thrill from committing murder, the exercise of the power of life and death over a helpless victim, and slow poisoning enabled him to enjoy the process over a long period of time. Chapman was undoubtedly sane; he even had a copy of the memoirs of James Berry, the hangman, so he was well aware of the possible consequences of his actions, but he was also arrogant and over-confident, and as time passed and his murders remained undetected he must have thought he could do as he wished with impunity.

Was Chapman Jack the Ripper? He may have lived in Whitechapel at the time of the Ripper murders, and it has been suggested that brutal murders of women in Jersey City at the time of his stay there could have been his work, but it is unlikely that the individual who obsessively strangled and disembowelled prostitutes made such a startling change of both method and victim. Descriptions of a man seen with the Ripper's victims shortly before they were found dead all give an approximate age as late twenties to mid-thirties. Chapman was twenty-two at the time of the murders.

29

SUTTON

In the Heat of Passion

William Wittman was an exciseman who, over the years, had amassed 'a handsome independence', the income from which was easily sufficient to support himself, his wife and child. The Wittmans had been living in Penton Place, Walworth, Southwark, but on William's retirement, probably in the mid-1820s, they took a 'neat cottage' known locally as 'the White House' (not to be confused with the substantial Whitehall) in the quiet rural village of Cheam. The Wittman family would have appeared comfortable, even affluent, but there were 'frequent quarrellings and bickerings' and their friends and neighbours in Walworth had been well aware that it was an unhappy household. The quarrels continued after the move to Cheam, and it soon became obvious to their new neighbours that the Wittmans led a turbulent and miserable existence. They were an unusual couple since Wittman was small and afflicted with a hunched back and 'labouring under general bodily weakness', whereas Sarah was a robust hearty woman, easily stronger than her diminutive husband. It was rumoured in the village that Wittman was very jealous of his wife, and that on the fatal night of Friday, 12 December 1828, they had both been drunk.

Matthew Steadman, of Nonesuch Park, had been at the cottage of a Mr Willis at about twenty minutes to eight that evening when he heard someone scratching against the side of the house. He went out to see who it was and found William Wittman looking distressed and agitated. 'Holloa,' said Steadman. Wittman said that his wife had struck him twice with a poker and he had then shot her and she was dead. There was blood running down his face. He asked Steadman to go to the house with him, which Steadman at first refused to do, instead going to raise the alarm, but on his return Steadman agreed to go with Wittman after getting some other men to accompany him.

William Perkins, a farrier, and David Deacon, a servant, had been working in Mr Willis' barn that evening. At about half past seven they had heard what sounded like the report of a firearm, coming from the direction of Wittman's property. Knowing that Wittman liked to shoot at birds in the garden they thought nothing of it, and went on with their work, but a few minutes later Steadman came to the door and said that Wittman had just told him he had shot his wife. All three went to investigate. At the gate of the premises Wittman said,

> For God's sake come in. I fear I have shot my wife, but before I did she struck me twice on the head with a poker, and the blood from the wounds you now see streaming down my face.

They followed Wittman into the garden and when they asked where his wife was, he asked them to come with him into the house. He then entered the house by climbing through the parlour window, and the others followed without questioning him about this unusual mode of access. There was nothing amiss in the parlour, but when Wittman took a light from the table and led them into the kitchen, it was all too clear that his story was true. Sarah Wittman lay face down on the floor, in a spreading pool of blood. Perkins stooped and felt for a pulse. 'It does not beat,' he said. 'She is quite dead.' Perkins asked Wittman where his gun was, and Wittman said, 'here it is', producing it from behind the parlour door. Perkins sensibly decided to take charge of the weapon, which he could see had been recently fired. Wittman repeated several times that his wife had twice struck him on the head with a poker. He said they had quarrelled, although he didn't say about what, and that in the heat of the moment he had shot her. Perkins could clearly see two distinct wounds on Wittman's head.

Deacon at once went home and informed his master what had happened. Samuel Tarrant, a local surgeon, was sent for and arrived at about half past eight. He confirmed that Sarah was dead, having received the contents of a firearm loaded with powder and small shot full in the face from close quarters. Her face was shattered and death would have been instantaneous. Underneath the body was a large poker. He asked Wittman if he had loaded the gun for the purpose of killing his wife and Wittman said it was previously loaded, adding, 'I am very sorry, but I have had great excitement and provocation.' Tarrant also saw the contused and bleeding wounds on Wittman's head and thought that Wittman must have been running towards his wife when the blows were struck as he had been hit with the middle of the poker and not the heavy 'bit' at the end. Mr Harris, the village constable, was sent for, and placed Wittman under arrest. Wittman, who had made no attempt to escape, immediately surrendered himself into the custody of the constable, repeating his story of provocation, describing the 'state of excitement approaching to phrenzy [*sic*] under which he had laboured at the moment he had snatched up the fatal weapon.'

On the 13 December, an inquest was held at Mr Wittman's cottage, before Mr R. Carter, the coroner for Surrey. Steadman confirmed that when he entered Wittman's cottage there was no servant there and the only other occupant was the Wittman's child, a little boy of about 6. An important witness was William Prosser, a plumber and painter who had lodged with the Wittmans for three months. On the day of the murder he had dined with Mrs Wittman and the child in the kitchen while Wittman sat by the fireside. Prosser went out to work just before two, and returned to the house at twenty past five. Both Mr and Mrs Wittman were at home, and Mr Wittman bought a goose at the gate and gave it to his wife. Prosser thought that Mrs Wittman was drunk and she had admitted that she was tipsy and shortly afterwards went to bed. There was some gin on the kitchen dresser and Wittman had a glass of it. Shortly afterwards, Prosser left the house and spent the evening at the Harrow public house. He returned home at a quarter to nine to find several people in the house and Mrs Wittman dead on the floor. When Wittman gave the coroner his account of the incident, saying he had shot his wife in a passion, Prosser retorted by asking him if he had loaded the gun in his passion, and Wittman replied that he did not as it was already loaded. Unfortunately Prosser did not state whether the gun was normally loaded or not, but his question to Wittman certainly suggested that he did not expect it to have been loaded.

Once the evidence was given, Wittman, described by the *Morning Chronicle* as 'a short, deformed man, of sallow complexion, and a general expression of misery', heard the witnesses' depositions read over to him. He was asked by the coroner if he wished to say anything with reference to the serious offence alleged against him. Wittman, with tears rolling down his face, said he had received the greatest provocation before he took up the weapon and fired, and expressed his strongest regret for what had occurred. The jury conferred for a few minutes and returned a verdict of 'wilful murder' against Wittman, who was committed on the coroner's

Horsemonger Lane Gaol.

warrant to Horsemonger Lane Gaol. In view of his injuries, he was placed in the infirmary under constant observation as he was felt to be a suicide risk. Wittman said he was sorry for what had happened and expressed his gratitude for the humane treatment he had received from the governor, Mr Walter.

From the very first, all public sympathy went not to the murdered woman but to her killer, the newspapers reporting that 'the unfortunate man remains in a most deplorable state. He labours under excessive agitation of mind, attended with great depression of spirits.' The chaplain of the gaol, Mr Mann, attended him zealously throughout his incarceration and Wittman repeated to him his tale of provocation, but with a significant alteration. Wittman now said that it was his wife who had initially seized the gun after she had struck him with the poker, and that he, in a paroxysm of rage from the violence he had suffered at her hands, had wrenched the weapon away from her and shot her. He also claimed that she had been unfaithful to him on many occasions, and that only two or three nights since he had actually discovered her in the arms of another man. As the days passed, the prisoner's manner became more composed and he looked forward to the outcome of the trial with some confidence.

The Times sent a correspondent who must have been permitted to interview Wittman, for on 20 December it published a full account of the tragedy which it said came from the prisoner's own mouth, and again there had been a subtle change to the story. According to Wittman, his wife was a woman of ungovernable temper and extreme violence. On the Wednesday before the tragedy she had destroyed all the silver spoons, and on the following day she destroyed three family pictures which hung in the front parlour. Between six and seven o'clock on the night of 12 December, he and his wife had been sitting in the back parlour in conversation when he had mentioned the fact that she had been in bed with another man the previous night, that man being William Prosser. On his mentioning this she jumped up, enraged, and seized the poker, which was in the fireplace, and inflicted the blows on his head. One of his guns was standing loaded in the corner of the back parlour, which she seized, and he took hold of it to prevent her firing it at him and in the struggle the gun went off. Wittman said he owned two guns, a long gun which he invariably kept by his bedside and a smaller one he had bought the previous October, which he used occasionally to shoot birds in his garden for his amusement, and was always kept in a corner of the back parlour so as to be handy. Previous to his buying this gun he had kept the long gun in that place, but some time ago his wife had tried to shoot him with it, and was only prevented from doing so by the intervention of another person who happened to be in the house at the time and who struck her arm down when she pointed the gun at him, so the contents lodged in the floor. Wittman did not explain why, despite this incident, he still chose to keep two loaded guns in the house.

Over the next few days *The Times* correspondent uncovered more facts. When Prosser had gone to carry out plumbing work at Wittman's house there had been a female (presumably a servant) named Clark living there, and Prosser had paid his addresses to her. This girl had been discharged by Mrs Wittman. Shortly afterwards, Prosser moved in, and he and Mrs Wittman became lovers. When her husband discovered this, he remonstrated with her, and she behaved violently, breaking chairs and destroying anything within reach. Sarah Wittman's sister was a frequent visitor, and witnessed many quarrels between husband and wife. On one occasion she had been sitting in the kitchen and heard them quarrelling in the parlour, and went to try and calm things down. There she saw Sarah with the gun in her hand, with which she motioned her husband to leave the room. Before he could do so the gun went off, and the shot entered the floor. This account sounds very like the story told by Wittman and may well refer to the same incident, except that Sarah's sister did not mention whether the gun firing into the floor was as a result of her intervention. Once the shot had been fired, Sarah had got up from her chair, saying, 'fetch me the other gun and I will shoot him with that.' Wittman had at once gone to get the second gun and discharged it in the garden. It is scarcely credible that after this occurrence Wittman continued to keep a loaded gun where his wife could pick it up.

Mrs Wittman may not have been Prosser's only amorous interest. An unsigned letter, addressed to Prosser at the house probably from a cast-off mistress, threatened to expose him as a 'gay deceiver' who would 'walk with many'. The writer had heard he was courting a virtuous girl but, 'you, false man, intend serving her as you have served me.'

The Times correspondent visited the Wittmans' house and reported that the best parlour was very neatly furnished. The body of Mrs Wittman was still there, just prior to burial, which was to take place on 23 December. In one corner of the room were portraits of the husband, wife and child, cut to pieces as Wittman had described.

Wittman at last explained why he had been obliged to enter his house through the window. He said that after his wife had been shot, he had tried to leave by the back door to give the alarm, but found it was locked and the key missing. The front door was normally kept locked.

On the morning of 22 December, Wittman was visited by many of his friends in prison. He was still in the infirmary and the surgeon believed it was absolutely necessary that he remain there. Wittman, his manner and appearance exciting the sympathy of all who saw him, claimed that he was unable to remember how or when he had been conveyed to the prison. The accused, reported *The Times*, 'expressed a wish to see his "poor boy" who is a very interesting child; but when told that, under the circumstances, his friends thought he had better not at present, he nodded assent; but we could perceive the tears gathering in his eyes.'

The trial took place on 29 December and Wittman now provided yet another version of his wife's death, since his defence was that he had no recollection of having cocked and fired the gun. Mr Justice Burrough observed that if he had had recourse to the gun solely for self-defence then there would be no offence, however the prisoner's initial statement was that he had acted in the heat of passion. The jury without any hesitation acquitted Wittman of murder but found him guilty of manslaughter. The judge stated that while the prisoner had received great provocation, he was not justified in using a gun to avenge himself. He did not believe, however, that it was a case calling for heavy punishment. Wittman was sentenced to three months in the House of Correction.

30

TOWER HAMLETS

The Terror

It began on 7 August 1888, when the body of Martha Tabram, a 39-year-old prostitute, was found lying in a pool of blood on the landing of George Yard Buildings (now Gunthorpe Street), Whitechapel. It was a murder of uncommon savagery. Martha had been stabbed thirty-nine times, the wounds penetrating her heart, lungs, liver and kidneys.

Even in Whitechapel, where violent crime and screams in the night were commonplace, this was a shocking event. Crowds who clustered to stare in horror at the bloodstained landing wondered how such an atrocity could have been committed in silence – the killer vanishing without a trace. Although it was not at first believed that Martha Tabram's murder was connected with any other crimes, there had been three previous cases that year of women being assaulted by strangers. On 25 February a 38-year old-widow, Annie Millwood, was brought to the Whitechapel Infirmary with multiple stab wounds on her legs and lower body. She said that a man had suddenly pulled a clasp knife from his pocket and attacked her. She left the infirmary on 21 March but died, from apparently unrelated causes, ten days later. Early on the morning of 29 March Ada Wilson, aged 39, who worked as a machinist, opened her door to a man who demanded money. When she refused, he stabbed her in the throat with a clasp knife. Her loud screams scared him off.

On 2 April, 45-year-old Emma Smith, who lived not far from the site of Martha Tabram's murder ,was set upon in the street by three men, robbed, and beaten. She was found to have a torn perineum from a brutal assault with a blunt instrument, and died of peritonitis two days later.

Following the murder of Martha Tabram there was a meeting of local men, as a result of which the St Jude's Vigilance Committee was formed, with the object of promoting better security in the streets. As the events of the next few months unfolded, there would be more such committees.

Early on the morning of Friday 31 August, the body of 43-year-old Polly Nicholls was found in Bucks Row, her skirts pulled up to her waist. The light of a policeman's lantern revealed that her throat had been cut. The full extent of her injuries did not become apparent until she was examined at the mortuary. Her abdomen had been cut open by a jagged slash of a knife. Her face and neck were bruised, suggesting that she had been silenced by being throttled before she was killed. Polly had parted from her husband in 1880, and spent most of the intervening years in workhouses or cheap lodgings. On the night of 30 August she had been turned out of a lodging-house in Thrawl Street as she was unable to pay. She was last seen in Whitechapel Road, where she hoped to be able to raise the price of a bed by prostitution.

As the news spread, and morning light illuminated the scene, crowds gathered in Bucks Row to see the scene of Polly's murder. Onlookers commented that the victim was to be pitied, whatever her character, and the women had their own views as to what they would do to the villain if they got hold of him. Uppermost in their minds, however, were fears for their own safety, and that of sisters and daughters, who might need to be out after dark for perfectly respectable reasons.

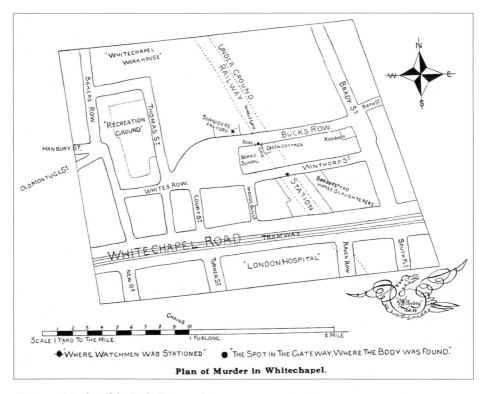

Plan of Murder in Whitechapel.

Contemporary plan of the Bucks Row murder.

Newspaper reports started to link the murder of Polly Nicholls with those of Emma Smith and Martha Tabram. Although the wounds were different, all the killings were unusually savage and targeted prostitutes, which suggested to some the activities of a gang trying to extort money and murdering the women who refused to pay. Another more worrying theory was that the murders were the work of a madman, which meant that no woman was safe. The *Star* in particular, an evening paper which had declared itself to be the champion of the poor and underprivileged, saw the murders as an opportunity not only to highlight the terrible living conditions in the slums of the East End, but to increase its circulation with sensational articles.

Scotland Yard sent one of their most able officers, Inspector Abberline, to co-ordinate the hunt for the killer. The police learned that Whitechapel prostitutes were afraid of a man called Jack Pizer, also known as Leather Apron, who had been demanding money from them, and beating them when they didn't comply. The *Star* described this sinister character as a 'monster' with glittering eyes and a repellent grin, who prowled the streets after midnight. The article resulted in a frenzy of public excitement in which Pizer suddenly seemed to be everywhere. He was obliged to go into hiding in case he was torn to pieces by the mob.

In the early hours of Saturday 8 September, Annie Chapman, a 47-year-old prostitute who had spent the last of her money on beer, set out to earn enough for a bed in a lodging house. Her body was found at 6 a.m. in a secluded yard at the back of 29 Hanbury Street, a decaying three-storey property which was home to seventeen people. It was assumed that Annie had taken a client there. Annie had been strangled, for her face was swollen, the tongue protruding between her teeth, but she had also been horribly mutilated, her throat deeply cut, her body slashed open and part of her intestines removed. A section of the wall of her abdomen and some internal organs were missing. The news flew around the district, and crowds of angry, frightened people gathered around Hanbury Street. That evening there was an unprecedented demand for newspapers, most of which only served to whip up the terror. The *Star* wrote of a 'ghoul-like creature . . . drunk with blood'. Even the sedate *Times* predicted that unless the fiendish murderer was captured soon, he would go on to kill again. Anyone could be a suspect, and any arrest in the area for other crimes started up a rumour that the killer had been caught. Crowds would pour out onto the streets to exact their own variety of justice, and were dispersed only with some difficulty. The district was alive with gossip and speculation – mysterious messages were said to have appeared – men had been seen with bloodstained clothing, or behaving in a suspicious or threatening manner. The smallest incident triggered rumours of another atrocity. At night the normally busy thoroughfares of the East End were almost deserted. Residents fitted new locks to their doors and kept them firmly closed. The streets were now the preserve of the police, and the poorest of the poor who had no homes.

Detectives drew up a list of suspects, men with a history of violence and/or insanity, and these were investigated, but no evidence could be found to link them to the crimes. The failure of the hard-pressed police to make an arrest excited anger in the community and was deplored by the newspapers, whose reporters were frustrated by not being given full access to the scenes of the crimes. The police, in their turn, believed that the activities of reporters who followed detectives about and then interviewed the people they had spoken to not only impeded their enquiries but helped to maintain the mood of hysteria.

Both the newspapers and the public expressed the view that the murders were so horrific that no Englishman could have committed them. To the alarm of the Jewish community, which had made great efforts to build up respectable businesses in the East End, the killing of Annie Chapman sparked off a wave of anti-Semitism. Any Jewish family which had escaped the pogroms would have been terrified that it was all going to start again. Samuel Montagu, the Jewish Member of Parliament for Whitechapel, offered a reward of £100 for the capture of the murderer. On 10 September the Mile End Vigilance Committee was formed, many of whose members were Jewish tradesmen. They lobbied the Home Office to offer a reward for the capture of the killer and when the Home Office refused, started to collect funds.

At 1 a.m. on Sunday 30 September the body of 44-year-old Liz Stride was discovered in Dutfield's Yard, off Berner Street (now Henriques Street). Her throat had been cut, but her clothing was undisturbed and there were no mutilations. About forty-five minutes later a police constable found a second body, that of 46-year-old Kate Eddowes, in Mitre Square, a quiet area where prostitutes were known to take their clients. She too had died from a cut throat, and her clothes were pushed up to reveal her stomach, which had been slashed open, and the entrails pulled out. The murderer had had time to mutilate her face. There was a deep gash on one cheek, and her nose had been almost sliced off. A later examination showed that her left kidney and womb were missing.

The rapidity with which the murder had occurred, the audacity of committing the crime while the police were making searches only yards away, the silence with which it had been carried out and the gruesomeness of the mutilations which surpassed any that had happened before, struck new terror into the population. The police, faced with two simultaneous murder enquiries, swept the area and made an important discovery. About 300 yards north east of Mitre Square lay Goulston Street, where a piece of bloodstained cloth, cut from Kate's apron, was found, presumably used by the murderer to clean his hands. Nearby, some words were chalked on a wall. 'The Juwes are the men that will not be blamed for nothing'. No one recalled having seen the writing before,

Mitre Square today. Kate Eddowes' body was found near this spot.

and the police believed that the murderer was trying to deflect blame onto the Jewish community. In a few hours it would be daylight and the streets would be crowded. Afraid that the words would provoke an anti-Semitic riot, with property destroyed and possibly lives lost, Superintendent Arnold decided that after written copies of the inscription were made, it should be wiped away.

Within hours the news was all over Whitechapel and people left their homes and converged on the murder sites, which had already been cordoned off by the police. The narrow streets were packed with crowds, and many people paid to get a better view from windows overlooking the area. Street vendors homed in, and as the first newspapers arrived, sales were brisk, and those able to read regaled horrified listeners with the details. As the night closed in, it was a different story. The streets emptied as terrified people stayed indoors and all but the most desperate or the homeless ventured out. The weather was getting colder, and there was an icy wind. Girls unable to raise their doss-money were evicted from lodging houses and were obliged to shelter in doorways, half-frozen and afraid. There was an outbreak of suicides by people obsessed with the idea that they were wanted for the murders or that the killer was after them, and matters were not helped by jokers who delighted in terrorising people by brandishing knives and claiming to be the killer.

The press saved the most vitriolic of its denunciation for the Home Secretary but many newspapers, frustrated by the refusal of the police to supply information about the progress of their enquiries, condemned the entire detective department as useless.

On 27 September a letter was received by the central news agency purporting to come from the murderer and signed 'Jack the Ripper'. It was one of many such letters, but it was the first one with this signature. It was regarded as a hoax, but it was followed by a postcard with the same handwriting and signature postmarked 1 October, referring to the double murder. This one was taken seriously and the letter and card were reproduced in a poster in a police campaign, asking the public if they recognised the handwriting. They didn't, but the name caught on and the police were inundated with copycat letters.

The Mile End Vigilance Committee still met regularly and on 3 October began to send men out on patrol. The police were unimpressed by this effort, especially when they wasted time keeping suspicious characters under observation only to find they were amateur vigilantes. Further confusion was caused by an influx of plain clothes detectives and reporters on the lookout for a story, one of whom disguised himself not very successfully in women's clothing.

The mood in Whitechapel was described by a *Daily News* reporter, who made regular visits to the area and wrote:

> While the visible excitement over the murders actually perpetrated is of course dying down somewhat, the awe-stricken dread of this mysterious being who thus strikes and vanishes is deepening as the hours run on and reveal the absolute help-lessness of the police and the impotency of heavy rewards.

The people remained jittery – rumours constantly swept the area, becoming more detailed as they passed from person to person, and if a woman accused a man of molestation, this was enough to start a full-scale hue and cry. All these stories and incidents had to be investigated by the police.

On 16 October the chairman of the Mile End Vigilance Committee, George Lusk, received a parcel containing a letter and half a kidney, which had been preserved in spirit. It was supposedly the kidney removed from Kate Eddowes, but it was impossible to prove that this was the case.

The additional numbers of men out looking out for the murderer may have acted as a deterrent. Weeks passed; the police were exhausted and dispirited, and the vigilance men were tired and running out of funds. Prostitutes started drifting back onto the streets.

At 10.45 a.m. on 9 November, landlord John McCarthy sent his assistant, Thomas Bowyer, to collect overdue rent from Mary Jane Kelly, the tenant of 13 Miller's Court, just off Dorset Street. Bowyer knocked, but getting no reply he pulled aside the curtain on a broken window and peered in. The room looked like a butcher's shop – blood, lumps of flesh, and a figure on the bed which had been stripped of any semblance of humanity. He ran to the police, almost incoherent with fright. One of the first policemen on the scene was a young constable, Walter Dew, later to achieve fame as the man who arrested Crippen (*see* chapter 19). Mary had died from a cut throat, but the murderer, operating without fear of disturbance, had removed substantial portions of flesh, which lay on a table, and the abdomen had been emptied of viscera. The soft tissues of the face had been cut away.

It was the day of the Lord Mayor's show and large numbers of people were already lining the main thoroughfares to watch the parade. The news carried rapidly by word of mouth and soon reached the waiting crowds, who abandoned the show for the greater excitement of another Ripper murder. Prevented by the police from entering Dorset Street they remained in the surrounding streets, which soon became impassable. When a cart was sent with a coffin to remove the body a crush of people tried to break through the cordon. That evening a man was arrested and taken to the Commercial Street police station, followed by a howling mob, but was later released. The area remained crowded for days and the slightest incident was enough to cause a panic. Any man with an unusual accent or foreign clothing was likely to be denounced in the street and pursued by a screaming crowd. On 11 November a man with a blackened face stood on the corner of Wentworth Road and Commercial Street and publicly proclaimed himself to be Jack the Ripper. He was attacked by a mob and might well have been lynched but for the speedy intervention of police. Numerous men were in custody after being reported as behaving suspiciously, but by the end of the day all had been released without charge.

Once again the murderer had vanished leaving no clue as to his identity, but the press and the public had long ceased to expect any resolution. Women of all sectors of society and in all parts of London were terrified. The police and the vigilantes continued to patrol during the winter of 1888, but when three months passed without incident, the police presence was reduced, plain clothes patrols were withdrawn, and the committees no longer met.

On 17 July 1889, the body of 40-year-old Alice Mackenzie was found in an alley near Whitechapel High Street with a cut throat and superficial wounds to her abdomen. The rumour spread that the Ripper had struck again. There were new patrols, more police were drafted in and the vigilance committees were reconstituted. Two days later, screams of 'Murder!' and 'Jack the Ripper!' brought vigilantes to East Aldgate, where they found a man wielding a knife and holding a woman by her hair. The man was disarmed and arrested, but by then the woman had disappeared. A mob soon formed, throwing stones at the man and were set to lynch him when the police arrived. The man claimed that he

Punch *cartoon satirising the police at the time of the Ripper murders.*

had acted in self-defence as the woman had robbed him. As she was no longer there to prefer charges he was released. There was increased police activity again in September when a female torso was found near Commercial Road, though it was later decided that this had no connection with the Ripper murders.

The last killing attributed to Jack the Ripper was that of prostitute Frances Coles, found with her throat cut but no other mutilations on 13 February 1891. Panic was averted by the rapid arrest of one of her clients, James Sadler, who had been at sea at the time of the 1888 murders. He was later released for lack of evidence. After that there were no other similar murders. In 1892 the police closed their file.

31

WALTHAM FOREST

The Walthamstow Mystery

At 1.20 on the afternoon of Saturday, 21 July 1888, William Barber, the manager of Edmund Hamilton's chemist shop in Markhouse Road, Walthamstow, sent his errand boy, 15-year-old Frederick Playle, to deliver a note. Nothing was written on the outside of the folded paper, which was sealed with wax, and the boy was under strict instructions to deliver it to Mrs French, a grocer's wife, who was a regular customer of the shop and lived at 208 Boundary Road, about five minutes' walk away. He was told not to deliver the note if Mrs French's husband was there. When Playle knocked at the door, Mrs French answered, but seeing that her husband was in the house, Playle went back to the shop without delivering the note. At 2.50 p.m. Barber sent the boy again, and this time Mrs French was alone. She opened the paper, read it, and said, 'Tell him yes.'

Playle's next errand for Barber was to get a shilling's worth of brandy, the second time that day he had been sent out to buy alcohol. As Playle left the shop he saw Mrs French arrive, and go into the back parlour with Barber. When Playle returned with the brandy the front door was closed, and he went to the side door. It was then about 4 o'clock, and Barber took the brandy and told Playle he could go home. The boy thought Barber's manner was unusually 'dull and strange'. Playle, who usually worked evenings, returned to the shop at six, and was astonished to find the premises closed and locked. Unable to enter by either the front or the side door, he scaled the wall which separated the garden from the footpath in Prospect Place, and got in through the back entrance. He knocked on the parlour door, and receiving no answer, pushed it open. The room was dark, but he was able to make out the figure of Mrs French, sitting on the sofa, her head leaning back. The buttons at the neck of her dress were undone, and she wore no hat or bonnet. She appeared to be unconscious.

Mrs French's visit and the suspicions of the errand boy.

On the table he saw a soda siphon, a brandy flask, a tumbler, a bowl of water with a pocket handkerchief in it, and a pair of Barber's trousers. He looked for the manager, but Barber was nowhere to be found.

Playle opened the front door, and spoke to Mr Patchett, the next-door butcher, who came in, and, taking the lady's pulse, confirmed that she was alive. Patchett called Mr Drummond, a nearby grocer, who summoned a local doctor, George Thorpe. Mr French was sent for and reached his wife's side at about 7 o'clock.

Mrs French's pulse was feeble, her face swollen, her breathing laboured, and there was an odour of chloroform about her mouth. Thorpe noticed that the items on the table included a bottle of toothache tincture and some cotton wool, and saw that on the mantelshelf were a ten ounce bottle of chloroform, a bottle of sal volatile smelling salts, and a six ounce bottle of carbolic lotion, an antiseptic.

He administered an injection of ether (then thought to be a heart stimulant and an antidote to chloroform) but by nine o'clock, finding no sign of improvement he summoned Dr Blight, who performed a tracheotomy. Although this eased the patient's breathing she did not regain consciousness, and artificial respiration was applied continuously. It was not until 11 p.m. that someone thought to call the police, and Superintendent Craggs arrived and sent for a police surgeon, Dr Chambers. The shop owner, Edmund Hamilton, was brought to look over his premises, and found that the till which should have contained some £6, had been emptied of gold and silver coin. Police were summoned from Lea Bridge Road station to search for William Barber. Throughout Saturday night and the whole of Sunday, doctors applied every known remedy to revive Mrs French, including electrical stimulation using a battery, but shortly before midnight, she died.

William Barber was said to be between 35 and 39 years of age, unmarried, and a native of Hitchin, but for some years he had lived in America, where he had taken his diplomas. He had been a manager at the shop since September 1886, and lived on the premises. Early in his employment he had occasionally carried out tooth-drawing, but Hamilton had ordered him to desist, and removed all tooth-drawing implements from the shop. Barber's papers were seized by the police and there was considerable anticipation that they would provide some startling information about his past. A description was issued of the missing man: 'height 5ft 8½ inches, complexion hair and moustache fair, near sighted dressed in a grey jacket dark trousers and a hard felt hat. He is splay footed.' Barber was known to be of a nervous and excitable disposition and his friends feared that he had committed suicide.

There had been two sightings of Barber during the critical time between 4 and 6 p.m. on the Saturday. Between 4 and 4.30 p.m., a Mrs Nellie Cashman had entered the shop and noticed that Barber looked agitated and flushed. At 5 p.m. John Patchett, the son of the butcher, saw Barber emerge from the front door, lock up the shop and walk towards St James Street railway station.

The deceased, Annie Mary French, described as 'a very handsome woman', was 22 years of age and had been married to 26-year-old Arthur George French for two years. A post-mortem examination of her body was carried out under the supervision of Dr Wellington Lake, divisional police surgeon for Walthamstow, at the mortuary, Walthamstow cemetery. There were no external marks of violence, she had not been sexually violated, and contrary to the rumours that were flying about, she was not pregnant. Her teeth were decayed, but there was no sign that any procedure had been carried out either to the teeth or the gums. It was suspected that she had died from inhalation of chloroform, but a final decision could not be made until samples taken from the organs had been analysed.

A coroner's court was opened at the mortuary on 25 July under the supervision of Mr C.C. Lewis, coroner for Essex. Arthur French said that he had known Barber for two years and had never entertained any suspicion of an improper intimacy between the chemist and his wife. Annie had visited the shop often to buy things for themselves and his mother, on whom she was in constant attendance. Barber visited them almost every day, and dined with them on Sunday. He was treated like one of the family. Annie sometimes complained of toothache and on the Saturday she felt another coming on, and had obtained a bottle of chlorodyne to treat it. It was however 'nothing to speak of'. She had been otherwise well and in good spirits and had eaten a hearty dinner. He was unaware that his wife had received a letter from Barber. He had searched for the one said to have been delivered but had not found it. A few weeks ago his wife had told him she 'utterly disliked' Barber and wished he would keep away from the house. Despite this, Barber continued to call and dine there. On the Sunday week when Barber had been at his house the chemist had remarked that he was very miserable, because he was 'too many hours alone'. French had thought Barber's behaviour 'very peculiar', and Mrs French had abruptly left the room.

Errand boy Frederick Playle revealed that Mrs French had been in the habit of calling at the shop at 11 o'clock every morning and again in the afternoon for the last nine months. She alone, of all the customers, was always conducted to the parlour behind the counter. When Barber and Mrs French were in the parlour the door was kept shut. Barber used to accumulate orders requiring delivery so that when Mrs French arrived the boy would be sent out with them. If Playle returned to the shop before Mrs French left he was sent out again. Barber did not do this when other people called. Although the boy had not witnessed any improper behaviour he was highly suspicious of the situation and had confided his thoughts to the errand boy at Mr Hamilton's other shop. Playle said that Barber had been drinking heavily during the last week, and he had often been sent out for bottles of whisky and Burgundy.

The inquest was adjourned, amidst growing pessimism about the chances of finding William Barber, however on the morning of Saturday 28 July a coffee house keeper named Hancock, of 379 High Street, Brentford, spoke to Constable Buchanan concerning his suspicions of a man who had been lodging there. The man looked harassed and anxious to avoid being seen. Buchanan

Scenes from the Walthamstow Mystery.

approached the lodger, who readily admitted that he was William Barber. He was immediately placed under arrest, and made a statement, in which he denied having administered any drug to Mrs French.

Barber said he had treated Mrs French for toothache a number of times by rubbing chloroform onto her cheek or gums, and had told her to come to the shop any time if she required further applications. The note he sent her on Saturday had been about some cigarettes which she used to make for him with a machine he had provided. On that day he had brought a bottle of muriate of morphia (morphine hydrochloride) into the parlour together with some water, intending to make a draught to 'allay nervous irritation'. He had then gone to attend to a customer and when he returned found that she had drunk the contents of the bottle. The brandy, the sal volatile, the bathing with water and the unbuttoning of the dress had all been to try and revive her. He had felt sure that she was dying and 'in the excitement of the moment I rushed away'. He said his first impulse had been to go for a doctor but he did not because he was 'so compromised by existing circumstances.' He and Mrs French had been great friends, he said, but there had been nothing improper between them. 'I tried to restore her, but failed, and ran away in the excitement of the moment. I didn't exactly know what I was doing.' How the morphia bottle found its way back to its accustomed position on the surgery shelf, where it was later found by Mr Hamilton, was never explained. In the middle of all this panic Barber had gone upstairs to change his clothes before making his escape. The reason why he had felt this to be necessary were not revealed, neither was the condition of the trousers abandoned on the table ever mentioned. He admitted stealing the money from the till, but said that it had been stolen from him the same night by a woman when he was the worse for drink. The police searched his pockets and found three bottles containing prussic acid, chloroform and laudanum. He did not say why he required them, but it was suspected that he intended to use them to commit suicide. Asked where he had been for the last few days, he said he had slept rough for three nights, and had wandered abut on the banks of the river and at Richmond Park. He had then ridden in a cab, where he had been robbed. On the following Monday Barber appeared at the Walthamstow police court charged on suspicion of causing the death of Annie Mary French.

The resumed inquest took place on 8 August at the Common Gate Hotel, Markhouse Road, where the Home Office analyst, Mr Charles Tidy, revealed that he had found substantial amounts of morphine in the viscera, stomach contents and urine. Mrs French might have inhaled chloroform, but only enough to make her dizzy. The cause of death was morphine poisoning. 'A murderous dose of the drug must have been taken,' said Tidy. If Mrs French had taken it herself he thought it was feasible for her to have replaced the bottle in the surgery afterwards. The coroner summed-up, describing the case as 'more and more difficult and mysterious.' He advised the jury that if a medical man caused death by administering an overdose of medicine through negligence then he would be guilty of manslaughter. If wilfully given, then it was murder. Alternatively, the deceased could have taken it, either with intent to commit suicide or by accident. The jury had no difficulty in returning a verdict that Mrs French had met her death through poisoning with morphia, but said there was insufficient evidence to determine if she had taken it herself or if it had been administered by another person.

On 11 and 18 August Barber appeared before the Stratford Petty Sessions charged with having caused the death of Mrs French. The main reasons for

Barber arrested and in the dock.

suspicion were his flight while Mrs French was still alive, and failure to fetch help, an action considered at best to be 'cowardly and base.' In his favour, however, was the obvious evidence that he had attempted several methods of reviving her, which strongly suggested that he had not intended her death.

The Bill of Indictment was finally brought before the Old Bailey on 21 September, but with minimal forensic evidence the case collapsed before it could start. Barber was freed without even coming to trial. His subsequent career is a mystery.

In 1892 Arthur George French married again. His second wife was Edith Emma Richardson, and the couple raised a family in Walthamstow.

How did Annie French die? There is nothing to suggest that she deliberately took her own life. She was not in serious pain from her teeth that day, so was unlikely to have impulsively swallowed a whole bottle of morphia. If she did, how did she know its usual position in order to replace it in the surgery? On the other hand, there is no evidence that Barber intended to kill Mrs French.

A possible scenario is that Barber and Mrs French had been engaging in a flirtation which stopped short of actual adultery. Perhaps he had asked for further intimacies or even suggested that they run away together, neither of which she would consider. She might well have asked for the relationship to end. This would have produced Barber's depressed mood and increased drinking and would explain Mrs French's sudden request to her husband not to ask him to the house again. Barber invited her to the shop possibly under the pretence of treating her teeth, but his intent may have been to drug her for sexual purposes, using morphine as a sedative, and chloroform for its known aphrodisiac effect. The fatal overdose was probably accidental, and Barber panicked when she did not regain consciousness. If Mrs French's death resulted from being drugged for a criminal purpose then even if Barber had not intended to kill her, he was guilty of murder.

32

WANDSWORTH

Mystery at the Priory

The marriage of 19-year-old Florence Campbell to handsome 21-year-old guardsman Alexander Ricardo in September 1864 was a glittering society event, full of the promise of a long and happy life together. The appearance was deceptive and the union doomed, for the young bride soon found that her new husband was sliding rapidly into hopeless alcoholism. Florence consulted several doctors, amongst them Dr James Manby Gully, a noted hydrotherapist of Malvern. Between treatments Alexander often relapsed into bouts of heavy drinking and *delirium tremens*, and by March 1871 Florence could stand it no longer and the couple formally separated. Alexander died in Cologne three weeks later, aged 28. Florence was still only 26 and a wealthy woman.

For consolation, Florence turned to a man she knew and trusted, whose company was soothing and pleasant, whose kindness and consideration was such a contrast to her late husband's dark and sometimes violent moods. Dr Gully was thirty-seven years Florence's senior, she was his patient, and he also had a wife, although he did not live with her as she was an invalid. The association caused tongues to wag and so, to preserve the appearance of decency, Florence employed a lady companion. Jane Cannon Cox was about 40. In 1858 she had married and settled in Jamaica where her three sons were born, but she had returned to England a widow in 1869. She had been working as a governess for Henry Brooks, Florence's solicitor, with whose family Florence had stayed after her separation. The two women soon became close and trusting friends. Mrs Cox was the perfect confidante; sympathetic, loyal and discreet. In November 1873 Florence became unwell, and was attended by Dr Gully, who later stated that he had removed 'a kind of tumour'. Although there is no proof, it seems very probable that he had performed an abortion.

The Priory, Balham, from a contemporary drawing.

In 1874, Florence found her perfect new home. The Priory, Bedford Hill, Balham was a delightful mansion with fifteen rooms set in ten acres of land. Dr Gully took a house nearby and the two continued to enjoy each other's company, although after the recent scare the relationship had become purely platonic. Later that year Florence was introduced to a young barrister, Charles Bravo. He was handsome and clever, and he soon professed himself devotedly in love with her. For the second time in Florence's life it seemed like the perfect match. Florence accepted Charles' proposal and broke off her relationship with Dr Gully, who, though unhappy about this, eventually accepted the situation with good grace.

The young couple were open with each other. Charles told Florence of a mistress and Florence told Charles all about Dr Gully. Both accepted that the past was the past, however Charles was adamant that his mother must never find out about Florence's transgression or the wedding might be vetoed. He also insisted that Florence must never see Gully again, even in friendship, and she readily accepted that condition. Most importantly, Charles agreed that Mrs Cox could remain as her companion. Shortly before the wedding, which would automatically convey all of Florence's property to her husband, Charles showed his true colours. When Florence proposed a settlement which would exclude her personal effects such as the furniture of the Priory, he flew into a rage and said that he would not live in a house where the chair he sat on was not his own.

Florence gave in, but she must have suspected that her new husband cared more for her fortune than he did for her. It was a terrible sign of what was to come. By then, it might have been too late to break off the engagement. Charles had been staying at the Priory overnight and Florence may well have been pregnant.

They were married in December 1875. Life at the Priory was extremely comfortable, but Charles started to worry about extravagance. He dismissed Griffiths, the coachman, who commented at the time that Bravo wouldn't last four months, a prediction he would come to regret. Charles also got Florence to dismiss her personal maid, and sell her ponies. He noticed that Florence was unduly fond of a drink and rebuked her for it. He even began to suggest that Mrs Cox's salary was an unreasonable expense. In January, Florence suffered a miscarriage. Later that month, Florence confided to a doctor that Charles, presumably frustrated by her temporary ill-health, had resorted to sodomy.

Florence Bravo, from a
contemporary photograph.

Charles Bravo, from a
contemporary drawing.

One morning early in March, Charles unaccountably began to feel very ill after eating breakfast. He had a glass of brandy and set out for work, but on reaching Balham station he was violently sick. He got the train but was obliged to take a cab to the home of his mother and stepfather to rest until he felt well enough to go to work.

Florence had another miscarriage in April. During her recovery Charles slept in the guest bedroom, next door to the main bedroom which Florence shared with Mrs Cox.

On Tuesday 18 April, Florence was up and about for the first time since her miscarriage. That afternoon Charles decided to take one of the horses out for a ride. He returned home tired and muddy, saying that the hose had galloped so hard it had shaken him up. He took a warm bath, then he Florence and Mrs Cox dined at 7.30. Charles drank four glasses of burgundy during dinner, but Florence and Mrs Cox polished off two bottles of sherry between them. Florence had not yet done drinking for the day. She got ready for bed, first sending Mrs Cox for a glass of Marsala and water and then, just before she retired, asked the maid, Mary Ann, to fetch some wine. When Charles saw this he spoke to Florence angrily, then marched back to the guest room, saying he would speak to her about it further in the morning. The bedroom doors closed. Mary Ann tidied up and was on her way downstairs when Charles suddenly threw open the door of his room. His face was pale, his eyes staring wildly, and he was gasping in pain. 'Florence!' he shouted, 'Hot water!'

Mary Ann rushed into her mistress's bedroom, but Florence appeared to be already asleep. Mrs Cox, awake and dressed, took charge of the situation. Charles was back in his room, vomiting out of the window, then, exhausted, he sank to the floor. Dr Harrison, who had previously attended Florence, was sent for. Charles was plied with mustard emetics and strong coffee, but he was barely able to swallow. When he vomited into a basin, Mrs Cox arranged to have it taken away and emptied. Mary Ann woke Florence, who went to see her husband. Astounded that Harrison had been sent for as he lived an hour's journey away, she ordered that Dr Moore of Balham High Road should be fetched at once. Moore arrived to find the patient almost unconscious, his skin cold, the pulse barely perceptible. Mrs Cox said that she thought Charles might have swallowed chloroform as there was a small bottle on the mantelpiece which was empty, but Moore was unable to detect any smell of it on Charles' breath. Mustard plasters were applied to his chest and feet, and they tried to give him brandy. Dr Harrison arrived and both doctors agreed that the patient was dying. Florence asked if she could call in Dr Royes Bell, a cousin of Charles', and he arrived together with Professor George Johnson of Kings College Hospital. All four doctors were convinced that Charles had taken some irritant poison. When Charles was lucid enough he was questioned, but said that all he had done was rub his gums with some laudanum. Mrs Cox then asked to speak privately to Bell. Outside the sickroom, she imparted that when Charles had first been taken ill he had told her he had taken poison but that she was not to tell Florence. Bell angrily asked why she had said nothing before and she replied that she had told Harrison. Mrs Cox repeated her information before Johnson and Harrison, but Harrison denied that she had ever told him more than her own suspicions. When Charles was challenged with Mrs Cox's statement, he seemed puzzled and denied that he had ever said he had taken poison.

Throughout the night Charles lingered on in terrible pain. He knew he was dying and dictated his will, in which he left everything to Florence. On the following day he worsened and the family gathered around him. Another doctor arrived, Henry Smith, who was also a personal friend. Finally, in desperation, Florence wrote to Sir William Gull, one of the most eminent doctors in London. Sir William had his own way of getting the truth out of a patient. He told Charles bluntly that he was dying and demanded that he tell him what poison he had taken. Despite this Charles continued to say, 'before God I've taken only laudanum! If it wasn't laudanum so help me God I don't know what it was!' His desperation had the ring of truth. Charles eventually lapsed into unconsciousness and died at 5.30 on the Friday morning.

The post-mortem found massive ulceration and inflammation of the intestines. The inquest took place at the Priory, where it was revealed that the cause of death was antimony, usually available as a preparation called tartar emetic, which was used to make a lotion for horses. It was also then a common treatment for alcoholism, dissolved in alcohol to induce disgust and nausea in the patient. It is readily soluble and tasteless. The court heard that Charles had been in good spirits on the day he had been taken ill, and there was no reason to suspect suicide. The jury, unable to determine how or why Charles had swallowed antimony, delivered an open verdict. The families were left in a state of simmering dissatisfaction. Florence's father had hoped for a verdict of suicide, while James Bravo, Charles' stepfather, suspected that Charles had been murdered. He and a barrister friend of Charles' went to Scotland Yard, the press got to hear of it, and by mid-May the mystery was in all the newspapers. Florence now found that all the intimate private affairs of her life had become a matter of public speculation, as the facts were raked over, theories proposed, and a campaign mounted for a fresh enquiry.

Mrs Cox had her own urgent concerns. She had known since 1874 that her aunt Margaret, who lived in Jamaica, was very ill and had willed her a substantial estate. Margaret had recently written to her niece urging that she come to Jamaica, concerned that if she were to die, her banker would move into the property unless her legatee was there to make her claim. Despite this, Mrs Cox remained in England to give her support to Florence.

At the end of May, Mr Stephenson, the treasury solicitor, started questioning witnesses. Both Florence and Mrs Cox had new revelations. Florence said that on the Tuesday Charles had been in a temper over finances and had threatened to cut his throat. The couple had also quarrelled over Dr Gully. During dinner, she said, Charles' face had had a strange yellow look, as if he was about to go mad. Mrs Cox, resigned to the fact that she and Dr Harrison would continue to disagree about what she had said to him, now testified that Charles had told her he had taken poison because of Dr Gully. She said she had not mentioned it at first to avoid a scandal, and she knew that Charles would be angry if he recovered. She added that Charles had told her that he did not want to live with Florence any more and wished he was dead.

Florence and Mrs Cox must have hoped that by introducing the figure of Dr Gully, and embellishing Charles' mood swings, they would put the case for suicide beyond any doubt. They had not reckoned that they had also supplied a possible motive for murder. A fresh inquest was ordered, which opened on 11 July at the Bedford Hotel, Balham. Charles' coffin had been exhumed and

THE BRAVO ENQUIRY

JURY VIEWING THE BODY

Viewing the body of Charles Bravo.

the jurymen were taken to Norwood cemetery, where, through a hole cut in the coffin lid, into which a pane of glass had been inserted, they viewed the blackened face of the deceased. Back in court, Charles' letters were read out, showing that he was in good spirits shortly before his death. It had been theorised that the antimony was in the burgundy Charles had drunk at dinner, although it was then pointed out that had that been the case, he would have been taken ill much earlier in the evening. A new possibility emerged when the maid, Mary Ann, told the court that Charles liked to have a carafe of water beside his bed and it had been filled afresh that morning. Griffiths, the coachman, heavily embarrassed by being questioned about his prediction of Charles' death, confirmed that tartar emetic had been kept in the stables.

The verdict of the jury was that Charles' death was not suicide or accident, but wilful murder, although the jurors felt unable to name a suspect. No one was ever arrested or tried for the murder of Charles Bravo. In the intervening years there have been many theories: that Charles swallowed the poison by accident having intended to use it on Florence to curb her drinking habits, that he committed suicide in a fit of jealous madness, that he had been murdered by

Florence, or by Dr Gully or by Mrs Cox, or any two of them in collusion. Other suspects are Charles' discarded mistress, and the dismissed coachman, Griffiths, though both would have needed confederates at the Priory.

Florence and Mrs Cox had undoubtedly colluded at the Treasury enquiry to increase the possibility of a verdict of suicide, although that is not proof of guilt, and Mrs Cox's behaviour must lead to grave suspicions. She must have heard Charles' call for help, as the two rooms were only a few feet apart, but did nothing until alerted by the maid. She then delayed the arrival of medical attention by summoning Harrison, disposed of the contents of the basin, and tried to confuse matters by suggesting chloroform. She almost certainly invented Charles' supposed admission to taking poison. On balance, however, Mrs Cox was probably an accessory to murder rather than a murderess. A woman expecting to inherit an estate has no motive to murder if she fears losing her place as companion. One thing that is without question is her loyalty to Florence.

It was later rumoured that the body of Florence's first husband had been exhumed and antimony found. Whether or not this is true, it is not unlikely as he could have been given it medicinally, but he and Florence had been apart for months when he died. Florence may have turned to antimony a second time to rid herself of her intolerably mean and bad tempered second husband, the sexual practices which disgusted her, and the danger of being weakened by repeated miscarriages until she died. Charles' sickness in March may have been a trial run. If Florence had poisoned Charles, 18 April was the ideal day. Charles was weakened by his horse ride, and she may have hoped his death could be attributed to a heart attack. There was time to poison the water bottle when Mrs Cox went downstairs to fetch her drink. The devoted companion, either guessing or being told what Florence had done, rallied to her aid, and did everything she could to protect her.

In June, Mrs Cox departed for Jamaica. Florence was left alone, and sought increasing consolation in brandy. The Priory, with its unhappy memories, was sold in 1877 and she moved to an isolated villa in Southsea, where, in September 1878, she died of a stomach haemorrhage brought on by excessive drinking. Dr Gully's career and social status did not survive the scandal. He died in 1883. Jane Cox went to Jamaica and inherited a substantial plantation from her aunt in 1879. She later returned to England and died in 1917, aged 90.

The Priory still stands at No. 197 Bedford Hill, though the coachman's and gardener's lodges have gone and the grounds are covered with modern housing. The mansion itself is now divided into flats.

33

WESTMINSTER

The 'Lamentable Catastrophe'

Shortly after 5 p.m. on 11 May 1812, there were about twenty men in the lobby of the House of Commons. Some were discussing the main political concerns of the day: the grant of £100,000 made to the Prince Regent, the prospect of war with America, and the activities of the Luddites. Others were simply passing through on their way to the public gallery. One man stood alone by the door, glancing about him anxiously, his right hand thrust into the front of his coat. No one, neither the officers on duty nor the men who saw him as they passed, thought anything of his presence, since he had been a frequent visitor in the last few weeks. Many would later recall that they had recently sat with him in the public gallery or spoken to him in the lobby. A Commons enquiry was taking place that day, and the Prime Minister, Spencer Perceval, was expected at any moment.

Spencer Perceval was 49 years of age. He had married in 1790 and was the father of twelve children. After an early career as a barrister he had entered parliament in 1796, where he quickly made an impression, rising to Attorney General in 1802 and Chancellor of the Exchequer in 1807. He had been Prime Minister since 4 October 1809. It was a turbulent time politically and Perceval had made some unpopular decisions. He was especially noted for his anti-Catholic bigotry, which was considered extreme even in his own day.

At about quarter past five, William Smith MP had paused to speak to a gentleman in the lobby, when he heard a shot. He turned and saw a crowd of people gathering around a spot near the exit door. Several voices were crying out to close the door and let no one escape. A man staggered from the crowd, looking about him, then with a muffled cry of 'Murder!' he reeled suddenly and fell face down to the floor. Smith and another gentleman helped to turn him over and it was only then that he recognised the stricken man as Spencer Perceval.

The assassination of Spencer Perceval from a contemporary print.

Blood on his shirt and waistcoat showed that he had been shot in the chest. They carried him into the office of the Speaker's secretary and sat him down where he could lean on a table, and elevated his legs by supporting them on two chairs. His eyes were open, but this and a barely fluttering pulse and a few convulsive sobs, were the only signs of life. William Lynn, a surgeon of nearby Great George Street, was summoned, and arrived within a few minutes. He felt for a pulse but by then it was clear that the man was dead. Opening the shirt, he saw a puncture wound just above the left nipple. He probed the wound, but was unable to reach the ball, which had gone deeply into the chest cavity.

Meanwhile, in the lobby, the assassin was sitting quietly on a bench to the right of the fireplace, sweating with agitation. Someone pointed to him, saying, 'That is the man,' and solicitor Henry Burgess went over to him. The man's left hand rested on the bench but in his other was a pistol. Lt General Isaac Gascoyne, who had raced down to the lobby from the committee room on hearing the shot, saw the man raise his hand and, convinced that he was about to shoot himself, seized the arm and pushed it down. Burgess at once took charge of the pistol, which was still warm. The man did not resist. 'What induced you to do such a thing?' Burgess demanded. The assassin said that it was the refusal of the government to redress a grievance. Burgess sensibly asked him if he had another pistol in his pocket, to which the reply was 'yes'. 'Is it loaded?' demanded Burgess. Again the answer was 'yes'. Vincent George Dowling had been in the gallery when he heard the shot but arrived in the lobby in time to take the second pistol. It was primed and loaded.

Several people were putting their hands into the man's pockets and taking charge of the contents. Burgess removed a penknife, a pencil, a bunch of keys and some money and Gascoyne found a bundle of papers tied in red tape and handed them to another MP, Mr Hume, for safekeeping.

Shortly afterwards the assassin was taken into custody, and, together with the witnesses, was conducted upstairs to be examined before a magistrate. By the time he was ready to be questioned he was perfectly calm. He gave his name as John Bellingham, and said he had no personal hatred of the man he had just killed.

John Vickery, a Bow Street officer, was sent to Bellingham's lodgings at 11 New Millman Street, where he found a pair of pistol bags, a powder flask, a pistol key that fitted the murder weapon, a mould and some pistol balls.

There was never any doubt that Bellingham had shot and killed the Prime Minister, but the question was why had he done so? Many, on hearing the news, must have suspected that the assassin was insane. Bellingham, however, while he might fairly be described as a man obsessed, was not insane, he was simply very, very angry.

The body of Spencer Perceval was taken to 10 Downing Street, while Bellingham was placed in the custody of the Keeper of Newgate Gaol until his trial, which took place only four days later at the Justice House, Old Bailey. There was only one possible defence, insanity, which, despite the prisoner's opposition, was put forward at the insistence of his friends and family. After asking for the return of his papers, Bellingham was allowed to address the court in his own defence on the subject of what he described as the 'lamentable catastrophe' for which he was on trial. He made it clear that he had 'no personal or premeditated malice towards [Mr Perceval]; the unfortunate lot had fallen on him as the leading member of that administration which had repeatedly refused me any reparation for the unparalleled injuries I had sustained in Russia'.

There followed a lengthy account of Bellingham's grievances against the government, which, if true, were ample evidence of why he had reached the end of his tether, and if untrue, could only suggest that he was in the grip of a serious delusion. No one, not even the Government officials and ministers who were present to hear his speech, came forward to claim that his story was all in his imagination. Lord Gower was in court and learned that if Bellingham had met him first, it was he who would have been shot and not Perceval.

John Bellingham was born in London around 1771, the son of a land surveyor and miniature painter. He was brought up first in St Neots, Huntingdonshire and later in London. His father died insane in 1780. As a young man, he had lived

Contemporary statuette of a Bow Street Runner.

an unsettled life, trying a number of different business ventures. He is believed to have made his first visit to Archangel in 1800, acting as an export agent for a Russian merchant. He returned to England, and worked in Liverpool as a broker. In 1803 he married Mary Neville, the daughter of a merchant. A son was born to them, and when in the following year he again travelled to Russia on business, Mary and the child accompanied him. He had been about to return to England in November when, without warning, he was arrested and thrown into prison. His arrest, he discovered, was connected with the fate of a Russian ship, the *Sojus*, which had been insured by Lloyds of London, and had been lost with all its cargo in the White Sea. Lloyds had received information that the claim was fraudulent, and had refused to pay the owners for their loss. The ship's owner, Solomon van Brienan, suspected that Bellingham was the informant, but having no proof, had had him arrested on a charge of being liable for a debt of 4,890 roubles. Bellingham appealed to the British Ambassador, Lord Granville Leveson Gower, who wrote to the Governor of Archangel, but on being told that the prisoner had been detained for a legal cause declined to assist him further.

In November 1805 Bellingham was able to join his family in St Petersburg, but in June 1806 he was once more arrested. Mary Bellingham, who was expecting her second child, remained in St Petersburg, hopeful that her husband would be freed, but eventually, in the eighth month of pregnancy, she was obliged to return to England. For two years, Bellingham was moved from prison to prison, kept in filthy conditions and subsisting on bread and water, but when at last he was permitted to make a case, he obtained judgement against the Governor of Archangel and the Senate. Instead of being freed, however, he was sent to another prison, and a demand was made on him for another debt of 2,000 roubles. Bellingham refused to pay a debt which he said he did not owe, and as a result he was declared bankrupt and remained in prison. Eventually he was handed over to the College of Commerce. Lord Gower still refused to help him, and Bellingham continued to refuse to pay the debt, or even part of it. He was afraid that if he paid anything at all this would be seen as an admission that the debt was just and he might then be accused of bringing a false claim against the Governor and Senate and sent to Siberia. Eventually his determination not to capitulate paid off. One night in 1809, the Senate sent him his discharge from prison and a pass to enable him to return home. He was at last reunited with Mary, who had been obliged to take up the trade of milliner in Liverpool. A son, Henry Stevens Bellingham, was born to the couple on 11 May 1811.

John Bellingham felt that he was entitled to some compensation from the British Government, which had so far refused to help him. The same relentless determination which had seen him through six years of unjust imprisonment was now brought to bear in his fight for redress. He first sent a statement of his grievances to the Marquis of Wellesley accompanied by documentary evidence. Wellesley referred the matter to the Privy Council, who referred it to the Treasury, and finally it was placed before Mr Perceval. Bellingham also sent a petition to the Prince Regent. No one would agree to assist him. 'I was plunged into ruin and involved in debt,' he told the court,

> ... and the learned Attorney General has admitted there was not a spot on my character until this fatal catastrophe, which when I reflect on it, I could burst into a flood of tears. I was totally refused any redress. Gentlemen, what would be your feelings – what would be your alternative; as the affair was national, and as his Majesty's Ministers recommended me backwards and forwards from one to another.

Six weeks before he shot Spencer Perceval, Bellingham had written to the magistrates at Bow Street accusing the government of having 'closed the door of justice' and asking them to approach the ministers to do what was right and proper. If this was denied he would feel 'justified in executing justice myself'. Having been told he could expect nothing, he was 'driven to despair, and under these agonizing feelings ... impelled to that desperate alternative.'

On 25 April, Bellingham asked his tailor, James Taylor of 11 North Place Greys Inn Lane, to carry out a small alteration. Showing him a dark-coloured coat, Bellingham asked Taylor to attach a new pocket inside the garment. He provided a piece of paper about nine inches in depth to show the precise size of pocket required. He was anxious to have the job done by that evening, and Taylor was able to oblige. The coat was later taken from Bellingham after the assassination and at the trial, Taylor identified it as the one in which he had sewn the deep pocket.

Treasury minute books show that only days before Bellingham shot the Prime Minister, he had received a reply to his most recent petition for redress stating '... it does not appear that this government could interfere in [your] case, even if this country were in amity with Russia.' It must have been the final straw.

At Bellingham's trial, the defence brought witnesses to say that they had believed the accused to be 'in a state of perfect derangement', although all were obliged to admit that he had been conducting his business as usual, had never been confined for insanity and no medical man had ever been called to attend him.

There followed an emotional scene in which Chief Justice Sir James Mansfield addressed the jury, during which his voice became faint with distress and he was briefly unable to speak. As he referred to Perceval as 'a man so dear and revered' he broke down and sobbed, an outburst in which he was joined by many of those present. Recovering, he said that the only question for the jury to decide was whether the accused had committed the crime. His grievances

John Bellingham from a contemporary print.

were not a justification and should be disregarded. There was no proof that the prisoner was insane at the time the act was committed, and by his own testimony he clearly demonstrated he was a full and competent judge of all his actions. The jury retired for only fourteen minutes before returning a verdict of guilty. Bellingham was sentenced to death.

On 16 May the body of Spencer Perceval was interred at the family vault at St Luke's Church, Charlton. The execution of John Bellingham was to take place at 8 a.m. on 18 May, less than one week from the commission of the crime. *The Times* deflected any possible sympathy for the man by describing him as a 'turbulent, untractable, profligate adventurer'. Bellingham awaited his fate in Newgate, praying, consuming only bread and water, and expressing no regret for what he had done.

It was originally suggested that the execution should take place in Palace Yard, Westminster, the nearest public place to the spot where the crime was committed, but perhaps to avoid the crowds choking the streets as they followed Bellingham being brought there from prison it was decided that the place of execution would be before the debtors' door of Newgate Gaol. There were fears that a catastrophe might occur because of the number of spectators, so the military were drafted in and handbills were distributed, reminding the public of the tragedy that had attended the execution of Haggerty and Holloway in 1807, when thirty people had been crushed to death. This and the wet weather served to reduce the number of onlookers to manageable proportions. In prison, Bellingham, who had once felt hopeful of acquittal, was resigned to his fate. He was brought to the scaffold before an unusually hushed crowd, although there were a few cries of 'God bless you!' as the cap was fastened over his head. There was perfect silence as he dropped into oblivion, the executioners holding onto his legs to speed his departure.

The body hung for an hour then it was cut down, placed in a cart, covered with a sack, and driven away. As it progressed up Newgate Street, passing windows thronged with spectators, the executioner removed the sack two or three times so that the body might be seen. It was finally delivered to St Bartholomew's Hospital to be dissected.

Mary Bellingham, comforting herself that her husband had been insane when he committed 'the dreadful act', struggled to support her three children. It is believed that she reverted to her maiden name of Neville. She received some assistance from public subscriptions but her business failed later that year and she was left in poverty.

BIBLIOGRAPHY

GENERAL SOURCES

Contemporary national and local newspapers
The Proceedings of the Old Bailey, accessed http://www.oldbaileyonline.org/
Family History records, accessed www.ancestry.com
International Genealogical Index accessed www.familysearch.org

SPECIFIC SOURCES AND FURTHER READING

BARKING AND DAGENHAM
Stratmann, L., 'The Dagenham Outrage', in *Essex Murders*, (The History Press, Stroud, 2008)
Rhodes, L., Shelden, L., and Abnett, K., *The Dagenham Murder*, (London Borough of Barking and Dagenham, 2005)

BARNET
Butler, I., (ed.) *Trials of Brian Donald Hume*, (London, David and Charles, 1976)
Williams, J., *Hume, Portrait of a Double Murderer*, (London, Panther, 1961)
Jackson, R., *Francis Camps*, (London, Granada, 1983)
Totterdell, G.H., *Country Copper*, (London, Harrap, 1956)

National Archive papers
PRO MEPO 3/3144
PRO DPP 2/2889
PRO DPP 2/2906
PRO CRIM 1/2033

BRENT
National Archive papers PRO CRIM 1/97/7

BROMLEY
National Archive papers PRO ASSI 36/14

CAMDEN
Ellis, G., *Ruth Ellis, my mother*, (London, Smyth Gryphon, 1995)
Farran, D., *The Trial of Ruth Ellis*, (Manchester, Manchester University Sociology Dept, 1988?)
Goodman J., *The Trial of Ruth Ellis*, (Newton Abbot, David and Charles, 1974)
Hancock, R., *Ruth Ellis*, (London, Arthur Barker, 1963)
Jakubait, M., *Ruth Ellis: my sister's secret life*, (London, Robinson, 2005)
Marks, L., and Van Den Bergh, T., *Ruth Ellis: a case of diminished responsibility?*, (London, Penguin, 1990)

National Archive papers
PRO CRIM 1/2582
PRO DPP 2/2430/1
PRO DPP 2/2430/2
PRO MEPO 2/9888

CITY
Anon, *The Battle with the London Anarchists*, (Edward Lloyd, London, 1911) Accessed via National Archives online catalogue, reference JML/1987.57, Jewish Museum of London.
Rogers, C., *The Battle of Stepney*, (London, Robert Hale, 1981)
Rumbelow, D., *The Houndsditch Murders and the Siege of Sidney Street*, (London, W.H. Allen, 1988)
National Archive papers PRO MEPO 3/191

CROYDON
Hyde, H.M., *Trial of Christopher Craig and Derek William Bentley*, (London, William Hodge and Co., 1954)
Trow, M.J., *'Let Him Have It, Chris'*, (London, Grafton, 1992, originally published by Constable in 1990)
Yallop, D., *To Encourage the Others*, (London, W.H. Allen, 1971)

National Archive papers
PRO MEPO 2/9401/1
PRO MEPO 2/9401/2
PRO HO 291/225
PRO HO 291/226
PRO PCOM 9/2312
PRO CRIM 1/2282
PRO LAB 8/1845

EALING
McLeave, H., *Chesney: the Fabulous Murderer*, (London, Mark Goulden Ltd, 1954)
Tullett, T., *Portrait of a Bad Man*, (London, Viking Press, 1956)

National Archive papers
PRO MEPO 2/9542
PRO DPP 2/2338

ENFIELD
Will of Benjamin Couch Danby, National Archives PRO PROB 11/1795

GREENWICH
National Archive papers PRO DPP 4/7

HACKNEY
National Archive papers
PRO CRIM 1/58/5
PRO HO 144/1540/A61535

HAMMERSMITH AND FULHAM
National Archive papers
PRO CRIM 1/14/2
PRO J 77/282/8310

HARINGEY
Collier. P., *Secrets of the Tottenham Outrage*, (Patricia Collier, 2007)
Harris, J.D., *Outrage! An Edwardian Tragedy*, (Wilson Harris publications, 2000)
Jagger, D., 'An Outrage that Appalled a Nation', in Newsletter, February 2009, of The Friends
    of the Metropolitan Police Historical Collection

HAVERING
Evans, S.P., *Executioner: The Chronicles of James Berry, Victorian Hangman*, (Thrupp, Sutton, 2004)
Smith, Lieut-Col Sir H., KCB, *From Constable to Commissioner*, (London, Chatto and Windus,
    1910)
Rhodes, L., and Abnett, K., *The Romford Outrage: The Murder of Inspector Thomas Simmons, 1885*,
    (Barnsley, Wharncliffe Books, 2009)

HOUNSLOW
National Archive papers
PRO CRIM 1/1366
PRO DPP 2/910

ISLINGTON
Connell, N., *Walter Dew, the man who caught Crippen*, (Gloucestershire, Sutton, 2005)
Young, F. (ed.), *Trial of H.H. Crippen*, (Glasgow and Edinburgh, William Hodge and Company
    Ltd, 1933)

KENSINGTON AND CHELSEA
Camps, F.E., and Barber, R., *The Investigation of Murder*, (Scientific Book Club, 1966)
Kennedy, L., *10 Rillington Place*, (London, Panther Books, 1971)
Eddowes, M., *The Man on Your Conscience*, (London, Cassell, 1955)
Simpson, Prof. K., *Forty Years of Murder*, (London, Granada, 1980)
Eddowes, J., *The Two Killers of Rillington Place*, (London, Warner, 1994)

LAMBETH

Moulton, H.F. (ed.), *Trial of Steinie Morrison*, London and Edinburgh, William Hodge and
    Company Ltd, 1922)

National Archive papers
PRO CRIM 1/119
PRO HO 45/22261-64, 66—68
PRO MEPO 3/202
PRO PCOM 8/101

LEWISHAM

Thorwald, J., *The Marks of Cain*, (London, Thames and Hudson, 1965)

National Archive papers PRO CRIM 1/98/5

MERTON

Adam, H.L., *Trial of George Henry Lamson*, (London Edinburgh Glasgow, William Hodge and
    Company Ltd, 1951)
Hawkins, Sir H., *The Reminiscences of Sir Henry Hawkins* (London, Thomas Nelson & Sons,
    1904)

National Archive papers PRO CRIM 1/13/3

NEWHAM

National Archive papers PRO MEPO 3/77

REDBRIDGE

Ellis, J., *Diary of a Hangman*, (Glasgow, True Crime Library, 1996)
Weis, R., *Criminal Justice*, (London, Penguin, 1990)

National Archive papers
PRO CRIM 1/206/5
PRO DPP 1/70
PRO HO 144/2685
PRO MEPO 3/1582
PRO PCOM 8/22
PRO PCOM 8/436
PRO PCOM 9/1983

RICHMOND

O'Donnell, E., (ed.) *Trial of Kate Webster* (Edinburgh and London, William Hodge & Company
    Ltd, 1925)

National Archive papers PRO HO 144/36/82518A

SOUTHWARK

Adam, H.L., (ed.) *Trial of George Chapman*, (Edinburgh and London, William Hodge and
    Company Ltd, 1930)

Glaister, J., *The Power of Poison* (London, Christopher Johnson, 1954)

Gordon, R.M., *The American Murders of Jack the Ripper: Tantalizing Evidence of the Gruesome American Interlude of the Prime Ripper Suspect*, (The Lyons Press, Guilford, Conn., May 2005)

National Archive papers PRO CRIM 1/84

TOWER HAMLETS

Begg, P., *Jack the Ripper, the Definitive History*, (Harlow, Longman, 2004)

Fido, M. *The Crimes, Detection and Death of Jack the Ripper*, (London, Orion, 1993)

Rumbelow. D., *The Complete Jack the Ripper*, (London, Penguin, 1988)

Sugden, P., *The Complete History of Jack the Ripper*, (London, Robinson, 2002)

WANDSWORTH

Bridges, Y., *How Charles Bravo Died*, (London, Reprint Society, 1957)

Jenkins, E., *Dr Gully*, (London, Penguin, 1974)

Ruddick, J., *Death at the Priory*, (Atlantic Books, London, 2001)

Williams, J., *Suddenly at the Priory*, (Penguin, London, 1989)

National Archive papers PRO MEPO 3/123

WESTMINSTER

Hanrahan, D.C., *The Assassination of the Prime Minister*, (Stroud, Sutton, 2008)

Wilson D., *The substance of a conversation with John Bellingham the assassin of the late right hon Spencer Perceval on Sunday may 17 1812, the day previous to his execution together with some general remarks*, (London, John Hatchard, 1812)

National Archive papers
PRO 30/29/6/11
PRO T 29/116 p. 747
PRO T 29/117 para 5215

INDEX